D1389948

⁴/₈₇. THIS BOOK SHOULD BE RETURNED ON OR BE. ... LATEST
DATE SHOWN TO THE LIBRARY FROM WHICH IT WAS BORROWED

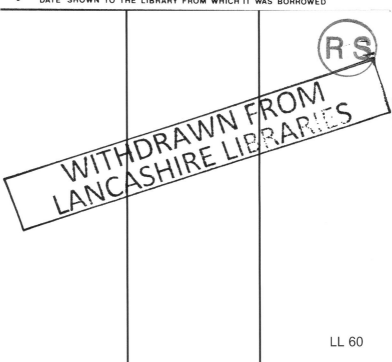

R·S

WITHDRAWN FROM LANCASHIRE LIBRARIES

LL 60

AUTHOR

MURRELL, H   578.0941/ H1L

TITLE

Hilda Murrell's nature diaries, 1961-1983

Lancashire
County
Council   \\.

THE LANCASHIRE LIBRARY.
Library Headquarters,
143, Corporation St.,
PRESTON PRI 2TB.

a30118 027102221b

HILDA MURRELL'S
NATURE DIARIES

Hilda Murrell on 9 August, 1975 making a speech at the White House,
Aston Munslow (owned by her friend Miss Constance Purser), to celebrate ten
years of the house being open to the public.

HILDA MURRELL'S

NATURE DIARIES

1961-1983

EDITED BY

Charles Sinker

COLLINS
8 Grafton Street, London WIX 3LA
1987

02710222

First published in Great Britain 1987 by
William Collins Sons & Co. Ltd
London · Glasgow · Sydney · Auckland
Toronto · Johannesburg

© The Estate of Hilda Murrell 1987
© The Introduction Charles Sinker 1987

All rights reserved. No part of this publication may
be reproduced or transmitted in any form or by
any means, electronic or mechanical, including
photocopying, recording or any information storage
and retrieval system now known or to be invented
without permission in writing from the publisher.

BRITISH LIBRARY CATALOGUING IN PUBLICATION DATA

Murrell, Hilda
Hilda Murrell's nature diaries.
1. Horticulture – England
I. Title   II. Sinker, Charles
635'.092'4   SB98

ISBN 0 00 412186 4

Photoset in Linotron Ehrhardt by
Rowland Phototypesetting Ltd
Bury St Edmunds, Suffolk
Made and printed in Great Britain by
Butler & Tanner Ltd, Frome, Somerset

CONTENTS

Acknowledgements

It was the late Diana Moss who first suggested that the Diaries might be worthy of publication, and who persuaded the Shropshire Branch of the Council for the Protection of Rural England, through its Amenities Committee, to accept responsibility for this undertaking; her tragically early death prevented her from seeing the work completed.

I am deeply grateful to Joan Tate for involving me in this enterprise, and for encouraging, nudging and helping me in so many ways through every stage of the work; I could certainly not have done it without her support.

Many people have responded to our enquiries with information and suggestions, or have assisted in other ways: I should like to thank them all, and especially Phyllis Bishop, Mary Briggs, Rex Cartwright, Elizabeth Dibb, H. D. G. Foxall, Mary Hignett, Lucy Lunt, W. E. Morris, Dorothy Paish, Trina Paskell, Con Purser, Violet Schwerdt, Margaret Sinker, Ruth Sinker, David Smith, Alicia Symondson, Clive Tate, Stan Turner and Charles Warren. Rebecca Sinker collated the edited manuscript, and Odette Murray helped to compile the Index.

Members of Hilda Murrell's family have given their enthusiastic backing from the start: I am particularly grateful to Robert Green and Stella Chick. Robert has gone out of his way to provide me with facts and ideas that would otherwise have eluded me.

I would like to thank Caroline White and everyone else at Collins for all their help.

Thanks are also due to Richard Banks of Kington and to John Llewelyn Jones of Clevedon for permission to publish extracts from a report and a letter respectively, and to John Murray (Publishers) Ltd for the use of the quotation from *The Zodiac Arch* by Freya Stark (see p. 8).

CAS

Publisher's Note
It has been necessary for the purposes of reproduction to reduce the size of some of Hilda Murrell's drawings.

The initial editing of this book for publication was made possible by the Shropshire Branch of the Council for the Protection of Rural England in part to mark the Diamond Jubilee of CPRE and to commemorate the work of Hilda Murrell and her successor, Diana Moss, who led the Branch Amenities Committee.

† This sign by the right-hand side of the text indicates where passages have been cut (see p.17).

'The advice for a good style is very simple. You must first have something you want to say. . . . The second virtue is accuracy or truth. Whatever it is you may want to say, you must say it as accurately as you can.

Freya Stark, *The Zodiac Arch*

INTRODUCTION

Each of us remembers a different Hilda Murrell. Her friends – and we are many – cherish our own portraits of her, private and precious. We may have little else in common, so wide were her interests. We do share, however, an obligation to put right the picture that now exists of her in the public eye: a nightmare-snapshot framed in the tragedy and squalor which attended her death.

The 'elderly rose-grower' of the press reports, and even the courageous absent witness at the Sizewell 'B' inquiry, are as inadequate descriptions of the real Hilda Murrell as the police poster with its big hat, its flat, Identikit-type face, its opaque eyes and its leftover smile.

Her end robbed us of much, and left us with little cause for gratitude. One thing, nevertheless, remains, transcending the flaws, the paradoxes and the missing dimensions in our personal memories of Hilda: her writing. The care and craftsmanship she devoted to the annual compilation of the catalogue put out by Murrell's Nurseries were well known and widely appreciated. Regular customers looked forward impatiently to each new edition, where they could savour the crisp and restrained eloquence of the fresh entries – even those dealing with modern rose hybrids that she disliked. While Murrell's catalogues were enjoyed by many, few indeed were the friends granted the privilege of reading – or hearing Hilda read aloud – selected entries from her other, and more permanent, literary legacy.

Hilda kept diaries and isolated passages of descriptive or contemplative prose, written at irregular intervals over a long period. In spite of their uneven distribution through the years and decades, these handwritten records were well ordered and often meticulously transcribed into fair copies. There can be no doubt, as I intend to establish later, that much of this material was written – and rewritten – with eventual publication in mind. She may have been modest and self-deprecating over most things, but she recognised and cultivated her talent for writing.

Her orderly attitude to the recording of her life, experiences and opinions led her to keep separate sets of personal journals, diaries on botanical and other natural history subjects, planting logs, and so on. The present publication contains the greater part of the natural history (predominantly botany) diaries alone, for the period 1961–1983. No direct reference has been made to the other parts of her literary *oeuvre*, though a few uncertainties over dates and people have been cleared up (with the help of Robert Green in particular) by cross-checking. This Introduction is emphatically *not* a provisional biography of Hilda Murrell. It is written with no more ambitious an aim than to provide a foreword to a body of writing which stands magnificently on its own merits, and to give a brief interpretative gloss on a few technical or geographical obscurities in the text.

THE DIARIST: MISS HILDA MURRELL
(1906–1984)

The name of Hilda Murrell – often mispronounced: the stress should be on the first syllable – is now very widely known, but not as a direct result of any effort or achievement on her part. On 21 March 1984 she was brutally assaulted in her home at Sutton Road, Shrewsbury; driven in her own car to an isolated lane about five miles east of the town; stabbed, several times; and left in a poplar plantation on the far side of a ploughed field, to die, alone. Her obituary in *The Times* ended 'It is an almost intolerable irony that a life so dedicated to peaceful pursuits, and to the pursuit of peace, should have been terminated by an act of mindless violence.' Her body was not found until three days later, in spite of the abandoned car in the lane. After a belated and apparently inept start, the police investigation of the case grew to become one of the biggest ever mounted. Allegations of a connection with the Sizewell inquiry (she had applied on 7 March to give evidence, and her application was accepted a few days before her death) or even with the *Belgrano* episode, and of secret service involvement, were made in the House of Commons and elsewhere. They remain unsubstantiated, and her murder, mindless or not, is still (at the time of writing) unsolved.

Hilda was born in Shrewsbury in 1906; she was the elder daughter of Owen and Lily Murrell. She was a pupil at Shrewsbury High School, and won a scholarship from there to Newnham College, Cambridge. Her father and his elder brother Edwin ran a successful and well-known rose nursery in the Belvidere area on the eastern outskirts of the town. Having no brothers, Hilda herself joined the firm and quickly developed her outstanding horticultural and business skills, although she was to confess later that she would have preferred an academic career.

During the Second World War, her energy and organisational skill proved a great asset in her voluntary work for the care and resettlement of refugees: she interested herself personally in several individual cases, making lifelong friends of some of those she helped. Her fund-raising efforts included arranging concerts by such notable performers as Myra Hess and Jelly d'Aranyi.

In the spring of 1961 the rose nursery moved, because of the building of the new Shirehall, to agricultural land beside the bypass near Sutton Farm. The business was under her sole management from that time until she sold it to Percy Thrower on her retirement in 1970.

She was a recognised authority on rose species, old and old-fashioned varieties, and miniature roses. In her time as manager, Murrell's Nurseries regularly won gold awards at Chelsea and Southport Flower Shows as well as at Shrewsbury. She sold roses and made friends in many parts of Europe. It is a curious fact, and perhaps a sidelight on her attitude to work and recreation, that she showed no interest in the native wild rose species of the British Isles until three years after her retirement (see below).

Walking in the country – especially hill-country – was one of Hilda's favourite leisure activities from an early age; during and after the Second World War her love of mountaineering and even rock-climbing continued, until arthritis in her ankles forced her to be less ambitious. It was no doubt another, less physical, aspect of the same passion that developed into a deep concern for the countryside and wildlife of the Welsh Marches.

She was a founder-member of the Shropshire Conservation Trust (now the Shropshire Trust for Nature Conservation), on whose Council she served for many years. She showed, on occasion, an understandable impatience with the Trust for its slow progress over local conservation issues, and what she considered its timid, parochial and ultra-diplomatic attitude on matters of wider importance. She gave forthright voice to her feelings, while remaining a loyal member; more recently, she found the

Shropshire Branch of the Council for the Protection of Rural England closer to her own way of thinking in its outlook and activities: she worked with her customary energy to promote its aims, and was responsible for the creation of its Amenities Committee, which she chaired.

Since about 1976 Hilda Murrell became increasingly concerned over the problems posed by nuclear power, in both its military and its civil aspects. She undertook, with characteristic thoroughness, to brief herself as fully as possible in a highly technical field. The publication by the DoE of its White Paper (Cmnd 8607) on Radioactive Waste Management found her ready to challenge the experts on their own ground. The fact that she was the first individual and independent objector to have a paper accepted as evidence by the Sizewell inquiry may indicate how seriously this challenge was taken.

Looking back over what I have written so far, I can see an unbalanced picture emerging: a rock-climbing business woman, a rose expert impatient for nature conservation, a thwarted academic obsessed by the threat of nuclear power. This isn't the Hilda I thought I knew – or only a small and unnaturally solemn part of her. So what do others think? How do her closer friends, and those of longer standing, remember her?

Among the many, helpful, comments I have received, three words or impressions recur most often: 'meticulous'; 'sense of humour'; 'everyone *liked* her'. The portrait grows in depth, colour and clarity with further brush-strokes: she was 'intelligent'; 'charming'; 'welcoming'; 'conscientious'; 'nervous of physical violence'; 'shy'. 'She had a ridiculous and enchanting giggle.' 'She never knew how to say goodbye . . . on the telephone.' She showed 'intellectual and moral incorruptibility'; 'clarity of thought'; 'a sense of purpose'; 'indomitable courage'; 'generosity and friendship', even to strangers such as hitchhikers. 'Truly, Hilda was a Renaissance woman.'

There is paradox and conflict in every one of us – even in the faces we show to the world. Hilda had her share of discord and inconsistency, but it all added up, in her writing as in her person, to a solid and integrated character of quite exceptional interest and charm. She was certainly meticulous and scientific in her observations, but at the same time a romantic; she was both passionate in her beliefs and fastidious in her attitudes; she liked nothing better than wilderness, but she dressed with a true sense of style; she subscribed with honest enthusiasm to the principle that the countryside was a heritage for all to enjoy – yet she 'fled' when she saw Porth Swtan's 'narrow sands . . . lined solid with Red-Indian-skinned bodies and royal blue and scarlet plastic'.

THE NATURAL HISTORY DIARIES
(1961–1983)

The late Diana Moss, who succeeded Hilda Murrell as Chairman of the CPRE Shropshire Branch Amenities Committee, was the first person to suggest that the Diaries (I shall use the initial capital hereafter when referring to the Natural History Diaries only) might be worthy of publication. She did not, however, feel competent to judge their technical merit, and sought advice from Joan Tate on where to get an opinion. It was through Joan that they came to my attention; my reaction is clear from the paragraphs that follow. I am only sorry that Di's untimely death, after a long illness, prevented her seeing them in published form.

My response to the CPRE's enquiry, communicated again through Joan Tate, indicated that I had been 'captivated' by the Diaries at first reading. The material sent to me consisted of two loose-leaf binders and an envelope of rough notes, unfinished drawings, and photographs, amounting in all to

'. . . some sixty thousand words of fair copy manuscript with many line drawings.

'The most expansive entries are day-to-day journals of holiday trips to Mallorca, Anglesey (more than once), Southwest Ireland and the Highlands of Scotland. Numerous but generally briefer notes record excursions made from her home in Sutton Road or her office at the nursery, to places as far away as Bath or Borth, or as near as Haughmond Hill. These visits are sometimes on nursery business but more often an escape from her work; sometimes on weekday evenings but more often on Sundays; sometimes with friends or botanical acquaintances, but more often alone.

'How deeply she felt about these interludes of freedom may be judged by the conclusion of the entry for 23 July 1961, after a weekend in North Wales: ". . . most perfect day . . . The sun and breeze tempered each other to a point of bliss and comfort rarely experienced. I left with desperate feelings about seven o'clock."

'Roughly two thirds of the text is taken up by lengthy and

meticulous botanical descriptions: word-pictures of wildflowers which she was seeing for the first time. As I would have expected, these accounts are thorough, accurate, graphic and lively; in the 330-word description of Bristly Oxtongue, for instance, she notes that the stems branch frequently "and at each joint there is a sessile leaf with cordate bases clasping the stem ferociously and reaching far back beyond it in a well-armed curve."

'It is, however, the vigour and beauty of her narrative style that has really caught my attention, whether she is recording her first impressions of a new place or plant, or expressing her joy at seeing again some well-loved view or bird or flower. Her drawings, too, some of which occupy a full page, surprised me by their precision and delicacy: I didn't know that the art of botanical illustration was one of Hilda's many self-taught talents.

'The Diaries are personal, but by no means private. One feels no sense of prying when reading them: indeed, there is evidence in the style and the corrections that Hilda was consciously writing for others to read. On the other hand, much of the botanical description is semi-technical and obviously written for her own benefit, as an aid to memory, but not of general interest – even to fellow-botanists.'

I have since revised my view on this last point, which I shall return to. Abbreviations and unfamiliar references have been explained; and detailed notes and cross-references have been added. I thought initially that 'Reproduction in facsimile would preserve much of the flavour of the original without being prohibitively costly.' Others disagreed, finding the photo-reduced manuscript difficult to read – especially so with its specialised terminology. The final decision to have the Diaries typeset has been based on publishing considerations: Collins believed they should be as easy to read as possible. Sample facsimile pages have been included (see pp. 212–215).

EDITING THE DIARIES

I had no doubt that the Diaries were worth publishing, in spite of the rather specialised character of their contents and the technical language used for the plant descriptions. This was why I had been approached in the first place. It was with some hesitation, however, that I offered to take on the responsibility of editing them: I had no previous experience of such work; I was engaged on another task which would have to be deferred – not for the first time; and although I had known Hilda for about 25 years, and respected her greatly, we were not really close friends. In the end two factors, one trivial and one weighty, made up my mind. The former was the fact that, in the 23-year period covered by the Diaries, Hilda had sought my botanical advice on only two occasions – and on both I had failed her! I owed her a professional debt, for her horticultural advice had been unstinted. The latter was the impotent anger I, and many others, felt at the manner of her death and its aftermath. As I wrote at the time:

'We owe her this memorial: a modest reflection of a marvellously unsullied person, and an antidote to the necrophagous [carrion-feeding] industry spawned by her tragic end.'

Volume I of the original Diaries contains 154 pages of manuscript, drawings and photographs (few of these, and mostly colour prints from transparencies): it covers the period 17 March 1961 (when Murrell's Nurseries were moving to Sutton) to 15 December 1963.

Volume II is 120 pages long, and runs from 29 December 1963 to 26 September 1983[?]. There are also some loose pages of untranscribed notes, mainly dealing with a botanical holiday in Savoy in May–June 1975 and a visit to Anglesey in June 1983, together with a few undated or unfinished drawings, a postcard or two, a letter from John Llewelyn Jones (see below), a quotation from Freya Stark (see page 8) and other miscellanea.

The distribution of this record over the 23 years, in number of pages per year, is strikingly uneven:

year	pages	year	pages	year	pages
1961	122	1969	1	1977	–
1962	25	1970	10 (retirement)	1978	2
1963	8	1971	15	1979	–
1964	39	1972	–	1980	2
1965	–	1973	6	1981	11
1966	4	1974	–	1982	17
1967	2	1975	[19 untranscribed]	1983	[12: 11 loose]
1968	2	1976	–		

The term 'Diaries' is hardly appropriate for so interrupted a record, but it has been common currency for this work among her friends, and is too late to change now.

Hilda presumably regarded the detailed botanical descriptions as the most important component in these two volumes – indeed, their *raison d'être*. Today, they are at once the main motive for publication and the greatest obstacle to reading the work. It is worth examining this paradox further.

For those not interested in plants, there is little to hold the attention through the wilderness of boredom between one purple passage of landscape description and the next. But the botanical notes are masterpieces of their kind. Because they deal with species which she has *not* met before, they are fresh and particular: they portray the actual specimen in front of her at the time, including its individual peculiarities. However, just as a photo of one's great-aunt Emily or one's nephew Gary is unlikely to provide a model for the 'ideal' *Homo sapiens*, so description of a single plant (however graphically written) cannot serve as the diagnosis for the entire species to which it belongs. Hilda's observation is truthful, precise, and she uses the technical language with easy skill: she was, after all, a professional rose-describer; but garden roses are bred for uniformity, and show far less variation than their wild relations.

The Diaries, then, are no substitute for a standard flora such as Clapham, Tutin & Warburg (1952, etc); so what was their purpose? I believe that, in the first instance, they were written to help Hilda herself to observe better, to remember, and to understand. So well did she succeed in this task that she came to realise she had created something worth sharing – and I agree with her. An interested reader can get pleasure and satisfaction from a well-written description of almost anything he or she can comprehend.

Deciding what to leave out and writing explanatory notes have been the main editorial functions. I have removed unfinished drawings; untranscribed records (rough notes and lists of species) for a visit to Provence in September 1970 and a holiday in Savoy in May 1975; records of a few relatively uninteresting business trips in England; incomplete descriptions; and an arbitrary selection of full botanical descriptions, some of them illustrated. I felt that the Diaries were more readable when pruned in this way. Fifty-five such entries survive, and are published in full; forty-five are still in as names only, with the descriptions amputated; approximately eighty have gone altogether. The omissions are listed at the end of the book, and † by the right-hand side of the text indicates from where they were omitted. The described inclusions are in the Index, under both scientific and English names.

Finally, at Collins' suggestion, I have divided the text into ten quite arbitrary 'chapters', so that the reader may pause and draw breath; each is headed by an appropriate phrase borrowed from its own contents.

SOME PERSONAL DETAILS

Hilda Murrell's eyesight was impaired: she had the use of her left eye only, the right having been irreparably damaged by an infection in infancy. She was always self-conscious about this, but did nothing to hide it. It did not inhibit her driving, but must have inconvenienced her in many ways. She used a monocular 'spy-glass' – not a telescope – for bird-watching, and a pocket lens (magnifying glass) for examining flowers: both referred to as 'the glass'.

The detail in her drawings and descriptions shows that her vision in the left eye remained acute as late as 1983. She had a professional interest in the exact observation of colours. It is possible, however, that her lack of binocular vision accounted, in part, for the difficulty she had in her fruitless search for Moonwort; and perhaps for her 'hostile' attitude to grasses, sedges and rushes: tall, thin green-and-brown plants are very hard to pick out against a brown-and-green-striped background without benefit of binocularity.

She was a photographer of intermittent enthusiasm but more than average competence, at least in colour. Her judgement of her own work must have been severe, for few prints found a place in the Diaries. She developed considerable skill at line drawing in pen or pencil, and showed some artistic flair. She was fanatical about the objective 'truth' of her drawings: having chosen the scale, she soldiered on, even if it meant running off the edge of the page.

Hilda was interested in the quality of her food and drink – as of so much else – but was neither a gourmet nor a glutton. Friends remember her as a skilful cook and an excellent hostess. She was not a vegetarian, though latterly she showed some sympathy with those who adopted the habit on moral grounds. Very few meals are mentioned in the Diaries, and none in detail, but she had a passion for brewing tea in the open air – at any time of day. This ritual is recorded many times. In the early days she 'boiled water collected in some wayside stream in an old enamel kettle over a much worn oil heating contrivance' (Con Purser); more recently 'she used a butane gas camping stove' (Robert Green), and got 'all her drinking water from the spring at Llanymynech' (Ruth Sinker). She particularly liked China tea, and she preferred it with milk, but she gave up taking sugar because 'it made her rheumatism worse' (Trina Paskell). Arthritis and migraines gave her a lot of pain. She dressed well, and with a real sense of style. She had, in particular, a passion for good fabrics, and would go miles out of her way to buy a skirt-length of Donegal tweed. She was also a keen collector of antique furniture.

One of Hilda's most innocent and endearing pleasures was her addiction to 'basking' in the sun in some sheltered private spot, often behind a hedge, on the edge of a field, and preferably commanding some magnificent view of distant mountains. If the site was well chosen and the weather tolerable, she would usually fall asleep for a while. Her basking was frequently associated with the tea-brewing ritual, and was not simply an antidote to fatigue. On 4 May 1972, she stopped no less than three times to bask or brew – or both – on the way from Shrewsbury to Beaumaris, a journey of less than one hundred miles on which she spent more than eight hours. Only once (p.91) does she record her basking being interrupted – by the farmer to whom the field belonged. She seems to have had no qualms about trespassing, nor about the possible dangers of this habit.

It would not have occurred to her to bask in company. Indeed, communal sunbathing on a public beach was an affront to Hilda's environmental sensibilities. Her enjoyment of her surroundings was enhanced by solitude and generally spoilt by crowds. A notable feature of the Diaries is the way they illustrate her capacity for solitary, incandescent joy – a truly spiritual joy which could be sparked by a view, a bird, a trick of light or weather.

PEOPLE IN THE DIARIES

Her Diaries give the impression that Hilda was never lonely, and that many of her happiest moments were spent alone. But she was solipsistic rather than selfish. She had several very good friends and devoted relatives, some of whom slip into the record almost unremarked – a casual christian name, an initial, a pronoun in the first person plural. They were welcome as companions on a walk or as drinkers of China tea, but they were not essential to her as sharers of her bliss.

She deeply appreciated the company of amateur experts: people who, like Hilda herself, had applied themselves to mastering a subject, and had reached a point where they could teach her something without displaying the impatient superiority of the professional. Edward Rutter, a retired railway executive who had made himself an outstanding authority on the birds and wild flowers of Shropshire, is a good example; Kim Dodwell, who retired from a tea-planter's life in India to become a skilled arboricul-turalist, is another.

She appreciated skill, dedication and enthusiasm wherever she saw them. In successive visits to Anglesey she records a growing but not uncritical appreciation of the wardens of several nature reserves. Nursery staff and gardeners are mentioned with affectionate respect. There is real depth of feeling in her references to the Morris family of Tynyfedwen, farmers in the isolated Maengwynedd Valley in her beloved Berwyn Mountains. Mr W. E. Morris still lives in this beautiful place; his wife died in 1974. Their eldest child, Ellen May, is married and now lives in a house not far away where Hilda used to spend weekends in the early 1950s. Maengwyn is the eldest son, Ellen May's younger brother.

Notwithstanding her love of solitariness, she enjoyed casual encounters and friendships made on the basis of common interests discovered by chance. She gives an impromptu lecture on megalithic monuments – one of her favourite subjects – to a no doubt rather bemused family party at Barclodiad y Gawres (p.172). In Scotland she picked up hitchhikers without hesitation, on one occasion inviting three of them back to her rented cottage for a meal.

In a handful of cases, she seems deliberately to pick on a local 'character' for more detailed description – almost as though she feels it is time to introduce some 'human interest'. Her treatment of these subjects is not unlike that of a botanical specimen or a bird (see, e.g., p.80). She would surely not have incorporated such passages – and the careful amendments to them – purely for her own edification.

PLACES IN THE DIARIES

Places were important in Hilda's world-view and philosophy. Her feelings about places were very strong: both as a transitory physical environment for her own spirit, and as the permanent home of the sort of people who live (and used to live) there.

She loved Wales with that deep but discriminating passion, not untinged by a glow of historical guilt, that is peculiar to the sensitive Saxon. Her feelings about Ireland (at least its mountainous southwest) were equally complicated, if less favourable. The Highlands of Scotland aroused her purest delight, and inspired some of her best writing.

She had a special fondness for deep views, and knew that a low viewpoint often commands a clearer and more satisfying panorama than a mountain-top: Snowdonia [Eryri] seen from the Pen-lôn dunes on Anglesey is a case in point. In spite of her useless eye, she had a sculptor's ability to visualise the three-dimensional structure of things, including the geological bones of the landscape (pp.125, 198). Her sense of history in the landscape was as sure as her instinct for geology. It is well illustrated by her visits to such places as Caer Din hill-fort in Shropshire, Glencoe and the Stones of Clava in Scotland.

Anglesey must have meant a great deal to her. She clearly knew it well before the start of the Diaries, and it takes up more pages than any other area. She usually stayed at the Bulkeley Arms in Beaumaris, or at Wern y Wylan. With its great variety of coastal habitats, and some very interesting mires, heaths and small lakes inland, Anglesey is an inexhaustible treasury for the naturalist. Besides Penmon near Beaumaris, she especially liked visiting Pen-lôn, Malltraeth ('the Cob') and Llanddwyn Island near Newborough in the south; South Stack and Porth Diana on Holyhead Island in the west; and Cemlyn Bay in the north.

Hilda's emotional roots, however, were always in the Welsh Marches, on both sides of the border. This country was close enough to escape into for less than a day: she could get away from work and worries into a sort of timeless childhood paradise, a fabulous land that was hers and hers alone. She could stand on the shoulder of Gyrn Moelfre and enjoy 'the swooping lines of the hills' to the west; around Glanhafon, at the head of the Tanat Valley, she could capture the afternoon sun; from Tynyfedwen farm, on the little river Iwrch, she could climb out of the valley into the heart of the Berwyns: the standing stone in Bwlch Maengwynedd, where her ashes are scattered on the open roof of Wales.

As the Diaries progress, an idea seems to be growing and taking practical shape in her mind: is she planning to make paradise her permanent home? On p.60 she visits Broniarth Hall near Guilsfield, and we read 'This is wonderful country' and 'The perfect house to my mind'. On p.70 she looks at Cefn Glaniwrch near Llanrhaeadr ym Mochnant. On p.112 she is cottage-hunting again, in the same area. In fact she had, by then, already bought the small steep plot of land [Maes Uchaf] at Fron Goch on the southwestern end of Llanymynech Hill, on which she was later to have a house built (1971 and 1974).

Maes Uchaf became her summer and weekend haven, but she never gave up the big house in Shrewsbury [if only she had!]. It is right on the Welsh border, high up under Offa's Dyke, and commanding a superb panoramic view to the west. Its immediate surroundings were equally appealing to her, for they provided an opportunity to make a garden on the Carboniferous limestone. This she did, over the years of her retirement, with such success that Richard Banks of Kington commented in September 1984: 'The choice of plants is quite exceptional in that so many of them are of special quality and character, and reflect the interests of a plantswoman of great perception and knowledge. The other outstanding feature of the garden is the combination of its beautiful and romantic setting with the choice and placing of the individual plants.'

The west-facing limestone scarp known as Blodwel Rock extends the hill northwards into Shropshire, where the names Llynclys Hill and Crickheath Hill are applied to it. The whole outcrop constitutes one of the richest botanical localities in the Borderland, and was a favourite haunt of Hilda's long before her 'shack' was built at Maes Uchaf. Edward Rutter knew it well, and may have introduced her to some of its most rewarding corners, whose biblical nicknames he himself had probably picked up from an earlier generation of amateur naturalists (members of the Caradoc and Severn Valley Field Club): the 'Holy of Holies'; 'Jacob's Ladder' (pp.49, 51).

HILDA MURRELL AS A NATURALIST

Although she would have regarded herself first and foremost as a botanist, Hilda's interests in natural history were catholic. Her approach to the study of animals and plants was serious and scientific, but she had a disarming way, in the Diaries, of making it clear which species were her favourites. Nothing gave her greater delight than to observe terns feeding (see pp.60–61). She also liked owls, and many of the smaller kinds of birds. Bird-spotting, in the first place, may not have been easy for her, but she was a patient and exact bird-watcher. This enthusiasm possibly introduced her to such friends as Edward Rutter, Frank and Hilly Gribble and, much later in her life, Charles Tunnicliffe and his wife. There is a painting in the Tunnicliffe Collection of two Guillemots (male) neatly inscribed 'Sept. 29th Obtained Menai Straits near Foel Ferry by Miss Murrell'. This may have been the work of which she wanted to obtain a copy (p.164), having been unable to buy the original.

Curiously enough, in spite of her impaired sight, her interest in birds seems to have remained primarily visual: she never developed a really good ear for bird song (though she was very fond of listening to good performances of classical music). She was fond of cats, from time to time adopting and caring for strays, but in general her attitude to animals was unsentimental.

Cobwebs figure prominently in some of her most evocative word-pictures (e.g. p.197), but as part of the fabric of the landscape, rather than as zoological phenomena. Her knowledge of marine biology was rudimentary, and on p.186 she seems to think an incrustation of barnacles is 'the small limpets which have holes in their tops'.

She was a very good botanist indeed. A natural aptitude for observing the significant detail in a plant specimen had been refined by her long professional experience as a rose expert. Though she was diffident about her knowledge and regarded herself strictly as an amateur, she had no hesitation in using the technical language which provides the necessary precision and brevity in the formal description of plant species, varieties and so on. [I do not intend to give a glossary of such terms in this book: the interested reader who is not already familiar with them can look them up in standard references such as Clapham, Tutin & Warburg (1952, etc.).]

Almost from the beginning of the Diaries (p.28), she shows a special interest in orchids and their strange [apparent] pollination mechanisms;

there is a good account of the Bee Orchid on pp.194–5. She is fascinated by the Purple-loosestrife (pp.61, 68–9, 70). Her discriminating taste would select an admired species (e.g. Tree-mallow) from a mediocre family (see p.76).

Spiny or shaggy composites [members of the daisy family, Compositae] held a particular fascination for her. The Bristly Oxtongue has already been mentioned; she devotes a great deal of attention to the Holyhead Island form of the Field Fleawort, *Senecio spathulifolius* (pp.100–102); she is still learning the thistles on pp.188–9.

Her belated attention to our native wild roses or briars – admittedly difficult to name, because they hybridise freely – may have been the result of her getting to know Mrs I. M. Vaughan of Cilycwm, the *Rosa* 'Referee' for the Botanical Society of the British Isles; she visited Cilycwm in June 1973, four years after joining the BSBI herself. She mentions this respectable body with a sardonic scepticism (pp.191–2); solemn gatherings of fellow-enthusiasts were not her cup of tea, and she preferred to slip away and brew her own.

Similar scruples, and her growing preoccupation with the threat of nuclear disaster, may account for the fact that she took no part in the ten-year-long survey for the Shropshire Flora (Sinker *et al.* 1985), though she could have been one of its most experienced and able contributors. She never enjoyed being organised by other people.

HILDA MURRELL AS A WRITER

Hilda kept diaries of one kind and another for many years. Nature Notes written in 1919 survive ('Today is cold and wet and windy – but our hen has laid thirteen eggs – the greatest number so far'). There is an essay, rich in atmosphere, dated 4 September 1941, entitled *Jelly d'Aranyi at Hereford*, which begins

> 'Dinmore Hill, willows by sleepy streams, a few oast-houses, red apples glinting in the orchard trees, grey village churches and half-timbered houses up to their ears in greenery: profound rusticity was the key-note of this country-side, utterly peaceful in the early autumn sun.'

By the start of the Natural History Diaries her style had matured. There is little real change over the twenty-three-year period covered, in spite of marked variation in texture and mood. She has developed and settled into a way of writing which, to some, may seem old-fashioned, unadventurous and over-embellished; but the florid surface conceals a strength and flexibility which serve her purposes well. They enable her to describe her botanical specimens fully and precisely; to deal with the flickering dynamics of bird flight; to capture the essential character of a landscape; and, through the winged lucidity with which she handles the intangibles of the atmosphere, to lead the reader into her private world of light.

In this, if not in her own religious beliefs, her line of descent is from the seventeenth-century metaphysical poets of the Welsh Borderland rather than from Wordsworth and W. H. Hudson. She read Traherne. She shared his capacity for sustained rapture of the intellect. Like his, her infancy was a world of orient and immortal wheat. She would have claimed, as he did, that in childhood 'The skies were mine, and so were the sun and moon and stars, and all the World was mine'; and that 'with much ado I was corrupted, and made to learn the dirty devices of this world: which now I unlearn'.

But the roots of her 'lyrical realism' go deeper still, and I have chosen an anonymous fragment from the mid-fifteenth century to compare (opposite) with one of her most limpid passages. Both exemplify the piece of advice for a good style by Freya Stark (see p.8), found in Hilda Murrell's handwriting on a slip of paper among her notes. There was much that Hilda wanted to say. Her ability to blend accuracy with poetry in her style gave her word-pictures more than mere precision: the best of them reverberate with truth.

Charles Sinker
Mytton, 1987

The marvels continued after dinner, when a huge moon came up over the shoulder of the Carnedds and floated behind an openwork fabric of cirrus cloud. The band where the moon was moved across it darkly with silver heavens behind: above and below, the tones were reversed and the clouds were ice-floes on blue-black depths. Below again was a solid band of softer cloud, dove-coloured like the mountains, and the silver path of the moonshine across the water.

HM 22 September 1961

Vpon a faire clere night ye skye garnyshed with sterres oute of number shynneth goodely: which and ye take hede ye may see them twinkle as it were a candle or a tapre brennyng and among them ye moone with hir full lighte glidinge softly: :: :: : be these not pleasant thinges?

Anon. 1451

I

FULL OF LUSTRE
AND PROMISE

March 1961 · Mallorca

17 March, Friday

By BEA Viscount to Palma, Mallorca. It was a wonderfully clear sunny day so that although we flew at 20,000 feet we could see everything – the Surrey pines and little hills, the irregular English fields outlined by dark hedges, then Eastbourne and Beachy Head – and we were over the Channel looking down on ships like tiny, white flies on the blue. France seemed very thinly populated after Surrey and Sussex, and the fields were an endless monotony of hedgeless rectangles. It was about two-thirds of the way down before we saw a French hedge, and soon afterwards we skirted the Massif Central and the geography became more interesting. We could see a whole river-basin with the tributaries cutting their way through green or grey hills which had a limestone look about them. Then the brown slopes began, and the Pyrenees came up towards us – first dark with white in the creases, then more solid white, and then the summit ridges with the peaks strung out along them, each a strangely flattened pyramid of three triangles, two white and one brown. In a snow-filled basin among them part of a stream showed like a thin black snake, both ends disappearing under the drifts so that from our eagle's view we could not tell which way it flowed. We passed right over Andorra, lying between two upfolds of the range, brown and bony and very sparsely inhabited, its tiny roofs scattered like square red beads on the bare earth. The southern mountain wall is not as high as the northern one but still had snow on it; after that we followed the brown slopes of Spain down to Barcelona and the sea.

A mat of white cloud was lying off Mallorca, lapping like waves against the cliffs which are the foot of the western mountain range. A splendid fine-pointed peak and a square-topped castle rose high above the rest. We passed to the south of them, and then over pine-covered foothills which ran down to the central plain of rich red earth as flat as the sea. It is thick with windmills, for the mountains send down no water, and the skies precious little either, as we found later.

All over the place was a handsome plant of the lily family with pink-tinged flowers in a tall spike – in the dusty roadside, in the walls, in the edges of the fields – in every possible nook and cranny – just like the garlic in Scilly. Euphorbia in solid yellowish clumps was another frequent roadside weed. We drove through the coastal part of Palma and back towards the southwestern tip of the island, through Paguera to Cala Fornells on its own little bay.

After tea we walked into the woods behind the hotel. They are almost entirely of a silver-barked pine with light foliage, *Pinus halepensis* (Aleppo Pine), the larger darker Corsican Pine growing only in ones and twos here and there. There is very little soil: the rock is a kind of brown tufa on the shore, running into a silvery limestone inland, breaking red-brown. Under the trees, the ground is a white dry gravel, sometimes sand, only partly covered with vegetation, in which the main plants are a yellow genista with silvery leaves, a pink cistus and a blue shrubby 'cornflower'.

The *Genista* grows 2–4 feet high, very erect, the stems and spirally-placed lanceolate leaves all silvered with what turns out under the glass to be a very fine and close tomentum, mixed with silky hairs. The flowers are in the eight or nine uppermost axils, six to eight on a ½-inch stem, with a bract at the base and a sienna-brown point at each side of it. The calyx is creamy-yellow with five fine points and long silky hairs. The flower is pure buttercup-yellow, the erect standard deeply creased in the middle and with three to five dark rust-coloured lines, but these vary. Wings fairly spreading, anthers pale cream. The leaves are trefoil, with the two side-leaflets less than half the size of the middle one. *Anthyllis cytisoides*? †

The cistus has flowers a good 2 inches across, of *Rhododendron ponticum* colour, each petal with a lemon-yellow base. A mass of deep gold stamens surround a pale green pistil, which has a deep gold boss of a stigma level with the stamens. Leaves sage-like, finely felted, sessile, meeting in pairs round the pale hairy stem. This too grows about 3 feet high. Here and there were Rosemary bushes in flower. The cistus is probably *C. albidus.*

Turning left and uphill, we came out on an open headland between the pinewoods and the cliffs. It was flat-topped, mostly limestone pavement and gravel in between, with all kinds of flowers and bushes growing so lavishly that it might have been a garden but for the lack of conscious arrangement, which made it all the more attractive. The ubiquitous lily swayed in the wind, and there were bushes of cistus and lavender and other maquis shrubs unknown, with tiny plants in the cracks of the rocks below them.

The lavender was *L. stoechas*, with fresh green leaves crowded at the base of the stem, silver behind and with tiny scalloping all around the edges and deep-cut veins. The flower-stems were square, each side grooved, and with silvery tomentum. The flowers in the spike were quite small, five petals joined in a tube with golden anthers in the throat. The spike has bracts in pairs – enormous bracts compared with the size of the flowers – each pair set at right angles to the ones above and below. Every bract has five flowers behind it, peeping over the edge like young birds out of a nest. At the bottom of the spike the bracts are dark brownish-purple with a scattering of white meal, but in the upper half they become even larger and have the colour and texture of petals, making a showy flaunting tip.

The 'lily' is *Asphodelus aestivus*, a most beautiful plant, with a tuft of Tritoma-like leaves at ground level. These have a sharp midrib below and turn to rich shades of brown and copper. The flower-stem is rounded with a hint of the triangular, glaucous with a copper flush, and ends in a branched spike; each branch has a long pointed showy bract. The flowers are on ½-inch stalks of pinky-brown. The six petals are clean white, each with a central brown vein which is edged with palest salmon-pink. The six stamens are placed exactly over the veins and are the same length as the petals. They are also pale pink with vivid orange anthers. The stigma is a long white thread. The final cluster of flower-buds is richly flushed with coppery-pink and lined with brown veins. The height varied from 2 to 4 feet according to the richness or reverse of the terrain.

In the limestone pavement were some *Orchis pyramidalis* varying in colour from white through blush to clear rose. It had a very fine long spur, double the length of the rest of the flower, and the two upstanding ridges at the base of the lip. There were no flowers of the strong magenta tone seen in *O. pyramidalis* at home.

All over the limestone pavement were plants of a small *Arum* which seemed to be able to push up through the hardest surfaces. The leaves were frequent, the flowers much less so. It was an evil-looking, cobra-headed thing, dusky nigger-brown at the hood, with dark stripes running down on a pale background and a pale green tongue hanging out. The leaves had white meal on the surfaces, and faded quickly to a very beautiful pale bronze colour. They lay flat on the ground, and we found them coming up in the middle of roads, under bushes, through the merest cracks in the rocks – all over the place. We found one or two spikes of green berries like Lords-and-Ladies. The flowers faded to a coppery-purple. This is *Arum arisarum* or *Arisarum vulgare.*

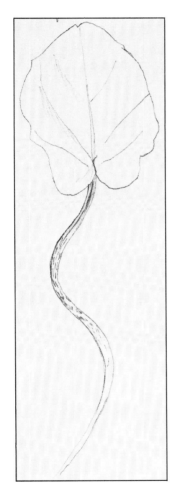 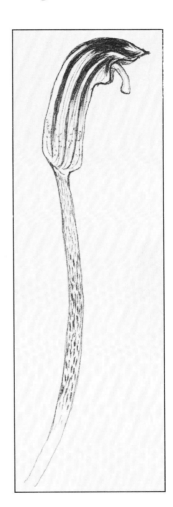

Arisarum vulgare (Friar's cowl)

Muscari comosum
(Tassel hyacinth)

Also in the limestone pavement was a strange-looking plant which we felt reminded us of a Grape Hyacinth, and we were right. It is *Muscari comosum*. It had about three very long folded leaves, glaucous, stained with crimson and withered brown at the tips. The flower-spike (on a round glaucous stem) had two quite distinct kinds of flowers. The top was a whirling Catherine-wheel of curved ½-inch stems in vivid violet, with darker buds, the uppermost no larger than pin-heads. Below these were larger flowers on ¼-inch stalks of pale green-primrose, the bells a wonderful shade of smooth yellow-brown, deepening towards the drawn-in mouth to grey-brown. The six little points indicating petals were primrose again. Below these were the withered flowers, dead ash-brown with a white stigma-tip protruding. The purple flowers are rudimentary and never mature – they just provide a panache of rich colour. The seed-vessel is three-sided.

At one end of the headland the limestone swept round in a beautiful curve to a dead pine tree with a tall white trunk. This became our landmark for a 3-foot bush near by into which a dim little Clematis had climbed.   †

A statuesque umbelliferous plant was the most decorative object on this hilltop. *Daucus aureus.*   †

By this time it was clear that every plant was provided with some means of protection against the semi-desert conditions, a scattering of white meal, or hairs, or succulent leaf-texture, or an all-over silver cast – any form of whiteness or thickness against the heat to come. Even if it was not apparent at the first view, it showed up under the glass.   †

18 March, Saturday

Sitting on the shore in the afternoon, I heard the same warbling birds as we had heard in the wood the evening before. They were very elusive, but in the end I did manage to get a glimpse of one with a grey back, black head and dark tail. It seemed likely that this was a Sardinian Warbler, but I did not feel I had seen enough of it to be sure.

In the evening I went up on the open limestone slope to the right of the road into the woods. These birds were singing all around me but I could never get a glimpse of them. Also several tiny greenish birds flitted from one pine tree to another: they must have been either Goldcrests or Firecrests, but as I couldn't see their heads they couldn't be recorded either. Bird-watching in these woods is not easy as the trees are thick with cones about the size of a bird.

On this slope I found several new flowers. There were small gladioli 6–9 inches high, very fine and dainty, with magenta flowers growing in the very driest spots such as cracks in the rocks. It seems this could be   †
Gladiolus illyricus.

In the same place was (Scarlet) Pimpernel of which only one plant was scarlet; all the others had flowers of strong gentian-blue, with a band of crimson at the base of the petals and a white throat. The leaves are sessile and spotted with chocolate below.

19 March, Sunday

We walked through the woods to Camp de Mar. These pinewoods have nothing of the dark-carpeted close gloom of the north – they are sparse and shot through with light, which is reflected from white limestone gravel or pale sand; the darkest note among the silver curves of the pine branches with their golden-green mops, and the carpet of silky-silver broom budding yellow at the tips, is the rich green and copper-brown of a heath still carrying its last-year's flower-heads. This must be *Erica mediterranea* – about 3 feet high.   †

We turned right on the footpath to Camp de Mar, which was spelled out in stones on the ground with a large arrow pointing the way. A few yards further on, MIMI and ⟜▷ in the same medium, advertised the attractions.

In the sandiest driest places were plants of a little rock-rose with golden-yellow flowers.   †

Only a few yards further on, we found our first orchid, just by the edge of the path under the pine trees. It was quite short – 1–2 inches, with a rosette of broad leaves spreading outwards at ground level and a narrow

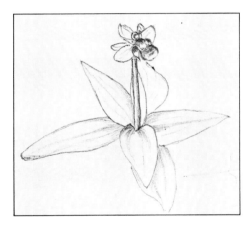

Ophrys bombyliflora
(Bumble-bee Orchid)

one sheathing the stem. *Ophrys bombyliflora.* It had two broad green side-sepals, the lip was chocolate-coloured, lighter at the tip. The small side-petals were also dark brown, and furry and were closely hunched-up like the legs of a bumble-bee. There was also a greenish 'head' with a vermilion stripe across it – the only bright colour in this very dusky flower. The end of the lip was not so tightly curled under as in the English Bee Orchid.

'I found a washed-up tree-trunk covered with barnacles that were both revolting and beautiful.'
(see p.46)

'We went round the coast to Llangelynin, where I got a good photograph of the church.' (see p.47)

Snowdonia with snow from Newborough Warren.

Hilly and Frank by wall – 'a wonderful sweep of country'. *(see p.64)*

A little further on were two really beautiful stems of a more colourful variety. There were three leaves at the base, 2–2½ inches long and averaging an inch wide. The flower-stem was 6 inches high and had one narrow short leaf near the bottom. The hood and sepals were pale green. The two small 'ears' (square-tipped) were more yellowish. The very large broad lip had three lobes, the middle one projecting and again indented. It was mainly reddish-chocolate with a greenish-yellow edge, with two elongated electric-blue marks in the upper part, and all velvety, mottled and scattered with meal. But not furry. The nearest to this is *Ophrys fusca* (in the green sepals and shape of the lip) but the blue patches are not mentioned. 'Orchids of Europe' produced the solution. This is *Ophrys lutea*. Quite a rarity.

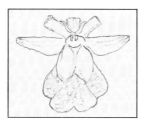

Ophrys lutea

We came down to Camp de Mar by a dry torrent-bed of a path and found the usual tiny *mas* with a tower like a Moorish fortress near it and two or three soaring graceful date-palms. The Asphodel was everywhere as usual, and here had a smaller sister growing with it – *Asphodelus fistulosus*. It averaged 2 feet in height, the leaves were fine and grass-like,

Asphodelus aestivus (Asphodel)

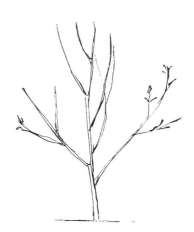

Asphodelus fistulosus

33

and three-sided. The flowers are *slightly* smaller, and the stamens, instead of being spread out evenly, one over the centre of each petal, are clustered together and bent downwards, and the pistil with them. The anthers are dark brown and the stigma only is bright orange. The branching of the flower-spikes is also quite different.

We had tea on the hotel terrace and then walked round to the north of the *mas* by way of a change on the return journey. There was a very large fig tree with silvery bark.

Then, in the broad verge of the road, we found another orchid with electric-blue in the lip, but this one also had fur: *Ophrys speculum*. The cap was green with brown shading, and the two little horns at the side were dark reddish-chocolate. The sepals were dirty white running to pale

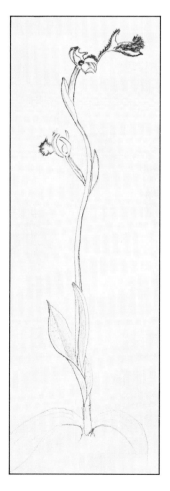

green at the tips, with chocolate bands. The pollinia were pale yellow and the semi-circle below them was black with a chocolate spot. The centre of the lip was electric-blue, running right up to the top, surrounded by tawny-yellow with hints of brown and green in it. The fur was rich chocolate-colour. The curled-under divided tip below the fur was light crimson.

Ophrys speculum (Mirror Orchid)

34

In the edges of the little fields there was an embarrassing profusion of flowers. Spurges and legumes were the most plentiful. One of the most interesting vetches had a broadly-winged leaf-stem which grew out of the blade of the leaf below so that, seen edgeways, it had a fascinating zig-zag pattern. The texture of the whole plant was smooth and slightly glaucous. The flowers were pale greeny-white with the faintest grey lines on the standards. Two pods developed at home in water, three weeks later, and were as individual in shape as the plant: they had a shoe, or ski, at right angles to the pod.

Coming back through the wood, I was browsing around where we found the first orchids, and noticed some beautifully marbled cyclamen leaves.

Lathyrus ochrus

These were the usual size for wild Cyclamen, perhaps 2½ inches across. The flowers were so tiny I nearly missed them, on thread-like stalks of perhaps an inch and a half, pearly white with the merest hint of shell-pink and about the size of one's little-fingernail. So tiny and so exquisite and in such arid ground. This is *Cyclamen balearicum* – the half-sized variety of *C. repandum* peculiar to these islands.

20 March, Monday

On Colonel Dawe's advice we walked in the afternoon to the cliffs beyond Paguera. Beyond the village there is a sandy bay without houses where I picked *Cakile maritima* (Sea Rocket).   †

We went on to the cliffs, which seemed a completely desert region with very little vegetation. There was *Fumana* (the yellow rock-rose) and cistus, but very little else. So we turned inland, into the pinewoods, and very soon found orchids. One was an *Ophrys* of the pink-sepalled group. It was 4–5 inches high, with the usual basal rosette of about three broad leaves, and one finer one enfolding the lower part of the stem. The flowers were the largest yet, about an inch from top to bottom. The sepals were all clear rose (including topmost 'petal') with just a hint of lilac in it, and a central green vein, all three back-swept. The two little pointed ears were the same colour. The small horny hood over the pollinia was dark purple at the base behind, running up to green between two bands of pale yellow at the end. The lip was very large, greenish-primrose with a large copper-red velvet diamond-shaped patch, cut at the top by two slanting double white lines. The velvet almost becomes fur at the bottom of the lip, which has a wide notch with a thick curled-up primrose horn in it. This grew in the driest most unpromising-looking places, in what looked like mere dust. *Ophrys scolopax.*

Of a green orchid in the same sandy pinewood, we found only two, but they were much less conspicuous, although taller – about 8 inches high. The sepals, back petals and ears were all clear green, like the stems, with soft yellow pollinia. The lip was flat, with three lobes, the central one square with a slight notch, maroon-velvet edged with a fine line of green, and with two cream-silk long pointed patches in the upper part. These patches in their turn were spotted with dull maroon. A smaller flower than the last, not of an exquisite clear-cut elegance. This is *Ophrys fusca.*

In the sandy pinewoods we found two new cistuses. One was short and

Ophrys fusca

spreading, and had sage-like leaves and pure white unspotted flowers about the same size as the *C. albidus*. I think this is *C. salviæfolius*.

The other was quite different – very erect, very bright green with very narrow long pointed leaves so that we wondered if it was a *Lithospermum*. It was not in flower but I found a fairly advanced bud and opened it and the petals were white. This must be *C. ladaniferus*. In a hollow beyond the first cliff, a little flock of Swallows was circling round.

There was a dampish ditch or cut running out to the sea in which there was Fennel.

We came out on the main road just opposite some fields with a *mas* behind. In the background was a beautiful peak of Matterhorn shape and in the fields a man was ploughing with a mule. I took photographs of this and also of a man in a mule-cart who came along just at that moment. I also took a group of four very large gum trees (eucalyptus) which were at one corner of the farm. On the opposite side were very large bamboos which had flowered last year but had not died. In the ditch by the road was an old friend, Alexanders. †

21 March, Tuesday

This was the hottest day of the whole week and we spent all the middle of the day lazing on the shore. After breakfast we went up to the Camp de Mar path to get details of the blue *Ophrys*, in case the photographs should be a failure. On the way we really saw the Sardinian Warbler – but not its red eye. It has a grey back, velvety-black head, slightly less deep black tail, and light underparts. This is the bird we have heard most of in the woods, a musical warble ending in a scolding note. It is always on the move, flicking from branch to branch, from tree to undergrowth, and from bushes to the ground, so that it is very difficult to get any continuous view of it. This proved to be my only Mediterranean bird!! after all the Hoopoes etc. which were going to hop round my feet.

We came back to the rocks by the hotel and I brewed China tea. While I was doing this, a huge butterfly flapped past; it was pale yellow with dark edges to the wings and dark markings and veinings. Swallowtail is as near as I can get.

After tea we went up to the limestone pavement to get photographs. I took the Clematis, and the umbelliferous plant silhouetted against the bare sea; there was a handsome and symmetrical plant standing alone just where the slope fell away. Also various other combinations of umbellifer, cistus and asphodel.

With the field-glass we could study some of the inland topography. There was a typical Spanish hill-village high on a hillside well behind Paguera, standing on a rather hollowed-out platform, with a windmill on each side of it higher on the ridge. We could see the church and its brown facade and longed to go there; it looked completely native with no tourist hotels or flats. We planned an expedition for the next day – I thought to this hill-village – but when we came to put the plan into action it seemed K meant somewhere quite different and a long geographical argument followed.

22 March, Wednesday

In the end we set out for Santa Ponsa, which was just as well, because the hill-village must have been Capdella and we could never have reached it. The hotel provided us with four *huevos*, meat, cheese and the usual hunks of bread, and we set out, first to Paguera, and from there on the main road to Palma. Soon it was making terrific loops which we were able to short-cut across dry clearings in the pinewoods. Any little hollow that had accumulated enough soil had been cleared of wild trees and planted with olives or almonds. The olives always seemed to have been mutilated: as soon as a limb reached a reasonable size, it was lopped off, so that the trees were in all sorts of contorted shapes, and often no more than twisted half-hollow boles; like the Holly forest on the Stiperstones, they had rock-like bodies of a thousand years which still could throw up young saplings full of lustre and promise.

Just as we were beginning to tire, a hotel bus came along, and an Englishwoman in it arranged a lift. In this way, we were whisked about five miles, into entirely different scenery. Where these roads met, we decided to get out, and a tip to the driver settled the question of fares.

We were now among the largest fields we had seen yet. The pine-covered hills had retreated into the background and we were in a region of rich red soil. The fields had widely-spaced rows of almond trees so that other crops could be grown in between. The almonds, which at home would be venturing some pink buds, had half-grown nuts; their blossoming must have been in mid-winter. The road south led to Santa Ponsa. In the angle between this and the Palma road was a brown *mas* with several tall date-palms waving over it. In the opposite corner was a mound, and on it a disused round windmill without sails. Near this was a sunny bank on which we decided to have lunch, after making sure there were no snakes.

This bank as usual had Asphodel growing on it. There was also the Scarlet (royal blue) Pimpernel. The rest I forget. We were hungry. K disposed of three *huevos* with ease, besides other oddments. We were also thirsty but as she did not approve of the *mas* for a water-supply we looked like remaining so. I settled down with the idea of a siesta, but was soon roused again by the sound of sheep-bells; a whole flock, raddled to a beautiful tawny-pink, with black and white lambs, was coming down the road. I rushed out with the camera, only to find that if I got in front of them so that the bells were in the picture, I was pointing straight into the sun. There was also a formidable cloud of dust. By the time I had got into the right position they were moving away from me into the field opposite. However, I took them, though the bells do not appear, nor the best lambs.

By the time this was over, K had discovered that the mill had a well. This was like finding an oasis in the Empty Quarter. Moreover it had a quite large, and quite clean, tin, on a 15-foot rope. We let it down, and drew up water that was clear and sparkling. The field-kitchen went into action forthwith, and while the kettle boiled, photographs were taken of this memorable spot. All round the base of the wall was a series of little fireplaces, two stones and an iron bar across, and scattered about were earthenware crocks, mostly black and broken. There was also a heap of sticks and brushwood. Perhaps the sheep-shearers met here, or the almond-pickers? We had our China tea, and I decided that of all the many places where I have brewed, this was the most delectable.

The windmill had a curving ramp leading up to a platform, from which we spied a *capella* about a mile away, at the foot of a little pine-covered hill; we decided to make this our objective, and set off along the straight tarmac road. It was much better than most tarmac roads because it had fairly frequent pine trees which gave shade, and because there were very wide earth verges with all sorts of flowers and splendidly-built dry walls separating these flower-borders from the fields. At the foot of the one on the left was a beautiful sprawl of *Convolvulus althæoides* – I think the loveliest of all the plants we found. The stem was hairy and mealy, the leaves roughly triangular but almost pinnate with irregular lobes, dull dark green, also hairy and mealy. The 2–3-inch flower-stalks grew from the axils, and were hairy, like the calyx, which was stained with black. The corolla was ravishing pure rose, with much darker feathering down to the base, which was white. The ribs on the outside of the trumpet were picked out in soft pale green. The five stamens were dark plum-rose, with a plush of pollen on the outer side of the anthers. The stigma was the same colour, and was in two long branches. There was a clump of yellowish *Euphorbia* on one side of this and of *Muscari comosum* on the other, with swirling violet heads.

We arrived at the Capella de San Jaime which marks the conquest of the island by King James of Spain in 1209. It was tiny, apsidal, nearly as wide as long and set with perfection against the hillside. The outer wall made a first platform and its broad flight of steps another; the pine trees framed and shaded it. We rested under them, and then set out on the fair number of miles that now lay between us and Cala Fornells, knowing quite well that we couldn't walk them all. We hadn't gone half a mile when the Paguera bus came along and, in a twinkling, we were sitting on the terrace of the Vilarmil drinking *té con leche*. Truly this was a lucky day. †

23 March, Thursday

In the afternoon we went into Paguera and then for a walk into the hills and woods to the left of the main road. Just beyond Paguera, before we turned off, we found two beautiful heads of *Allium roseum* ssp. *roseum* by the roadside, a foot from the tarmac. The stems were 18 inches high, slender and round. The spathe had divided in two. The individual flowers were on stalks about ¾ inches long. The petals were half an inch long, almost rounded at the tip, suffused with pale lilac-rose. Anthers dull gold on white filaments. No bulbils. Leaves prostrate or at any rate weak.

We climbed up and round the little hills by rough brown roads, and came to a *mas* which for once was painted white. It looked as if the road ended in a vast manure-heap, but both parts of this supposition were wrong: the road went on beyond – and it was no manure-heap, but piled up chaff on a threshing-floor, a very large circle of dry walling about 3 feet high. It was impossible to tell whether this was a platform with the floor at the level of the top of the wall – or a 3-foot enclosure filled to the brim with the debris of many harvests. The chaff and straw were of a kind I did not know – dead-leaf brown, and with a large fuzzy head. †

We went on into the hills beyond the *mas*. They were covered with the usual Silver Pines, cistus and broom; the soil was very thin and poor. There were no new flowers. I climbed up on a little crag from which there were fine views of the 'Matterhorn' and its neighbouring mountain, also very shapely, and took several photographs of them with silver pine-trunks in the foreground. On the way back I also tried to get the threshing-floor but there was no possibility of getting the whole circle. I could only get a small segment, which does not explain itself.

24 March, Friday

We left Cala Fornells in a car at 11.30, to make a short tour of the southwest corner of the island. The first place we came to was Andraitx, in a long wide scoop of a valley: the church stood out stark at the top, earthen brown and almost windowless. It had a cluster of houses around it which were visible, but below them the place was drowned in trees; one saw glimpses of red roofs, but the further down the valley they were, the deeper they were submerged. Higher up, and round the next hairpin bend, was the town's cemetery. This was a rectangular walled enclosure with many little alleyways in it, whose sides were compartments for funeral urns. Mallorca cannot spare earth for burial. Cypresses trimmed the corners: a neat and sensible place. Just beyond it was an orange tree of good size, blazing with hundreds of ripe fruit.

We crossed the next height and went down a long defile with the sea in a blue V at the bottom. Then we turned right on to a corniche road, which had its full share of Mallorcan twists and turns, and no wall on the outer side. Along here we met a herd of small mules and some foals, all with bells. Then we came into Estallenchs, a poorish-looking place where however we were bidden to go sight-seeing by the driver. Two climbing roses were flowering on the house where he stopped the car, and were growing with lustrous vigour. We went to look at the church, which was not remarkable. The padre came to talk to us; he wore a round pill-box hat with a peach velvet rim embroidered with flowers. It turned out that someone from Cambridge visited there every year and played the organ in the church! He picked flowers out of the minute churchyard and gave them to us. They were very like freesias but not freesias, copper-red with wonderful markings in the throat. (Tigridias?)   †

We were not far from Bañal Bufar when a patch of soft blue flowers made us stop the car. These turned out to be *Vinca major* (Greater Periwinkles), but much paler than usual – a clear light lavender, much prettier than the English version. What was our astonishment to hear the sound of running water – for the very first time in this parched land. It was dripping off the cliffs above and made a boggy patch beside the road, in which was a colony of garlic. This turned out to be *Allium triquetrum* – the variety which grows all over the Scillies. It had broad triangular stems with very sharp angles, a thin papery covering for the buds which split in two, and a head of exquisite flowers of long-campanulate shape. The six narrow pointed petals have green lines down the centre which do not quite reach the tips, and are arranged in a pattern of interlocking triangles (three outer petals and three inner ones). The six soft yellow stamens fit into the triangular space: There are nine to eleven flowers in a head, their stems ½–1 inch from the sheath.

Bañal Bufar also boasted a stream, and dozens of cultivated terraces and their blue-green reservoirs filled their recess in the mountain wall. Perhaps this was why it looked so much neater and more prosperous than Estallenchs. They grew tomatoes, and early potatoes – and a vine peculiar to the place which produces a huge golden grape. We had the wine from this at lunch, with wonderful local food; it was light and mellow and 3 shillings a bottle, so I bought one. The Mar i Vent Hotel rises like a cliff from the little terraces and is cool, stone-paved and interesting. There was a grandfather clock in a balloon-shaped painted case, brown with an edging of flowers. The dining-room was hung with antique majolica plates. The soup arrived in a large round earthenware crock with a slightly pointed bottom, so that it had to be stood in another bowl. The soup was wonderful.

All along this very steep, in places precipitous, coast, we noticed that the Silver Pine had become fastigiate, as though reaching desperately upwards for the morning light. This was all the more remarkable because it was not an upright or even pyramidal shape by nature. All the trees among the small foothills on the other side of the range tended to have round mop-heads on long spindly bare trunks, or even horizontally-spreading ones.

We left Bañal Bufar reluctantly. The road turned inland and worked its way through the mountains in a series of swoops and swirls which seemed to lead to nothing but another series. One saw a valley opening out ahead but found that to reach it the road had to contour round a side-valley, and then again in that one so that one was frequently facing almost backwards in order to progress forwards. When we really were getting down the other side we came to ancient olive-groves where the trees are said to be 2000 years old. The lopped, twisted, coiled and hollowed trunks looked incapable of passing upward anything so vital as sap – and the stony ground of supplying it.

We came to Esporlas, which was a sun-trap and comparatively lush, with ripe oranges and lemons in many gardens. A river-bed ran alongside the road. It had not a drop of water in it. We went on to Palma by the side-road, through more millenial olive-trees. The last miles into the city were one long string of mule-carts with barrel-shaped hoods, going in for the evening market. They had baskets slung on below, just like the Acton Burnell carrier's cart of fifty years ago.

Palma on the whole was disappointing. At the door of the cathedral we met Colonel Dawe, who was pathetically pleased that we had enjoyed the drive, which he had planned for us in every particular.

In an antique-shop next door was a bullfighter's cloak in heavy rich silk, vivid pink lined with gold. Price about £25. K bought a wooden figure of Don Quixote.

In the cathedral were many sight-seers and a tiny group of worshippers at the stations of the Cross (it was Friday). The priest arrived casually and opened his book, the people flopped down just where they were on the bare stone floor, with a beautiful spontaneity and quite oblivious of spectators.

25 March, Saturday

We went into the town and bought glass. From the bus I spied Bellver blocking the end of a street and thought the rest of the morning could be better spent up there than in the rather murky city (never washed by a good downpour). So we went up in a taxi. Bellver no doubt was built for defence and served its purpose: if it had been specially planned to please a photographer it could not have been more effective. At entrance level there were gun-emplacements, scalloped moat and fairy-tale towers – and the inevitable Asphodel growing in the ramparts. The next floor was a circular cloister with arches of ravishing design. From here a staircase-tower took us to the roof where the cloister-well and its ribbed tiles made a perfect foreground for the long harbour-mole and the headland beyond it, or the hills with roads zig-zagging to high-perched villas on the inland side.

We came down by a broad-stepped staircase cut in the hillside, to little alleys between villas and tantalising glimpses of shady patios with plants in huge earthenware pots. One garden had a huge Judas-tree in solid perfect bloom against the blue sky.

After a wonderful lunch at the Victoria (which has a terrace with pine trees growing through it facing the harbour-mole) we set off alas! for the airfield. I took three photographs of the windmills on the way. In the waiting-room I tipped over the basket with the three glass vases in. There was a horrible tinkle; I didn't look, I couldn't bear it. Not even to get them out of the country!

We hopped as far as Barcelona by Iberia. This is a very different affair from BEA. No word of comfort or encouragement, either written or spoken. Two engines instead of four. It taxied round the runway and then stood revving up with such a shattering noise and vibration that I wondered if I should survive the take-off, never mind the journey. K remarked that it was like a bull in the arena, roaring and pawing the ground before the charge. Once aloft, the pilot had no more regard for our tummies than he had had on the ground. Every now and then he noticed the mountain-range ahead and thought he had better get higher. Once we were out over the Mediterranean, progress was more even but seemed very slow.

At last we came to the Spanish coast off Barcelona. There is a dead flat stretch of country running inland, with a band of pine trees along the shore and a coast-road behind them. In this terrain the airfield was ready-made. The BEA Viscount was a welcome sight. Should we have the same luck with the Pyrenees? We climbed up and before long were over the foothills – and then in front of us was a great bank of cloud sloping up and up, furrowed and ridged and here and there with deep blue canyons – a wonderful sight in itself but not the one I had been hoping for. Then suddenly one of the canyons was not blue but bottomless – until in the grey-brown depth I realised I was looking at earth and tiny red roofs. Hope went up with a bound – this was Andorra, and the cloud was piled against the seaward wall. It thinned out and by the time we came to the higher range was providing a foreground of softest white and blue to all the giant heights to the westward, ridge beyond ridge, culminating in a superb group of peaks whose glaciers were flashing like glass in the sunlight. It was infinitely more beautiful than the outward view because it was more subtle, remote and mysterious. These mountains were entirely silver and floated in the sky.

2

I LEFT WITH DESPERATE FEELINGS

March – July 1961 · Mid-Wales, Shropshire & Marches, Anglesey

31 March, Friday

Afternoon to Corris via Dinas Mawddwy and Talyllyn. Greater Stitchwort in flower thick in all the hedge-banks. Came into a murk at Cross Foxes and had to travel with lights on over the pass to Talyllyn. Brynhyfryd a very nice house. Made myself very snug with camp bed and Dunlopillo mattress.

1 April, Saturday

Set off with Frank and Hilly to see if there was anything interesting in Borth Bog. Stopped at Furnace to photograph the old mill-building and the waterfalls.

In the bog we soon found *Andromeda polifolia*, a good deal of it in flower. This seems early. We crossed a number of dykes and arrived back at the car for a very late lunch. The clouds were down right on the foothills.

After this we went out to the end of the road beyond Ynyslas. We parked the car and walked through the sand-dunes on the shingle-bank. Here I found a washed-up tree-trunk (it looked like a pine) covered with barnacles that were both revolting and beautiful. They hung on stalks or tubes attached to the wood; these attachments looked like something between rubber and leather and hung flabbily. On the end was the shell, golden yellow at the hinge and all the rest dove-grey; this was exquisite, but a sinister claw peeped from between the pairs of shell, blackish-brown like the stalk and even more horrible. We took photographs of these sinister creatures.

We then drove through Borth to the cliff end of the village with a few stops. Scurvygrass was growing on the shingle near the station road. Hyfrydle looked very down-at-heel and in dire need of paint. The prospect was grey and cold wind blew. We walked along under the cliffs and I renewed acquaintance with the rocks, boulders and caves on and in which we used to play. The cliffs again were a mass of scurvygrass and there was a beautiful patch of *Veronica filiformis*. We had tea just past the railway bridge and then returned to Corris via Talybont, which is an attractive place. There was a wool-shop, but it was shut.

2 April, Sunday

There was great surprise at seeing blue sky and sunshine when we looked out of the window. The *Saxifraga oppositifolia* expedition was now on. We went round the mountain via Dolgellau and parked just past the Gwernan Lake Hotel; then took the footpath opposite to Llyn y Gadair. Here we turned left along the steep slopes above the lake and it was not long before we found the *Saxifraga oppositifolia* draping all the north-facing rocks. Why it should be called 'Purple' I can't think – it is a lovely warm rose. †

I took various photographs of these, some with Frank's help and some without. We had lunch on the slope below and then went down to the car and round the coast to Llangelynin, where I got a good photograph of the church. From here we went to Broadwater, where there was nothing special, but it all looked very beautiful in the evening light. Then back to Corris via Abergynolwyn and Talyllyn.

3 April, Monday

We went up Cwm Ratgoed and explored the old abandoned slate-workings, including a substantial Manager's house. Hikers had spent the night there; ashes were still warm in the grate and daffodils in a jar on the mantelpiece. There were supposed to be Choughs in the quarry above, but we did not see them. We crossed the range and came down through the forests (conifer) into the next valley. This was pretty in its lower reaches.

Then a desperate pack-up, clean-up and drive home. †

16 April, Sunday

A lovely day. Spent it on Caer Din (Bishop's Castle). The Blackthorn all along the top road was wonderful. I took two photographs. Had a blissful afternoon lying under the western side of the earthwork out of the wind. Built a screen against the bonnet of the car and had tea in glorious sunshine. On the way down to the Edenhope turn saw some Bitter Vetch in the hedge on the right, so having acquired a tripod and a close-up lens, I decided to photograph it. It was in a very attractive young stage with its tip soft and curved over and tinged with bronze. The photograph unfortunately turned out to be hopelessly over-exposed.

The hedge-banks on the long slope down to Mellington were wonderful flower-beds. Stitchwort, violets, the finest Lords-and-Ladies I have ever seen – all crying out for photographs – drifts of shining Crane's-bill – everything very lush I suppose because of the wet weather. At the bottom there were the last of the flowers of the *Petasites* and the first of the leaves – what a chance for a picture – but it was now too late in the evening.

30 April, Sunday

I intended to go to Llynclys Pool to see if there were any swans, but it turned out dull and drizzly and in the end I only got to Betton Pool. There was a pair of swans here; they both came across to investigate, the cob with wings high. There were also two pairs of Tufted Duck and a very watchful-looking Great Crested Grebe, so I suppose this was the male and his wife was sitting.

There is now not a trace of the gamekeeper's cottage. The garden is planted with larch. A Lilac bush and a spread of periwinkles were in full flower. I was standing looking at all this when I heard an unfamiliar bird-voice in the hedge and by good luck got on to the bird at once. It was a Whitethroat, popping up and down the hedge and in and out, its white patch very conspicuous, and its thin beak as it chattered away. Its back was warm chestnut. Another bird was circling round in the sky which to my great pleasure was a Swift – the first time I have ever seen one in April. Within a few minutes a Long-tailed Tit flew by with a mouthful of food, I think, rather than nesting material (we found nests with eggs two years ago at Llanyblodwel and this is an early year). I turned back to the Whitethroat but was diverted by a cock Reed Bunting in the hedge, very smart with velvety-black crown and bib. Another bird was hovering singing over the lane. I thought it was a Skylark but, when I turned the glass on it, it was the Whitethroat again, performing very sweetly. It soon returned to the hedge and its game of hide and seek. In the sloping field by the pool there was a yellow bird which walked like a Yellow Wagtail but it flew away before I could be quite sure. This seems an interesting place.

28 May, Sunday

A beautiful sunny day. Packed up and set off 11.20. From Grange Bank Berwyn was very clear, and it looked as if this was a day for seeing Snowdonia from the Bwlch. Went to look at Llynclys Pool for the swan-census, turned round before Llynclys via Morton – remembering suddenly the swampy pond by the railway where there had been a pair last year. The sides of the railway-track were full of flowers – the two vetches and Hairy Tare and *Scrophularia nodosa* (Figwort) among others. †

There was water-crowfoot in this pond; it turned out to be *Ranunculus peltatus* as usual. SRC shows the achenes of this variety without any hairs; CTW says they are hairy. This specimen definitely had a row of short hairs all up the backbone, and the shape of the whole head corresponded with the CTW illustration.

In the swampy parts round this pond (depth over my boots, thick with moss and grasses) was a white forget-me-not with small flowers (*Myosotis caespitosa*). There are two water forget-me-nots which have small flowers; this is the smaller. Calyx divided into lobes for over half its length, pedicel twice length of calyx in fruit. Stems, leaves and calyx covered with very much appressed hairs. Petals rounded.

There were no swans on this water, nor on Llynclys Pool, unless they were skulking on the far end by the farm. There was a pair of grebes; no young ones were visible. Yellow Flags were beginning to flower and there were sedges and rushes which as usual defeated me.

I moved up to the Holy of Holies. The hedge as usual was a brilliant flower-bed of Red Campion, veronica, buttercup, Herb-Robert etc. The hill was thick with *Helianthemum chamaecistus* (Yellow Rock-rose). The yellow is deep and rich, and deepens nearly to orange at the base of the petals. In some plants the petals had a semi-circular orange mark and a spot inside it; these were very beautiful. The plants occupied all the driest spots, such as old mole-heaps or outcrops of rock.

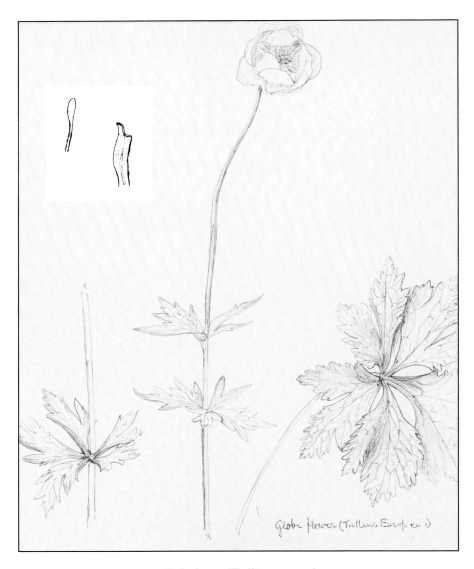

Globeflower (*Trollius europaeus*)

There were milkworts in deep blue, China blue and rose-pink which presumably were *Polygala vulgaris* but I was unable to check. Also Green-winged Orchid. And a minute *Euphrasia* in the driest places. As it is on limestone this is probably a form of *E. nemorosa*. Also *Arenaria leptoclados* (Lesser Thyme-leaved Sandwort). I spent a delightful afternoon in this lovely spot. Afterwards went down to the lane leading to the quarry. The house has been abandoned and the site is already beginning to be grown over. I found a handsome plant of *Helleborus foetidus* below it. Went along to the quarry. Not an orchid to be seen.   †

I went round to Jacob's Ladder to see if there were any Frog Orchids. The vegetation was much thicker than last year and I did not see any. I went into the thicket. There were Early-purple Orchids, and in deep shade I found a *Trollius europaeus* (Globeflower); a little further on was a clump of them. They were drawn up by the shade, 2–2½ feet high, with slender erect stems, finely ribbed and smooth. The leaves are palmate, the leaflets wedge-shaped, the middle one three-lobed with the division coming half-way down, and all the other leaflets two-lobed, unequally – as if it were one middle leaflet and one side one. All lobes again coarsely toothed. Surface covered with a complicated network of veins. There were three leaves sessile on the flower-stem, smaller and simpler the higher they were. Flower soft yellow, with ten concave petals. Six nectaries were buried away between the petals or among the very numerous stamens. There were twenty-five green carpels, each with a horn to one side. (The flower of course should not be open, but it was in a very advanced state by the time I was able to draw it.)

In the same wood, in just as deep shade, I found several plants of *Aquilegia vulgaris* (Columbine). They varied from dark blue to China blue and white.

On the way back along the cliff I stopped to get a piece of the *Sorbus anglica*.

5 June, Monday

Spent the afternoon with Lucy drifting about in Much Wenlock, Barrow, and along the Edge to Wilderhope. There are more and expanding lime-works along the Edge. We had a quick look at one of the dry limestone slopes above a quarry. There was bird's-foot-trefoil, some yellow, and some rich deep orange – Burnet-saxifrage, Yellow-wort not yet in flower, Mouse-ear Hawkweed, some lovely little clumps of thyme in brilliant flower, and a new plant to me – *Acinos arvensis* (Basil Thyme).   †

18 June, Sunday

Evening to Cowslip Hill (Boreton). The vegetation is getting steadily more interesting. Where before there was one tall statuesque Hemlock plant, now the bank is thick with it. Also with superb Musk Thistles. The Weld has also spread enormously and is growing tall and fine. I also saw a few plants of Hound's-tongue. There were fine spikes of mullein and the *Geranium molle* and *Erodium cicutarium* had greatly increased. The grassy slope above the road was thick with Lesser Stitchwort.

I found *Trifolium arvense* (Hare's-foot Clover)* about half-way down the inner slope. It has transparent stipules and red ribs on the calyx like my two Mallorcan trefoils. A long sprawling hairy stem branching from, or with flower-stalks in, almost every axil. The hairs become longer and thicker at the node. Stipules large and oval, of papery tissue edged with green, and with strong green ribs running parallel, and forking just before joining the green edge at the top. Unlike *T. stellatum* etc., this one's stipule ends in a long fine green point as long as itself.

Leaflets darkish green, a little lighter below, oval, pointed, covered on both sides with fine silky appressed hairs, leaf-stalks vary from 2–3 inches at the bottom to less than ½ inch at the top, the basal part of them having three strong ribs with pale tissue in between, like the stipules. The bract is a stalkless leaf with its papery pair of stipules, but these have shorter points and the ribs are crimson. The calyx is also ribbed with crimson, its pointed divisions are very short, about ½ mm, and the hairs minute, so

---

* Realised, by the time I had written this, that it could not be *T. arvense*. Calyx too short, no long silky hairs, leaves wrong shape. Seems it must be a hybrid. C. Sinker thinks *T. arvense* × *T. striatum* possibly. Leaves so *large* like a cultivated clover.

that the flowers stand clear instead of being embedded in silk as in *T. stellatum.* The keel and the base of the flower are white, the standard and upper part of the wings delicate rose. Length of flower from tip of calyx about 2 mm.

20 June, Tuesday

Spent the evening botanising with Mr Rutter in the Cound area. Parked at Cound Arbour and went back to the main road and got down to the brook on the left of the bridge (downstream). A vast mass of Comfrey along the bank, with occasional Hemlocks. A little further on I came upon a plant of *Scrophularia aquatica* (Water Betony) just coming into flower. Stem square and winged, making it look very thick. Leaves large, oval-pointed, slightly heart-shaped at base, coarsely crenate, doubly so in the lower part of the leaf (a large and a small together), each with a slight point. Scattered very short hairs on both surfaces. First pair of flower-stems in the axils of the uppermost pair of leaves; above that they are in opposite pairs with five small bracts. Lower and greater part of flower-stem is square and winged like the main stem but with a few hairs. Then there is a pair of bracts and the individual flower-stems branch off. These are round, and thick with chocolate-coloured glands. The five rounded sepals (united at base) have broad dark brown papery margins. The flower is greenish, stained with purplish-chocolate. Two overlapping lobes at the top project much the furthest, with the staminode in brighter colour attached below them. Three stamens rich with golden pollen were grouped at the bottom. The fourth seemed to be missing. This was the shape of the staminode: dusky maroon in front, green with maroon spots behind.

The shingle-banks which were thick with *Apium* last year only had one or two scrubby bits this year. Redshank and Curlew were in the rushy parts near the backwater. In a curving dike there was a lot of flag, and some *Scirpus sylvaticus* (Wood Club-rush). This had thickish stems (8 mm), triangular with rounded corners, sharper just under the flower-head. Three or four longish leaves (10 inches) 1 cm wide, with a sharpish midrib; all smooth except the edges of the leaves, which are rough when stroked downwards.

The flower-head is an irregular kind of umbel, growing from two long leafy bracts of unequal size. There are about five partial umbels on long stems, which bend downwards. In the middle of them grows a short spike with its branches all growing upwards. Each partial umbel repeats the pattern. Glumes green with black shading, anthers off-white.

We came to the end of the dike and I remarked on a large and lush plant of Water Betony, not yet in flower.   †

16 July, Sunday

Afternoon collected Joyce Haseler and took her out to Llynclys Hill. The rain had had a reviving effect on all the plants at the house-site. It was very interesting to see the difference in just a week. The Basil and Betony had more or less disappeared, but the Marjoram was full out and making the whole slope pinkish. Yellow Bedstraw had put in an appearance and there was a lovely colourful patch of these two mixed with Wood Sage. We visited the *Hypericum montanum*, which looked much fresher than last week.

We had tea by the tram-cut, after trying to find the way to the bottom of the quarry and being beaten by the jungle. After this we shot up to Glanhafon for a breath of hill air.

19 July, Wednesday

Had news of last week's botanical meeting on the telephone from Mr Rutter. The figwort at Cound that I had assumed to be the ordinary Water Figwort (see 20 June) is the rare *S. umbrosa*!! I went straight off to get a piece, and sure enough there it was. Now collapsed on its side but lush and flowering freely. I noticed that there were more and finer flower-stems than in the two common figworts, giving it a lacy look. *Scrophularia umbrosa*. The stem is square and very broadly winged. Leaves oval-pointed, and coarsely toothed. The pedicels spring from the axils and are thin and fine, and also narrowly winged. This part varies from an inch in length at the bottom of the inflorescence to half an inch at the top; it then branches into three with a very fine pointed bract at the junction. The middle of the three branches has one flower which comes out first; the two side ones branch again into three or more flowers, each with a minute pointed bract. The final pedicels have minute dark glands.

The sepals are rounded with narrow buffish scarious edges. Upper lip of flower dark reddish-chocolate, lower lip clear green and curved under. The staminode is this shape: and extends across the whole width of the flower. The notch is very clear-cut indeed.

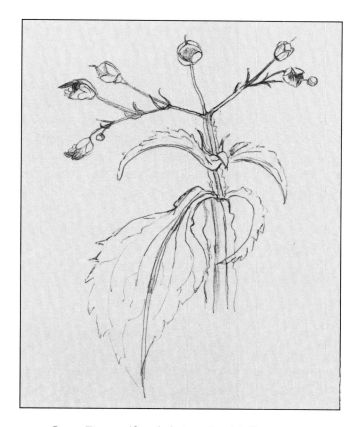

Green Figwort (*Scrophularia umbrosa*) inflorescence

22 July, Saturday

At Penygwryd. Decided to go round and look at the Idwal slopes. Found I had left the glass at home so had to go down to Betws to buy one – and the only one available was heavy, and gave a very small magnification. Betws was like Oxford Street.

Arrived at Ogwen 11.45. Went up past the slabs. The Parsley Fern started at the stone wall after this feature. Came to a stream in a deep cleft where plants immediately began to appear. *Solidago virgaurea* (Goldenrod), presumably var. *cambrica* as it was short, grew in the perpendicular rock-wall. All hairy flowers in a close head at the top, leaves wavy rather than serrated.

Another plant that soon appeared in an inaccessible place was *Oxyria digyna* (Mountain Sorrel). †

Mountain Sorrel
(*Oxyria digyna*)

23 July, Sunday

Grey skies over the mountains so decided to go to Newborough Warren. Sun began to come through at Llanberis, full out over Anglesey as usual. The way down through the forest to the Caernarvon road was vividly lined with Rosebay, ragwort, *Hypericum* and *Hieracium.* Arrived at Newborough in one hour flat from P y G.

Pen-lôn was wonderful – a sheet of flowers. All the dune-flora was at its freshest – solid mats of brilliant thyme, sometimes alone and sometimes mixed with Lady's Bedstraw grow-ing only a few inches high. Pink Centaury was all over the place in little clumps and there was a skittering of a minute White *Euphrasia* and *Linum catharticum,* the latter quite fresh. I would have expected it to be over. Quite a lot of Yellow Rattle in the grassier places, a few *Orchis fuchsii,* Bog Pimpernel in the slacks bleached very pale. The grassy part between the entrance and the mere was gay with yellow composites, Cat's-ear etc. and a little Meadowsweet, Bird's-foot-trefoil, mostly yel-low but a few of the very deep orange. Some of the Lady's Bedstraw on the other hand was very pale, making me wonder if the hybrid with *G. mollugo* had occurred. On the highest and driest spots were foot-high Carline Thistles, each with a central flower going to bloom in about a fortnight, and two candelabra-arms with less mature buds. In the grass was also Restharrow.

The first new plant to me was *Gentianella amarella* which grew on the top of small mounds rising 1–2 feet above the flats, usually coming through a tangle of the Creeping Willow. They were just coming into flower, and there were plants of all sizes, from 1–2 inches up to 9–10 inches. The stem is square and angled, purlish-chocolate, and dead

Autumn Gentian
(*Gentianella amarella*)

Twayblade flower

Twayblade
(*Listera ovata*)

erect, leaves in pairs, oval-pointed, the upper part also stained with dull purplish-chocolate. Calyx campanulate at base dividing into long finely-pointed segments (five). Corolla dull lavender with five nearly triangular petals springing from a longish tube, with a circle of upstanding paler fringe at the mouth. This fringe distinguishes *Gentianella* from *Gentiana*. I drew and photographed these plants. One had a flower with six petals.

Just as I was packing up after drawing the best and tallest plant, I saw a greenish orchis by my foot! I could so easily have stepped or sat on it. If the *Gentianella* hadn't been there I should never have seen it. This was *Listera ovata* (Twayblade). I went back and had lunch, and by a rubbish-dump not far from the car I found another but this was not such a good one and nearly over. After lunch I went to photograph this one as I had a good conscience in spite of having been warned by a local inhabitant of the awful things that were coming to me because I had no permit. The Assistant Warden (Reg Arthur) found me at this ploy and received me very courteously. The *Gentianella* drawing served as a passport, and I was let in. So I went back to the Twayblade which I had marked with a stick and two Oystercatcher's feathers, and drew it lying flat on my tummy. There were two other plants nearby – one had been picked (not by me) and the other was a non-flowering one. The stem is covered with short hairs and is light brownish-green. It grew up through a tangle of Creeping Willow in which the two large oval leaves were embedded. The lip is very long and two-cleft; there is no spur. The seed-vessel is rounded-oval. The flowers are yellowish-green and do not show up against the background of dune vegetation which is very much of this colour. I photographed it and various mats of thyme, etc. The various kinds of flowers tend to grow in colonies. Further on I found quite a drift of Grass-of-Parnassus. Violas grew more on dunes proper, in all colours – quite dark blue, clear yellow and most combinations in between.

This was the most perfect day I have ever known at Newborough. By the afternoon, the mountains cleared and their blue shapes provided a wonderful backdrop, especially the Rivals which were framed between two tall dunes at the end of one of the biggest flats. The sun and the breeze tempered each other to a point of bliss and comfort rarely experienced. I left with desperate feelings about 7 p.m.

On the way back towards Deiniolen I stopped to look at the hedge-bank which was a mass of flowers, chiefly enormous Harebells and Betony, both in richest deepest colour. Also took some photographs.

3

BASKING IN THE SUN

July – September 1961 · Shropshire & Marches

25 July, Tuesday

To lunch with Miss Jackson, Broniarth Hall.

This is wonderful country. Somewhere about Penrhos there was a splendid *Castanea sativa* (Spanish Chestnut) in the roadside hedge, very large and dark lustrous green, thick with catkins which were also scattered all around it. I picked up several. They were 9–10 inches long with fifty to sixty flowers spaced alternately but irregularly, so that they are often nearly in pairs. They consist of a furry calyx with a mass of stamens. Apparently the female flowers are few and placed at the bottom of the spike; mine seemed to have broken off above them for I could not see any.

Broniarth Hall is known to have been inhabited in 1680 and may be older. The perfect house to my mind.

29 July, Saturday

Decided to go to Stevenshill Wood in the evening. Stopped at Venusbank on the way to see if there was anything on the pool. The flowers were thick and colourful and the water low, so I went down to the central 'island' which had never been accessible before. All the birds betook themselves to the middle of the water – the swans and their six offspring, Coots and Dabchicks in plenty and a few Mallard. Suddenly I saw a tern; that wonderful flight, the Sand Martins which were skimming the water in dozens seemed clumsy compared with it. It winged slowly then stopped in one place, the beats going faster, then moved off with a steady deliberation, unlike the quick swing of a hawk that leaves its point in the sky as if released from a tension. At other times it would do a gannet-loop and plunge down to the water with wings and tail spread, usually with white underside towards me: this looked like a dive but was a superb parabola with the lowest point a mere touch of the water, and the upward swing as swift and effortless as the downward one. Once it took a high flight around and then came back to its hunting. The wings were slatey-grey above, darker at the fore-edge, white below but seeming a little dusky at the feather-tips. The back was a warmer brownish-grey. Dark beak, white forehead, black crown, white behind that and a black mark on the neck.

So 1961 has not passed without a tern.

While watching it I noticed a Great Crested Grebe among the Little Grebes etc. in the middle of the pool.

Lythrum salicaria (Purple-loosestrife) was the most conspicuous plant, just in its perfection; there were clumps all over the place but the far side was lined with it, gorgeous plants about 4 feet high. Stem square, with slightly irregular rib on the angles, which are tinged with red. It is covered with very short hairs. Leaves in opposite pairs; each pair should be at right angles to the ones above and below as they grow N and S and the rest E and W, but the stem has a slight twist from right to left so that the alternate pairs are not above each other. Leaves sessile, very nearly meeting round the stem, oblong, untoothed, more sharply pointed the further up they

Purple-loosestrife (*Lythrum salicaria*)

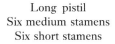

Long pistil
Six medium stamens
Six short stamens

Right
Six long stamens
Medium pistil
Six short stamens

Six long stamens (or five)
Six medium stamens
Short pistil

are. Flowers start in axils about half-way up; about four tiers above this the leaves could be said to be bracts, at the top of the spike they are minute. They have quite minute hairs on both surfaces. Calyx campanulate, two-thirds entire, one-third divided into six fine points, and with twelve well-marked ribs, covered with white hairs.

The six petals are long and narrowish, spread flat and separate, vivid Fuchsia colour with a darker vein in the middle, diameter 2 cm (of flower). In my shoot there are six long stamens grouped at the bottom of the flower, sticking right out beyond the petals, of a richer and redder colour and with purple-black anthers: in the middle a pale pink pistil with a large round pale green stigma, perhaps two-thirds the length of the long stamens; and above this, six very short stamens all down inside the flower, pale greenish-primrose. Apparently there are two other variations on the size and arrangement of stamens and pistil which occur in different plants. The petals are of a thin tissue, a little crumpled-looking, sometimes five and sometimes six.

30 July, Sunday

Turned right at Porthywaen and went on as far as Treflach Wood where I saw a quarry on the right. Quite near the opening was a large clump of mint nearly 1½ feet high. Stems pale green, squarish, thick with soft downward-pointing hairs. Leaves sessile, downy and markedly rugose above, paler and thickly hairy below. Flower-stems from four axils below the terminal spike, also thick with hairs. Bracts long and fine-pointed, purple and silky with hairs, not projecting beyond flowers. Calyx purple, with five more or less equal fine points, hairy. Corolla pale lavender with darker suffusion in upper lip, hairy on the outside. Stamens short, inside the flower. Stigma white, with a forked tip, double the length of the flower. Strong mint smell. This is *Mentha niliaca* (probably *M. nemorosa*). The Shropshire handbook only has one uncertain record.

The quarry was full of the usual limestone plants. The Marjoram was a splendid flush of deep purple-pink. Most of them were this colour, which is due to the dark Fuchsia-coloured bracts, but there were also paler plants in which the bracts were green.

There was also Yellow-wort just coming out (this has eight petals). Basil nearly over, two different kinds of *Hieracium* in the grassy bank, some splendid *Orchis pyramidalis* in a shady thicket, *Gentianella amarella*

Mentha × *niliaca*

just beginning to flower, a Bee Orchis just over. Several *Helleborus foetidus* in the floor of the quarry at the far end. Altogether an interesting place and worth further investigation.

Spent the rest of the day basking in the corner of a field.

6 August, Sunday

Went up to the larch forest towards Rhialgwm. The gate on to the open hill had a notice: 'Beware of the Bull' – however it was windy out there. I settled down in a gateway inside and had a wonderful afternoon basking in the sun. When the sun went behind the hill after tea, I packed up and went round by the Treflach quarry to get a fresh specimen of the mint. The entrance was blocked with a heavy rail and I could not take the car in. The clump of mint had a markedly silver look, what with the light-coloured flowers and the hairiness of all the leaves and stems. Also the basic green is very pale. I searched around for other plants but there were none. I picked a fresh bunch of Marjoram and counted seven *Helleborus foetidus* at the far end but found nothing fresh.

I brought a piece of the mint home, and was rather shattered to find that some of the flowers had projecting stamens – or at any rate thin and twisted filaments; there did not seem to be any anthers. Telephoned Mr Sinker, who disclaimed any knowledge of mints. This is all very awkward.

7 August, Monday

To Stapeley Hill with Hilly and Frank. Cadair Idris, Aran Fawddwy etc. all blue and clear – a wonderful sweep of country. We had lunch just beyond Mitchell's Fold in warm sunshine but could see the clouds piling up to the southwest, and every now and then a shower like a tight-stretched length of smoke-blue gauze from cloud to hill. However, these clouds travelled up to the west of us, hiding each range in turn, but when the mountains appeared again they were grey, not blue, and quite a brisk southeast wind was blowing. We walked over Stapeley Hill to the northern end. On the grass between the gorse bushes a bird was feeding with quick lively movements, running backwards and forwards and every now and then peering up and around like a partridge. We sat down and watched it and it turned out to be a Woodlark. The crown of the head was dark,

'Snowdonia from near Cerrigydrudion.' (see p.86)

'Tryfan, rearing its back like the most primitive armadillo.' (see p.72)

'Beaumaris, with blue mountains, pink clouds and everything perfect.' (see p.72)

'To Penmon and photographed the dovecote.' (see p.86)

with lines running over, then a light stripe through the eye. The upper breast was pale fawn with dark streaks, and the 'shoulder' was white, then dark, then white again, and all the rest of the underparts nearly white. The back and wing-coverts were rich brown, almost chestnut, with very dark brown blobs and streaks. The whole bird looked rounded, not with the long streamlined look of a Skylark or a pipit, and the tail was shorter.

We went across the Corndon road to get water and down the other side and so back to the More Arms, having circled the hill.

In the Hope Valley on the way home picked a Goldenrod – flowering there in profusion – being interested in the long slender spike compared with the stumpy Welsh one.

Goldenrod (*Solidago virgaurea*)

12 August, Saturday

Evening went out to Cound Pool to see if there was anything. Mr Harrison was sketching and gave me all the news: a Greenshank there, and Ruffs, a Spotted Redshank and Green Sandpiper at the sewage-farm. The Greenshank was to the left of the hedge, striding about in the water and feeding; it looked very large against the silver-white surface. I couldn't get close enough to see as much detail as I should have liked, but its upperparts were noticeably darker than in the Scilly and Cemlyn Bay birds. I went off post-haste to the sewage-farm, to the tip-lagoon, where somebody has made a hide of corrugated iron. A man with two children and two dogs was messing about and at first I thought I wasn't going to see anything. Then as they drifted away towards the river, I made out several birds in the edge of the grass in the middle of the lagoon. So I went to the hide, which has few amenities and plenty of smell. However, it served. I gradually made out the Green Sandpiper, with strongly-contrasted upper and lower parts; the back and wings were very dark, a sort of blackish dead colour, the underparts white except for a slight deepening to greyish-buff on the upper breast. The head was lighter and browner than the back and there was a conspicuous white eye-stripe. When seen full-face, these made a clear white V, rather flat and open, above the dark bill. This bird stood, or fed, by itself. In a group quite near were three other birds which turned out to be the Ruffs. They had warm reddish-brown backs with strong dark brown markings. This clear-cut pattern was the most obvious thing about them. As they fed, they turned up a white triangle under this rich brown at the tail. The rest of the underparts were buffish or soft pale brownish. Their heads were mid-brown without any stripes or markings, rather paler at the back of the neck. Beaks short and dark. Once the Green Sandpiper passed right in front of them; it was noticeably smaller, and more slender and graceful than they were. This disposed of my fear of repeating the howler of my first season at the sewage-farm when I put down some Dunlin as Ruffs. But the back-markings were too large and strong for Dunlin. On looking them up in Witherby afterwards, I found that these markings are character-istic of young birds, which are also the ones most often seen on passage in this country.

I did not see the Spotted Redshank.

19 August, Saturday

Evening to Cound Pool. The Greenshank was still there, and also three Ruffs; and two birds which I decided in the end were Green Sandpipers – the contrast between dark above and light below was very strong. Harvesting going on. It all looked most beautiful.

20 August, Sunday

Evening to Polemere, to find it completely dried up. Went on to the Hem, hoping to get some interesting plants from the ditch, but it had been cleaned out and the banks were bare. The Hem also was quite dry. Went up to Corndon and had a short walk and a breath of hill air. Collected another piece of Goldenrod on the way back, from which I finished the drawing.

2 September, Saturday

To Cound Pool evening. One Ruff and three or four Ringed Plover. It has gone down a lot; the water is now only covering half the mud-flats. Collected the three variants of Purple-loosestrife once more. Drew one of them, with the long pistil. The dominant plants now are the Trifid Bur-marigold and Whorled Mint.

I managed at last to draw the three variants of the loosestrife flower.

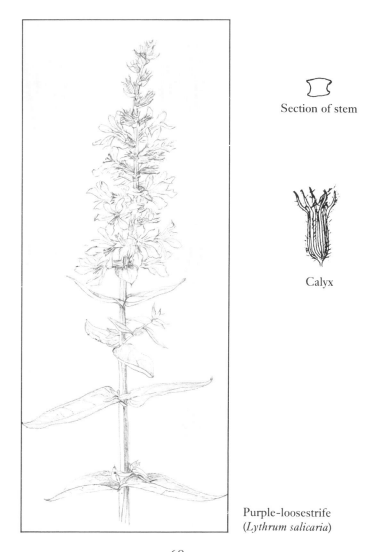

Section of stem

Calyx

Purple-loosestrife
(*Lythrum salicaria*)

Sometimes there are five petals and sometimes six, and the stamens also vary between 5 + 5 and 6 + 6. The twist in the stem is not always in the same direction; some plants have left to right and some right to left. The square stems also are interesting: N and S are convex and E and W concave, changing over to the opposites at each node. The calyx has six long fine points and six short triangular points alternately, the twelve ribs leading up to them.

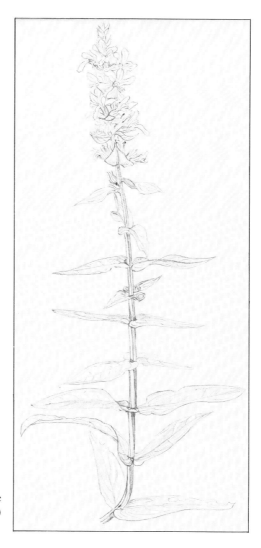

Purple-loosestrife
(*Lythrum salicaria*)
side-shoot

9 September, Saturday

A perfect day of calm sunshine. To Wellington to see Mabel in the early evening. Stopped at the Beet-factory flood-water on the way back and collected two more pieces of *Lythrum* from the stream or dike on the opposite side of the road. Discovered that the pollen is a most wonderful shade of vivid green, just a little bluer than emerald. This stage only lasts a short time so that there are only a few flowers with anthers of this colour on the spike; they then turn purplish-black. It might be fun to have a microscope and study pollen-grains?

10 September, Sunday

A grey day, very disappointing after yesterday. Took Ellen May's wedding present, looked at Cefn Glaniwrch on the way up. Had no cravings for it. Had lunch in the car just short of Tynyfedwen. Drizzle set in so decided to go home. Just before the dog-leg in the road, a Kestrel settled on a power-line pole. It was a female, a rich brown all over – just not red enough to be called chestnut. Her back was barred horizontally with dark brown, also her wing-coverts, but the bars on these were much smaller and closer. Long black wing-quills and a broad black band near the end of her tail, and a narrow band of white at the tip. Her legs were conspicuously rich yellow with black talons, and her eyes were large, round and dark. She stood so that I had a rear-right-side view of her, but a good deal of the time turned her head completely round to the back, through 180 degrees, and looked at me with her left eye – so easily that one could imagine her completing the turn right round to the front again without any difficulties. Her beak was greyish, darker at the tip. She kept her head hunched down on her shoulders and her feathers slightly fluffed out against the drizzle.

17 September, Sunday

A day of golden calm after raging winds yesterday. Evening went up on the Downton end of Haughmond. Had hoped to find some Lesser Skullcap to draw, but the cuts were dried up and hidden in rank vegetation so that walking over this part of the hill was hellish. Sneezewort was just going over. There was not a cloud over Wales. Berwyn and Aran Fawddwy both clear, ethereal grey-blue. The sun went down rich copper-gold just to the north of Breidden and reddened the twisting branches of the Scots Pines with its glow. The piled-up clouds behind the dark needles were rosy – it would have made a wonderful photograph.

4

MOONSHINE ACROSS THE WATER

September – October 1961 · Anglesey

22 September, Friday

To Beaumaris. Had tea by river just beyond the Rhûg Bridge again. From beyond Cerrigydrudion the Snowdon Mountains looked incredibly high, especially Tryfan, rearing its back like the most primitive armadillo (or some horny-backed cousin??). By the time I got near to it, the sun behind the range was casting up a halo of beams from its crest. I tried some photographs of this, with the yellow filter on, and hope I have something better than previous efforts of this kind! Took another on the approaches to Beaumaris, with blue mountains, pink clouds and everything perfect (or should be).

The marvels continued after dinner when a huge moon came up over the shoulder of the Carnedds and floated behind an openwork fabric of cirrus cloud. The band where the moon was moved across it darkly with silver heavens behind: above and below the tones were reversed and the clouds were ice-floes on blue-black depths. Below again was a solid band of softer cloud, dove-coloured like the mountains, and the silver path of the moonshine across the water.

23 September, Saturday

Really hot. Lay on the Green till I was over-heated. Moved along the coast to a little bay called Lleiniog where I lay about and had lunch. There was a thicket of *Sorbus* (variety to be checked) behind and a steep bluff of 20 feet or so to the shore. Below this was a group of plants of *Picris echioides* (Bristly Oxtongue). Roughly lanceolate leaves with stiff hairs, almost spines, on white warty bases. A branched inflorescence, yellow composite flowers.

Went on to the corner of Trwyn y Penrhyn and lay in the sun. There were mats of *Spergularia rupicola* (Cliff Sand-spurrey) on the wall and tucked against the rocks here.

Picris echioides (Bristly Oxtongue) – a plant of great character. It was clearly a biennial – there were several flowering plants and still more rosettes of basal leaves getting ready for next year. Leaves lanceolate, tapering off to a sharp point armed with a spine; wavy, rough, with bumps

Bristly Oxtongue (*Picris echioides*)

and boils and bristles all over, of all sizes, the largest with raised whitish circles at the root. Stem round with fine red ribs, covered with spines and bristles of almost transparent fish-bone colour and texture, and all sizes. All the spines on the stems branch at the very tip into three, turned outwards at right angles. The stems branch frequently and at each joint there is a sessile leaf with cordate bases clasping the stem ferociously and reaching far back beyond it in a well-armed curve. Flower-stalks from these branchings are similarly ribbed and bristly, and carry sometimes one flower, but more often three: each of these has a stalk ½–¾ inches and then a set of terrific bracts – looking more like a calyx than five bracts. They are more or less heart-shaped but with a long fine point ending in a spine, a broad midrib and wide-based wings, all with bristles. Inside these is the normal calyx of long narrow segments also ending in prolonged bristly points. The flowers are yellow and I found two types – one male only, with ligulate petals each with one stamen, thick and yellow at the base, black and two-branched at the top. The tips of the branches cling together when the middles have begun to separate, making a club-shaped organ with a gap in the middle. These male flowers had about five rows of petals, decreasing in size right down to the centre. The other type was hermaphrodite, with male ligules, for three to four rows, and a group of about a dozen female flowers in the middle. These were tubular and yellow of the usual disc-floret type, though hardly numerous enough to make a disc. Such splendid, if spiny, curves and rugged individuality called out to be drawn.   †

24 September, Sunday

Thick sea-fog lay against the mountains opposite till middle-day. Then the sun began to come through and there was another golden afternoon and evening. Went to Penmon and walked on to the headland beyond. Found two flowers of *Helianthemum chamaecistus* (Yellow Rock-rose) in the turf up there.

25 September, Monday

Went round to Aber and turned up the hill road. Went to the end of the tarmac two spurs to the west of the falls and got on the end of the Roman Road. Pylons spoil this hillside. Went up towards the lake. A tiny spring made a flush in which there were the typical plants – Blinks, Brooklime, *Ranunculus hederaceus*, *Ranunculus flammula*, all very small. A heron was drifting down the opposite mountainside and settled when he saw me, with neck upstretched, rigid like a garden ornament. After a good five minutes he began slowly and deliberately to walk uphill. The slope was quite steep, and it was comical to see this bird of horizontal landscapes and waterscapes mountaineering among the bilberries.

There were two multiple sheepfolds of a complicated design, like a five- or six-petalled flower, one on each side of the stream, about a quarter of a mile apart. In each section were small sheep-doorways connecting with the middle fold, and little gates to close them.

Arrived back at Beaumaris about 6.30 to find Mr Rutter had been there since 3.00. He had strolled along the road beyond the castle and on the shore below the first headland had seen a Purple Sandpiper when the tide was nearly out.

26 September, Tuesday

We went to the Cors at Talwrn – Cors Bodeilio. Almost at once there was *Serratula tinctoria* (Saw-wort) – mostly of course in seed, but a few flowers here and there. These plants were in the moderately damp parts near the edge – not in the real bog, but not out on the grass either. The shoots tended to occur singly or at most two or three together, looking as if they were having severe competition with the thick herbage. Grass-of-Parnassus was scattered about in much the same habitat. Also Angelica in the wetter places. I found about half a dozen hefty seed-heads of *Orchis*, all with narrow very pointed leaves, and one shoot of helleborine. The head had rotted off but there were four or five oval yellowed leaves. Pink Lousewort was still in flower here and there. There was an *Oenanthe*.

The wind was a nuisance. We managed to find a sheltered place by a high hedge at the end of the lane for lunch. We then went along the road to the east of Cors Erddreiniog and had a look at it but did not go down as it looked much the same as the last. We went on to Benllech and walked along under the limestone cliffs to the north. Just beyond the last cottage was a wonderful group of Tree-mallows, one enormous one with a five-fold spike of dead flower-heads about 6–7 feet high, and others in all sizes down to a foot high. The leaves were lush and brilliant green, wavy and velvety. There were a few flowers of a beautiful rich rose-pink, with a big flush of dark crimson at the base and a plushy pistil. I was astonished to find that this is a biennial. It would be interesting to follow the history of the various plants here. Must try to get a photograph at the height of the flowering next year.

A few hundred yards further on, just above our heads on a steep clayey bank were quite a number of flourishing clumps of the *Serratula*. These really were clumps, with a large number of flower-stems in each. The place was not noticeably damp. In cracks in the limestone cliffs, usually protected by an overhang, were a few elegant plants of *Asplenium marinum* (Sea Spleenwort) with richly shining leaves and spores in straight dark lines. In the flat limestone pavement below, just above the tideline and wedged in narrow cracks, were some rather battered-looking plants of *Crithmum maritimum* (Rock Samphire).

Tea by the roadside near Pentraeth. We came back to Beaumaris hoping to see the Purple Sandpiper, and took up our positions on the headland. The shore was swarming with Turnstones, all running around like little mice. There was a bird on the water's edge which could have been the sandpiper but the tide was too far out and we couldn't see properly.

The wind increased as the evening went on. About midnight as the tide turned it died down.

From my bed I could hear the Curlews calling as they fed on the ebb of the water.

27 September, Wednesday

Heavy dark clouds over Snowdonia and still some wind. We went to Newborough – *Erodium cicutarium*, *Viola curtisii* and tiny *Centaurium* only an inch high with one flower. This was the Pen-lôn end. There was a pair of swans with five cygnets, endless Coots, a Tufted drake and two ducks on the water, and a dozen Wigeon circling round the sky: these had very dull-coloured heads, we supposed in eclipse.

At the Malltraeth Cob lagoon there were several Shelduck, quantities of Lapwings, about a dozen Dunlin and twenty-five Golden Plover. Only one or two had traces of the heavy black on the belly. The whole of the upper plumage was of dark-centred feathers edged with tawny-gold. The upper breast was golden-buff and all the rest of the underparts white. The crown of the head was darkish but the light yellowish colour made bands above and below the eye. The beak was noticeably short and stumpy and the birds all had rather a hunched-up look and a nearly straight slanting line from the back of the head to the end of the short tail. While we were watching, a different wader flew in and settled in the middle of the water. It had a clear light grey back, all white below, long legs and a longish straight bill and, although we could not see the colour of the legs as a wild squall of rain came on, we felt pretty sure it was a Greenshank.

Every now and then a Golden Plover would make a dash at one of the Lapwings, or a quick little flight: this stumpy little bird then revealed its graceful long pointed wings, silvery white below and with a sketchy light wing-bar.

We called on the Warden at Malltraeth but he was not at home. However, Reg Arthur was, but without his beard. He examined the permit with care. There was a drawing of a bird on the table – a Little Egret – which had been in the marsh for several days and was last seen on Sunday. We decided to concentrate on this!

We had lunch in the car at the forest end of the Cob, while a wild rain-storm lashed outside. The meal and the storm ended together and we set off across the saltings. At first we could see nothing except large gulls on the furthest edge under the sand-dunes. The saltings had the usual plants: Sea Aster, Sea Arrowgrass, Sea-blite at the edge by the water: I had gone out there to find out if anything different grew. From here we could see a dike or stream which cut through the saltings, and on the further bank something white which looked larger than any gull. We rushed on through the jig-saw of little pools until we were near enough to be sure, after anxious inspection with glass and telescope, that we really were on to the Little Egret. It was standing in a typical heron attitude, with its head hunched back on its shoulders, and made a very staring white splash in the landscape. We worked forward steadily; there was no cover but we gradually came near enough to get quite a good view with glass and telescope. I could see the golden-buff tinge of the plumage on the lower parts of the wing-coverts or back. Suddenly it flew – but only just out into the water, where it came down and took a few stately steps, lifting each leg slowly and stretching it forward horizontally before planting it in the water again. These legs were black. I could not see the yellow feet – they could have been plastered with mud. After a bit it flew again: an enormous spread of snowy wings, more pointed and graceful than a heron's – but with the same unhurried dignity. It settled on the further shore under the dunes and hunched itself down in the same position as at first. When we left, it had an attendant heron on each side to keep it company. One longed to know just how it got here and how it was going to get back – if ever.

There was *Oenanthe* in the marsh near the road. We left news of the bird at Malltraeth and then went across to Traeth Dulas, where we had tea. This bay is a muddy, not a sandy estuary, and therefore does not attract visitors and their apparatus, and all the surroundings are natural. The birds were Curlew and Redshank chiefly. There was a nice collection of the tide-edge plants.

Halimione portulacoides (Sea-purslane), a silver plant. Under the glass the surface is rather warty and has a close network of little pits. Leaves blunt-pointed, oval. Stems similar but with a brownish cast and ribbed. Small shoots branch off from every axil. CTW says shoots are terete below; mine is ribbed all round. Terminal flower-spike in which it is difficult to distinguish anything. The clearest objects are thick with fleshy triangular bracts; after that I give it up.

Glasswort (I suppose *Salicornia ramosissima*). Quite a rich dark green with touches of red. Looks as if it has been stuck together in sections – nearest to a cactus in the British flora? Central stem and first section of side-shoots are always plain, and from them the scaly growths spring (these have a definite pattern of scales and buds). It grows right in the high-tide line. Was first told the name of this plant by Dai Morgan at Cemlyn. I put it down as *S. ramosissima* because of the slight flush of dull red – but I would have said the tips of the segments were blunt not acute: but then there is no sign of a flower.   †

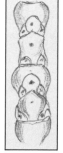

main stem   pattern of side-shoot

Glasswort (*Salicornia ramosissima*)

28 September, Thursday

A strong westerly gale. We walked along the front and over the headland, still looking for the Purple Sandpiper, but had no luck. I counted forty Turnstones on the shore below the cliff. They are almost invisible until they move, with backs now a soft streaky tea-brown. All at once they dart in little runs like mice, with bodies fixed and legs going like lightning, and you realise that the apparently empty shore is alive with them. Suddenly the whole flock gets up together with an excited twittering and circles low over the sea, comes nearly in as if to settle but swerves abruptly out again in another sweeping arc, all moving as one, as Starlings do. They flicker in and out of sight as they wheel, the broad white bands on body and long fine wings sometimes shining clear and sometimes disappearing along the light ripples on the water.

29 September, Friday

To Penmynydd to see the old house, the original seat of the Tudors. I do not think we found it. To Malltraeth. There was a Bar-tailed Godwit in the Cob lagoon. It had quite a lot of the copper in its neck and foreparts generally. Underparts pure white from the legs backwards. Eyes and beak dark. Not as good as the Rhosneigr one but still a very lovely bird.

A wild wind raging. We went to Aberffraw to see the island-church at Llangwyfan. We looked over the bay and decided to stay on the mainland and went down the lane by the Tree-mallow instead. My three plants had increased to something like a dozen, and had spread both up and down the lane. I notice they always grow where they have good shelter from the west wind. We went down to the bay and then came back and sought a sheltered spot for lunch. Afterwards we went up to Cemlyn. This lagoon had hundreds of Mallard and a few Tufties. We walked on the seaward side of the shingle-bank, which makes a perfect curve. The tide was just beginning to ebb, and it was fascinating to watch the swing of the water round this wonderful arc, the terrific pull out of the celestial face, and the little slap back on the stones of the piled-up sea. The Sea-kale was also on the way out – good clumps of crisp wavy leaves had a mat of pale brown dead ones round them, and the dead flower-stems in a blown-over thicket carried a few seed-vessels, as round as sea-washed pebbles and as hard.

We retreated to the car and drove round by Amlwch, finding the shelter of a high hedge somewhere for tea. This northeast corner is pretty desperate.

30 September, Saturday

A beautiful morning with glorious sunshine. Mr Rutter went home, having been rather unlucky in the weather. I set off for Benllech with the idea of drawing the Tree-mallow. A bulldozer and a pneumatic drill were working on the shore. I picked several pieces with flowers on and put them in water. At this point the bulldozer etc. stopped work so I tried to find a sheltered sunny corner in which to settle down and draw. This was an impossibility and the plant wilted anyway. In a frustrated mood I went round to Cors Goch, and walked round the south side of it. About the middle is an outcrop of rock and near this I found *Cladium mariscus* (Fen-sedge). It was conspicuously handsome, 4–5 feet high, with rounded stems tending to triangular. The leaves were bluish, quite wide, with a sharp midrib and very rough edges. The flower-spike had long bracts, the lowest a foot long; there were three axillary flowers besides the final one. The pedicel was a semi-circle, one side very flat and smooth, and the curved side ribbed. There were brown small bracteoles also at the branching of the spikelets.

In the afternoon the rain came on. I was sitting in the car when a man came along, struggling against the wind on a bicycle. When he saw me, he thought this was a good excuse for a rest and a chat. His words came in quick sharp bursts, like volleys of machine-gun fire. He had a bunch of lemon-yellow Dahlias which he was taking to a cemetery to put on the grave of a farmer's wife who died of leukaemia a year ago, aged only forty-one. He had cycled all the way from Caernarvon and kept the flowers undamaged in the violent wind. Afterwards he was going to see her parents who were eighty-one and eighty-six. He was feeling real bad – got a cold on him – here he spat vigorously – it was all across his head. Wouldn't like to live here – nothing going on – now in Caernarvon there was music – and singing – he was going back to it tonight. He himself played the trombone and the euphonium and another instrument which I forget. He performed in a brass band. But you wanted a fortune to live these days – at least £10 a week. He was arrayed in a heavy khaki army coat and a round knitted cap of an indefinite buff-brown with a small bobble on top and a large feather stuck through it – a turkey-feather at least. No hair could be seen but his eyebrows were gingery and his eyes blue, and if his musical performance was as spirited as his speech he would certainly carry the brass band to victory at the Eisteddfod. Clenched in his teeth was an old briar-pipe, knotty and black.

At last he rounded off the conversation with another good spit and went on his way. I decided that this district had become insalubrious and moved down the road before brewing tea.

1 October, Sunday

A beautiful day, sunny nearly all through. Spent it in Newborough Warren making lists of everything I could see for the card-index. There was an umbelliferous plant which I saw when I had no book and conscientiously did not pick – and never found again. *Erigeron acer* (Blue Fleabane) I had not seen here before – and only at the Buildwas gravel-pit.

Blue cloud-shadows travelled over Snowdonia. There was no wind; this was a heavenly day. †

2 October, Monday

A duller day – more or less overcast but with gleams of sunshine now and then. Warm and fairly calm. Called at the Cob lagoon but there was nothing much – a lot of Dunlin, some with black smudges, and a few Ringed Plover.

Decided to go out to Llanddwyn Island. Found the road in Newborough which goes past the church. After this it degenerates into a track in the sand until it joins a forest road. Continued making the list. Had a short walk along the shore before lunch and found one good clump of *Cakile maritima* (Sea Rocket) last seen in seed on the beach at Paguera in March. This plant on the contrary was very fresh and in full flower with dozens of unopened buds!

After lunch walked on to the island. On the far side looked over at the rocks and seeing some samphire went down to investigate. In the same clefts and ledges found *Inula crithmoides* (Golden Samphire). Round the next bend was a beautiful bay with a sheltered cleft in the rocks almost entirely lined with it. Here there were luckily two fresh flowers so I was able to record it. †

Along this bit of coast there were two rocks offshore of a rich purplish-crimson colour. Opposite these were rocks covered with mustard-yellow lichen and carpeted all round thickly with Thrift. This is a clear case for a photograph when the flowers are out and the sea a deep deep blue!

On the inner slopes by the lighthouse I found another new sea-plant – *Limonium [Statice] binervosum* (Rock Sea-lavender). There were rosettes of very clear-cut oval leaves, with a tiny red point; these were flat against the ground, and the wiry flower-stems were dead, a rich brown. They varied from 2 to 6 inches high, mostly 3–4. They were all over the slope and on the rocks, where they were mixed with another colony of the *Inula*. Another photograph when these two are out together! Couldn't find a single fresh flower so could not record this. However, this trip produced three interesting and uncommon plants, all rather wonderful at this date. Surface of leaves slightly glaucous.

Back to the Cob lagoon. Still nothing. Had tea at the forest end of the Cob and then went out on the saltmarshes to try to settle the *Oenanthe* question. First plant was *Oe. fistulosa* but I think the next was *Oe. pimpinelloides*.

Cakile maritima (Sea Rocket) makes a sprawling bush about 3 feet across. The central stem buried in the sand (it had blown into it and made a mound). The branches emerge horizontally and then turn upwards, all entangled together. Stems and leaves are clear pale green, smooth and succulent. The flower-stems are ribbed; the calyx pale greenish-buff, slightly saccate and erect. The corolla-tube is creamy, slightly longer than the calyx. The petals are pale lilac, arranged two up and two down round the six soft yellow stamens which come just level with the top of the tube. The pistil is pale green and shorter than the stamens, enclosed in the tube. My plant was clearly an exceptionally late one. I found others which had entirely gone to seed and were shedding it. In all cases only the upper cell of the seed-vessel had developed (cf. the Mallorca one). It contained one brown seed. My plant was visited by bumble- and other wild bees.

Sea Rocket (*Cakile maritima*)

3 October, Tuesday

To Llanddwyn Bay to draw and photograph the Sea Rocket. Did about two-thirds of the drawing, and realised afterwards that I had taken the photograph with the yellow filter on.

Went round to the Cob saltmarsh to settle the *Oenanthe* question – which I did to my satisfaction: there is *Oenanthe fistulosa* with smooth soft hollow stems and no bracts (but a few bracteoles) and also *Oenanthe pimpinelloides* with practically solid stems, quite hard and markedly ridged, and with a few fine bracts at the main umbel. Also the seed-vessel is longer, and has longer horns on one side than the other, as shown in SRC.

4 October, Wednesday

To Malltraeth morning to give in my list. We went all through it and I was able to add ten to the record of plants.

Reg Arthur said the Little Egret was still in the marsh on Monday so I decided to go through the forest and try to verify the *Ranunculus hederaceus* and see the bird. It started to drip. I found Hare's-foot Clover. I searched the slack under the look-out but could find no *Ranunculus.* Nor could I see the bird. The rain became a downpour. I sat on a dune under the oilskin and as soon as it slackened a little made a dash for the car, but the way was long and wet. Had some tea and went home.   †

5 October, Thursday

Went to Llanddwyn Bay to finish the Sea Rocket. Took another photograph without the filter! Then walked south, found several more of these plants all in the leafless seed stage; mine must have been a late freak. These were a mass of seed-vessels, half of them dead-ripe and dropped; all only had the upper cell developed.

Beguiled by the guidebook, went to have a look at Rhoscolyn. Got down to the horse-shoe bay only to find it hedged in with notices of 'Private', 'No Parking Here', 'This Runway must be kept clear' etc. It seemed impossible to penetrate to any wild coast. There were Tree-mallows. I should have gone to Trearddur Bay and walked south from there. The drip started again. I came back via Llanynghenedl, Bodedern and Llan-gefni. This was beautiful unspoilt pastoral country.

6 October, Friday

To Malltraeth Forest to draw the little clump of *Parnassia* on the rock. Lovely sunny morning. Found the circular dikes and mounds where the Little Egret might have been and walked all round it with camera at the ready but had no luck. Had lunch on the Cob. Became overcast afternoon. Dealt with *Spergularia marginata*, of which there was a nice plant in the stones near the samphire. Went to Pen-lôn to look for *Crepis nicæensis* but did not find it.

Grass-of-Parnassus (*Parnassia palustris*)

7 October, Saturday

To Talyfoel with ideas of walking along the coast westwards but it looked stormy so I didn't. Took several photographs instead as the tide was at the full and the surface dead calm and silvery, with wonderful reflections of Caernarvon Castle etc.

A cloud, flat and very high (clear of Snowdon), had hung over the Beaumaris end and across to between Talyfoel and Pen-lôn. It now began to move back so I went to Pen-lôn where the sun came out and the sky was unbroken blue for the rest of the day. What luck for my last! Had a walk round before lunch and found the *Crepis nicæensis* which was a great relief. Wrote up some notes, lay in the sun and walked round again. Found five more plants for the list. Decided that two tiny centauriums about an inch high which were flowering just where I had tea were *Centaurium littorale*. All the leaves were very narrow and strap-shaped, and the basal ones had only three very dim veins. The fine long-pointed calyx sections came right up to the top of the tube. These, and the leaves and two at any rate of the corners of the stems showed a minute but bristly ciliation under the glass. I suppose this is what CTW means by 'scaberulous'. The seed-vessel projected well beyond the calyx in the brown ripe stage. I looked at a number of other plants after this; they were nothing like so clear-cut, and I can't help thinking that there are a whole lot of transitional types growing here. Took in a second list for the card-index, and found that Musk Thistle was not in.

8 October, Sunday

Packed up and started along the coast to Pen-lôn. Picked a fine piece of Bristly Oxtongue to take home to draw. Then wrote up the *Spergularia rupicola*. To Penmon and photographed the dovecote. Drove through towards the lighthouse and had lunch at the top of the slope facing Puffin Island. Afterwards climbed down to the shore and found a piece of cliff draped with samphire. And a whole lot more of the Tree-mallow near the cottage. Took photographs of the lighthouse and Puffin Island.

Then to Benllech to get the *Serratula*. There were no flowers left now. I picked two pieces but was never able to do anything with it as the leaves curled up and the Ox-tongue absorbed all the time and energy there was. Had tea in the Nant Ffrancon between storms – it looked very black and threatening – and arrived home just after dark.

19 November, Sunday

At Widcombe Hall, Bath. Going round the garden, noticed Dog's Mercury in flower all over the place! This seemed extraordinary. Took a plant home and found it was the annual variety, which I didn't know existed. *Mercurialis annua.* CTW gives July–Oct. as flowering season. It was branched, and the joints were rather swollen like balsam joints. Leaves more shiny than the perennial one's. I put it in a bucket in the yard and it remained there until the frost killed it off at Christmas – in quite good condition all those weeks, but I never had the time to draw it.

26 November, Sunday

To Monksfields to collect blackberries, which I did after a little argument. Afterwards had a walk along the road west of the pub. Sun set, and cast up a vertical beam of light like a searchlight, which caught a small cloud and made a completely circular rainbow on it, like a tiny Brocken without the spectre. This beam was white at first but gradually deepened in colour until there was a glorious sunset sky, with pink clouds and a green gap low down and a rosy ribbon of aeroplane vapour right across it. I took a series of photographs of this sunset which turned out quite well.

23 December, Saturday

Started freezing hard. By 27th river was frozen over. Fog every day. Freezing on windscreens. Five inches of snow on 30th.

5

THE TRAIN OF THE PROPHET

January 1962 – April 1964
Shropshire & Marches, Anglesey

2 January, Tuesday

About twenty degrees of frost in the night. Milk frozen in the larder. Washing-up bowl stuck to the sink.

3 January, Wednesday

The change came and a slight thaw started.

4 January, Thursday

Went to take photographs of the frozen river – last chance. There was a solid line of tracks across the ice just below the Port Hill Bridge, where people had walked across.

27 January, Saturday

Afternoon went round Pitchford road etc. looking for leaf-mould to pot lilies in. Went into the dip by Pitchford Hall. There wasn't any, but saw the first weak-looking soft shoot of Dog's Mercury pushing through. Found gorgeous black mould under oaks by the wall round the back of Acton Burnell Park and scraped up several buckets full.

28 January, Sunday

To Maengwynedd. Walked half-way up the slope to the Bwlch. Have seen no interesting birds in Maengwynedd this winter – because there are no berries at all.

4 February, Sunday

To Camlad with Mr Rutter to look for the geese. Soon found about 150 in fields to right of bridge – then about 450 further in. Went round to Forden Crossroads and from there saw some hundreds more – we reckoned 1,000 plus altogether. Had lunch on Montgomery road. Nothing at Stalloe. Went round to Leighton – nothing much on Severn meadows. Up on to Long Mountain and after some messing about found the way into the redwoods (Greenwood Lodge). A mass of Snowdrops just inside. Had a very pleasant walk in these woods. A grey and drizzly day.

18 February, Sunday

To the Snowdrop valley above Pulverbatch. They were just perfect, full-spread but quite fresh. I took about half a dozen photographs, two of them close-ups, and one in the 8–15-foot range. There are not enough of the flowers to be really thrilling – perhaps they have been over-picked; but it is delightful that what there are are really wild. They seem to like being near the stream, and grow in pretty groups by the hazel bushes. Further up were handsome clumps reaching up through the dead bracken. The spreading outer petals have about eight delicate veins. Their bases are narrow so that the inner ones grow between them. These are of thicker texture; the bright yellowish-green makes a horse-shoe round the notch, and inside three thick vertical lines each side of it and an indication of a fourth. The veins between them are positive grooves and the whole pattern has an edging of cruddled white. Six orange-yellow stamens are tightly grouped round a fine-pointed pistil which only just protrudes beyond them. The young leaves are glaucous.

Alder saplings were coming up by the stream. The bloom on the fat young buds was nearly as blue as wood-smoke.

I went round to Habberley and seeing the Holly forest obviously in good health and preservation (which was the other object of the day's expedition) decided not to go round to the Minsterley side. I went up the Gatten road. In a field on the right was a flock of sheep several of which had Magpies on their backs! A bird would run along to the top of the sheep's head, half flop over its nose and then run back to the tail end again. I watched this performance several times, and tried to photograph it out of the car window, not daring to get out. Just hope one of them may be clear enough to enlarge.

Turned up the rough road to Lower Vessons Farm. The owner directed me to Upper Vessons from which one can motor right over to Snailbeach. I left the car just through the upper gate and walked in the forest and took more photographs. Berwyn was clear, and Aran Fawddwy and Cadair Idris could just be seen over the western rim.

4 March, Sunday

To Maengwynedd. There was an inch of snow at home, so telephoned Mr Morris to find out what the road was like. It was reported clear. As I went westwards the snow became a mere skittering and at Knockin the countryside was suddenly green. Took several photographs in the Tanat Valley, including the lime avenue at Llangedwyn.

At the dog-leg in Maengwynedd I photographed the little waterfall and its pool, with icicles glistening in the sun. In the afternoon I also took the bigger waterfall, which was lined with snow and icicles, with the white-seamed black mountain in the background. Gleams of sun came through occasionally. The stream in its flat channel above the fall was bridged over with snow, which had rents in it edged with transparent pitted ice. I took this too, and when the picture came, I couldn't make out which way up it should be.

Maengwyn said the Llanrhaeadr fall had been a really spectacular sight with 10-foot icicles.

18 March, Sunday

Men stock-planting, the soil is just wonderful. Started late (about 12.35). Stopped on Knockin Heath for lunch, got over the hedge and found it so warm in the sun that I had it out under the bank. The sandy soil was warmer than my hand. Curled up and went to sleep, from the depths of which I was aroused at 2.20 by a honking, to find a tractor nearly upon me with a huge double Cambridge roller. Removed self and effects with all speed.

In a hedge-bank facing southwest near Llynclys I found the first two Celandines of the year. One had eight petals, the other eleven, overlapping, highly varnished, vivid yellow except at the base, where the opaque yellow gives way to an almost transparent pale green. The backs of the petals are streaked with purplish-brown except at the base. A thick cluster of golden stamens crowded in the middle. This would be the fertile variety. CTW says that the bulbil-producing one has the stamens and carpels less numerous and less fertile, and grows in shadier places. This warm bank had all sorts of tender shoots pushing through its yellowish moss: there were leaves of Lords-and-Ladies tightly rolled but thrusting several inches up; Dandelions reaching out but not spread flat; furry blobs of Ground-ivy on thread-like stems not much more than an inch long; and tiny tips of vetch of less than an inch, with spear-head leaves folded close together, glaucous-grey with hair-streak veins below. All these so small and so soft one wondered how they would survive another night of thirteen degrees of frost if it came.

From Morda turned into the lanes and by Trefonen and Llansilin to Moelfre. The lake was frozen except at the roadside edge. Went round under the western end of the Gyrn and walked up a little way. Found a little rill flowing from under the roots of a hedge-bank willow, cutting a 2-inch bed through a mat of golden-saxifrage. A day of superb sunshine and a kindling of life in spite of the cold. Heard a Curlew on Knockin Heath.

15 April, Sunday

To Clun, Bucknell etc. with Mr Rutter. A really bitter east wind raging. We went up by the church in Clun and turned left, and up the road to Fiddler's Elbow. From here there is a wonderful view to southwest and we found a spot under a bank which sheltered us from the east wind and so were able to have lunch out. A Raven croaked around; the nest was in the wood above us. We walked up to have a look at it, a huge mass of sticks in the top of a larch. Unfortunately the other Raven was lying dead at the foot of the tree; presumably it had been shot.

We went on down to Bucknell, and then up the valley to Stowe, a hamlet in a cul-de-sac facing south. We had a very pleasant walk in this lovely place. Below us on the other side of a running ditch was a glowing golden patch of Alternate-leaved Golden-saxifrage – and a little further on a smaller one of the Opposite-leaved kind, about half the size in all its parts.

We did not see a single Buzzard all day.

22 April, Easter Sunday

Lovely sunshine all morning; didn't believe it would last. Planted row of broad beans out. Had lunch in loggia; sat in corner by it for a short time afterwards. This is a good spot. 2.40 decided to go out. Went via Marton to Caer Din, Bishop's Castle. Lay in the hedge till tea-time, then went up to the earthwork. All the Welsh mountains visible from Berwyn to Cadair Idris. Lying against the bank, with a sheep's-eye view of the grass in front of me, I saw all the gossamer glinting in the sun; there was a slight breeze, which made silver shimmers run to and fro along the threads like a fairy telegraph. When I stood up it was all invisible, though the whole field was enmeshed in it. The only green patches in the hedges are Lilac, Gooseberry and Honeysuckle.

23 April, Monday

Walked up to feed the poultry owing to the unbroken line of cars on the road. Heard a Cuckoo up in Mottram's Wood. Collected J. Haseler and went to Caer Din again. Not quite so good as yesterday; there was a brisk east wind but we settled on the west side for lunch and lay all afternoon in lovely warmth. Learnt that Edenhope is pronounced Edenop, and forthwith a woman came down the road to the Dog and Duck where we were having tea and said she lived at Edenop Barn, pointing to the opposite slope. This structure however was invisible to both of us. She had a long pink-and-white-striped skirt with black apron over. We walked on Edenhope Hill towards Two Crosses. Came home via Mellington where I took photographs of Butterbur and golden-saxifrage.

24 April, Tuesday

Evening to Grinshill to see Downes. There was a Cuckoo in the wood, calling incessantly. Also a Green Woodpecker calling and drumming, and another loud repeated bird-call which I did not know, unless it was a Nuthatch – but repeated half a dozen times instead of three, as at Linley. Some chestnuts just spreading their leaves.

25 April, Wednesday

About 6.30 a.m. heard a Cuckoo from my bed, to my great pleasure. Also a warbler – my first this year – about twenty days late.

26 April, Thursday

This morning heard a distant Curlew from the office, from the Sharpstones direction. In the afternoon went out to see the men hoeing in the rose-field. Harry Jones had avoided rotavating a Lapwing's nest with four eggs in it. It was just a shallow hollow lined with a few roots; the eggs were very dark and not easy to see. Thorn hedges have turned green since Sunday. There is quite a lot of Blackthorn in the hedge between the 5-acre and the 8-acre, just coming into full flower.

28 April, Saturday

The Swallows have arrived at the buildings. Hope they approve of my arrangements for them. Fetched various plants from the old nursery; was putting *Iris stylosa* in under the house-wall when the owl, which hoots by day as well as by night, flew round and settled in the gable by my bedroom window. This was about 4.30. All the thrushes etc. set up a terrific clatter, and in a few minutes it flew off to the limes.

To the Mansells at Mytton for sherry. Montford Bridge is in a smother of damson blossom.

29 April, Sunday

Wonderful sunshine all day, but a cold northeast wind. The lawn and the next-door shed were white with frost at 5.30 a.m. Put some plants in, then got away at 12.20. Went to the house-site on Llynclys Hill. Violets, Cowslips and Ground-ivy were the first flowers that met the eye; a rich clump of Marjoram growth. Had lunch in a hollow out of the wind, leaning against a huge grassed-over mole-hill. Afterwards went more to the right than I have done before and found half a dozen really splendid plants of *Helleborus foetidus* in a small quarry about 5–6 feet deep. They seem to like shelter, and to be nearly on the rock. Took photographs. There was one particularly beautiful plant with a simple flower-stem, poised above a band of limestone, with its leaves fanning downwards, and its flowers richly tinged with purple. †

The thickets were full of warblers and I saw one hopping about the bottom of a thorn bush. A Whitethroat, on the other hand, shouted his presence from the top-most branch of any tree or bush he alighted on. A Curlew went over in particularly full-throated song soon after I arrived. I also heard a Chiffchaff at last.

On the dry edge of the quarry, where all other plants had given way to rock, were several groups of *S. tridactylites* (Rue-leaved Saxifrage) in full flower – just 2 inches high, with tiny flowers of finest white, petals separate, rounded, with a central vein, ten pale cream stamens; the red glands which covered the stems and calyx and edged the leaves glistened fiery in the sun. Took a photograph but do not suppose 3½ feet could be close enough for such a fairy plant, although the patch more or less filled the picture.

Had tea here, then went on up to the western end of Gyrn Moelfre. This time I went up to the top of the shoulder and came down the ridge on the northern side of the stream. What a perfect piece of country, with the swooping lines of the hills ('the train of the prophet'), and all its beauty unspoilt.

1 May, Tuesday

Was pruning the roses (!! Nevada etc.) at 7.30 in the evening, when a flock of Swifts flew screaming round the church. Tel. Frank Gribble – but he saw one somewhere about the middle of April, before the Swallows!

4 May, Friday

To Beaumaris by easy stages. Started about 11 a.m., stopped in the crossroad between Knockin Heath and the A5 and had China tea. Glorious sunshine. Berwyn had attracted the usual cloud and there was heavy rain in the Vale of Llangollen. Came out of it at Corwen and had lunch out in warm sunshine in the usual place by Rhûg Bridge. Got out the bed and had an hour's siesta. Shopped at Capel Curig, then went up to Penypass where I had tea and a chat with old Owen, now eighty-six and on his feet again, but says he hasn't been out of the house for three years. There is a very good simple slate tablet in the porch to 'Geoffrey Winthrop Young. Mountaineer and Poet' and the dates of his eighty-two years.

After this the sunshine was so wonderful that I went up the Pyg Track a little way and lay on a grassy slope sheltered from the east wind, and really basked! It was after 7 p.m. when I trailed into Beaumaris at last.

5 May, Saturday

The wind went right round to southwest and the clouds piled up. Went to Malltraeth to present my permit but no one was at home. Dunlin, Ringed Plover, Shelduck and Redshank in the Cob lagoon. Went back to the end of the Cob and had lunch and afterwards went out on the marsh. Nothing to be seen but Dandelions – in fact, there was far less than last October. Went to Pen-lôn to see what was there. The most conspicuous plant was the Meadow Saxifrage, flowering beautifully all over the place. On the dry slopes was *Saxifraga tridactylites* – minute plants, much smaller than the Llynclys ones – mixed in one place with equally minute chickweed and veronica. Must track these two down. The Dwarf Willow was covered with golden catkins. The marshes towards Newborough had Marsh-marigolds, and Bogbean just beginning.

6 May, Sunday

Grey, blustery and drizzling, a good deal of the day. Went to Cors Bodeilio. Nothing but Marsh-marigolds and sedges. A good deal of the bog had been burnt and cut over. It was a problem to find a sheltered spot for lunch. In the evening went to Llanddona and got on to the rough hill north of Red Wharf Bay. It was very beautiful with thickets of Blackthorn, clumps of Gorse, Bluebells under both and little hollows with Marsh-marigolds. There were Mallard in some of them. Took the car down to the bottom of the road and found it came out on the natural shore; no houses, and a good sheltered spot at the bottom of the lane with high hedges – just what had been so badly wanted on other visits!

7 May, Monday

Weather much the same. Went to Plas Newydd Nursery in the morning; bought stocks which were a joy in the dull colourless room. Just past Plas Newydd found a dead Tawny Owl on the road, still warm. No head, not much body. Wings and feet perfect. Wings barred in tawny-brown and very dull dark brown on the upper side, off-white below but with the dark bars showing through. There were a few white spots on the main quills above. The legs were covered with 'fur' right down to the claws, of which there were three forward and one behind, all long, very curved and sharp, shiny black. The 'palm' of the claw was quite fleshy and folded, pinkish-buff and very finely scaly. The 'fur' on the legs was off-white with a few dull brown flecks. I sent the wings to Stella.

Went on to Malltraeth. Tried the Warden's house twice but he seems to be away. Walked on the marsh and back through the forest; found *Taraxacum laevigatum* with the protuberance on the sepals, rather a horn on the midrib than a duplicated lip – but also others with the very finely-cut leaves which had not got it. Wonder if there are not hybrid swarms between this and the Common Dandelion. There were no seeds yet, which I suppose would settle it.

'Took photographs of the lighthouse and Puffin Island.' (see p.86)

'Frozen Severn, Port Hill, Shrewsbury.' (see p.88)

'Malltraeth with rainbow.'

Anglesey: South Stack headland. (see p.99)

8 May, Tuesday

To Bodnant; went along the coast. Twice round Conway, which is altogether too medieval for motor traffic, before finding my way out. Had lunch at Roewen, a lovely village, secluded and unspoilt. Beautiful gentians and tree-heathers at Gilfach, from where there is a superb view up the Conway valley. Bodnant had suffered badly from the frost and there were not nearly the glories I had expected. *Azalea augustinii*, *Camellia* J.C. Williams and Donation, *Azalea albrechti*, a lovely deep pink tending to carmine, and the very free-flowering *Azalea chasmanthum* were the highlights. There was also an exquisite double azalea in a mauvey-pink, loose-growing, 2½–3 feet, whose name I didn't get. The paper-barked Birches, and the deep-copper-barked one, *B. alba sinensis septentrionalis*, were also thrilling, and the *Arbutus andrachnoides*. The sun blazed all day and it was almost stuffy in that deep garden. Came back via Llanrwst, Betws and Nant Ffrancon. A much better route. The Conway valley is entirely unspoilt, and there are no frustrations.

9 May, Wednesday

A great improvement in the Anglesey weather – sunshine nearly all day, although the southwest wind was still cold. After calling at the Plas Newydd gardens, I went to Llanddwyn, and in the afternoon to the island. There was no trace of any Sea Rocket; it must germinate very late. Thrift was about half-way out and very fresh and colourful; luckily there were a number of patches together in full bloom so I took photographs. The Squill was also out, very short and close in the turf, on the inner sheltered side on the whole and the Thrift on the outer rocky side. So I could not get them together. On a tump in some fine scree were some tiny white flowers which I assumed at first to be more *Saxifraga tridactylites*, but luckily looked closer and they turned out to be *Sagina subulata* (Awl-leaved Pearlwort). †

As I was coming away, two Linnets scolded from the abandoned garden. The hen was very demure, but the cock was in splendid plumage: rosy forehead and breast, rich chestnut back and white flash on the wing.

Had tea in the Llanddwyn car park, then went round to Pen-lôn, with the intention of taking photographs of the Dwarf Willow in flower. Did this, but the richest yellow had already faded since Saturday; the moment must be snatched with this plant. The snowy drifts of Meadow Saxifrage are increasing; took these too, and the views of Snowdonia and the Rivals that I never can resist, though I have them already.

10 May, Thursday

A wonderful sunny day. To morning coffee with Mrs Crichton. Met Mr Owen, who showed me on the map where gentians grow at Bodafon – autumn ones – I hope they won't turn out to be *Gentianella*??

Went on by stages to South Stack. There was a Common Tern at Four Mile Bridge, just to keep up the tradition. The Gorse was nothing like the blaze of two (three?) years ago. All the banks beyond Trearddur were an off-white haze of *C. officinalis* (Scurvygrass). The slopes near the lighthouse steps were a mixture of this and Thrift and Sea Campion just beginning to come out – the beauty spoilt by litter. Managed to find a sunny corner and lay in bliss for a time. Went down the steps, took photographs. There was a man from Denbigh with a telephoto lens taking the birds. He gave me long directions how to find six pairs of Fulmars on Penmaenmawr, which I had no intention of doing and am afraid my expression became rather fixed. Took a view of the stacks just beyond him; he said I should want to get in the 'castle' at the top, but as it is a very pseudo construction I did not do this either. He said the view of the curved strata from the lighthouse was good; this piece of information appealed to me more, third time lucky.

I went back to the car and had tea, and afterwards wandered over the top looking for the Annual Rock-rose but could not get a glimpse of the smallest shred of it. Lay for ten minutes in a sunny flowery hollow and wished I had done this all the time – it would have been more profitable.

11 May, Friday

Grey, cloudy, rain in the morning. Mist down to the roots of the mountains all day.

12 May, Saturday

To Pen-lôn. Cloudy, and wind now in the north and very cold. Found a hollow behind a south-facing dune; a gap came in the clouds and the sun shone through; it seemed a miracle. Lay and basked all afternoon, then went down to Llanddwyn to finish description of *Sagina*; had difficulty in finding it as the flowers were shut – just two remained open enough to get details. There was a pair of Common Terns in the bay; they called to each other with a quiet, conversational 'chip, chip' which drew my attention to them.

13 May, Sunday

Grey though a little warmer at Beaumaris. Collected the milk at Plas Llanfair Farm and suddenly decided to go to South Stack. Clouds thinned and there was glorious sunshine in that area. Stopped at the Four Mile Bridge antique-shop and got involved. Took Thrift in great clumps in a cobble wall, King-cups below the rubbish-tip and Sea Campion against a blue sky. After these diversions went down to the headland. This turned out better than I had ever dreamed. The coast is a succession of deep clefts and small stacks; at the head of one of the clefts I found a grassy hollow just below the level of the moor and facing the sun where I lay and basked and put on another layer of tan. Half-way through the afternoon I began to explore, and take photographs. The stacks had nesting Herring Gulls and one pair of Black-backs. There were also nests in the cliff below me. I was able to photograph one which was only a few feet down. I could easily have taken the single egg; this gull must have been inexperienced, they usually put them in inaccessible places. There was another a few feet below this; by craning my neck I could see the bird sitting on it but to photograph her would have put my life in peril. I wandered on round the headland until I was facing South Stack lighthouse: I saw a yellow blob and having been disillusioned so often decided it was a Dandelion. Took Holyhead Mountain with the white farm and sloping fields and a blue sea, and started to wander back towards the car when I realised there was a colony of strange composite plants all around me, very much wrapped up in cotton wool but with a few open flowers here and there. I took a number of photographs, all close-ups ($3\frac{1}{2}$ feet or $3\frac{1}{2}$–$4\frac{1}{2}$ feet) because I had to; it was exasperating to think what a golden mass there would be in about a fortnight, and what a picture that slope would be. They were on the lowest part of the headland, towards the outer end but facing South Stack lighthouse, growing in nice cosy grass. All the rest of the headland is stony and covered with a close carpet of heather and gorse. I wondered what on earth I had got and went back for tea and enlightenment from CTW. What was my surprise to discover that I really had got a rarity this time. *Senecio spathulifolius*, which only grows here and on Mickle Fell in Westmorland. Went back fully armed with notebook, CTW etc. Tried to draw it, but there wasn't time to do it properly. CTW says the basal leaves are '± coarsely toothed'. Minus seems to have it in this case – I couldn't see a single tooth anywhere. If *S. integrifolius* didn't stop at Gloucester I should really wonder if this were not it – 'grows in calcareous grassland', whereas *S. spath* 'grows on maritime cliffs'. What with the glory of the day, the complication of the table at Four Mile Bridge, and this problem, decided to come back tomorrow instead of going home. (There was *Inula crithmoides* in one of the clefts, NB.)

14 May, Monday

Arrived at the headland 11.45. Took several photographs of the banks of Squill, then went down to the *Senecio* path. I found a plant with three flowers out and started to draw it. The sun had begun to come through just after Gaerwen, and there was wonderful sunshine all over Holyhead Island, with a cold northwest wind however. In the little bays of Trearddur the sea was deep blue with dark streaks, but not by the Stack. I found a comfortable little hollow behind a rock for lunch and was really warm. Finished the plant about 3.30, then photographed it. All this was blissful.

About 4 p.m. I went up to South Stack and took photographs of various flowers – tried Stag's-horn Plantain, Portland Spurge, Bird's-foot-trefoil, and a lovely bank by the steps with everything flowering at once. Then I took the Guillemot-shelves and the arching strata. The noise here was like the din in a row of pig-stys at feeding time – groans, squeals and grunts in every key. I then went down to the lighthouse but there was not the view of these strata that I had been led to expect. However there was another set on the other side of the bridge that made up for it. There are 401 steps from the bridge to the top.

These last two days, particularly, made up for the rather gloomy beginning of the holiday.

Field Fleawort (*Senecio spathulifolius*)

Senecio spathulifolius. The grassy slope had a generous colony of these plants in all stages of development, varying from two or three leaves, and big clusters of leaves, through to plants with flowering stems. All had their basal foliage tight down in the grass so that it was difficult to see at first that the stem was longer than (or even as long as) the blade, but I did come to believe it in the end. These rosette-leaves were of a long irregular oval shape, the blade curving in abruptly and then running down the stem in a narrow wing. The stem-leaves were more elongated and sessile. They were all of a deep lustrous green, almost shiny, above, but with short scattered hairs and with strands of white cotton stitched across them. Below, they were white-felted with a thicker covering of cotton. The central vein was broad and pale green.

The flower-stem stood erect, nearly 1 cm thick, pale green and some-times ribbed with dark reddish-brown. It was thick with tomentum. The flowers are grouped at the top in a rough umbel, but branch off alternately, the lowest with a leafy bract, the higher with a long fine-pointed scale. All the branches, buds and bracts are enmeshed in loops of white cotton of the finest spider-web gauge – at the young stage in which I found them, some parts of the head disappeared in it entirely. The receptacle is goblet-shaped and the sepals are in a single row, green, and bound together with cotton for two-thirds or three-quarters of their length, but separating at the tips into fine recurving points tinged with dull purple. I measured the fully-developed flower at the top of my plant; the ray-florets tended to curve down, but when they were flat it was 1¼ inches across. These florets were of the deepest buttercup-yellow, broad and pointed or with one notch at the tip. There were twelve to fifteen in the ones I counted. The disc-florets were a deeper orange-yellow.

With regard to 'teeth' on the basal leaves: by dint of very careful search, and if looked at from the underside (the edges of the leaves tended to be rolled under), a few pale points could be perceived, widely spaced, which could be interpreted as the tips of the teeth, but there were no indentations between them whatever; on the majority of leaves even these points did not appear.

My plant was 10½ inches high.

18 May, Friday

The Swallows approve my arrangements in the ex-cowshed and have built on a projecting plank – a huge blob of mud. This gives me great satisfaction.

19 May, Saturday – 25 May, Friday

Chelsea. Bitterly cold weather. The Oxford Ragwort in gay full flower in the hospital ruins, the bombed-site near Crosby Hall and railway banks and roadsides all the way down.

29 May, Tuesday

Susan showed me the Chaffinch's nest in the hedge opposite my window. The cock was shouting his song a month ago. Now there is a young fluffy family. The nest was wedged in the multiple fork of an Elder, very well camouflaged and built with the usual artistry.

A grey and drizzly morning. To Plaish to see about the supposedly ailing roses – found them in excellent shape but a little late. Hedges full of flowers – the parsley exquisite, Archangel Nettle, Greater Celandine etc. Approaching Plaish, I saw a patch of unfamiliar pink in the hedge on the left and thought there must be a garden escape of some kind. Investigated afterwards and found it was a plant with a pink-stitchwort flower but broad oval leaves like a campion. A man working on the hedge-banks was sure it was not a garden-plant. Poking through the hedge, I found it in great drifts all through a little wood, an exquisite dim rosy lace. I was completely mystified and wondered if a new hybrid had arisen between stitchwort and Red Campion. Took pieces home and found it was *Claytonia alsinoides* – with only two records for Shropshire, a C XIX one and 1938, the latter in the Plaish section of the county.

1 July, Sunday

A lovely summer day. To Llynclys Hill. Had a look at the Holy of Holies. There were two butterfly-orchids (but which?), both measly specimens on the left of the track near the entrance – and a few very poor *Orchis pyramidalis* just opening. The place looked scorched. Some sort of cultivator had been dragged across the open part, breaking the turf in places. Was deceived once more by *Pimpinella saxifraga*, into thinking I had found something new. Went to the house-site – this was also rather between-times – Marjoram and hypericums not out – only a few small *Orchis pyramidalis*. Hellebores looked very flourishing though nearly smothered in other growth.

Had lunch. The sun was really burning hot. Went up to Glanhafon. This was more temperate owing to a strong breeze from the west. Dog Roses and Foxgloves were coming out in the lower hedges, but the upper one by the hill gate was a big one of still fresh Hawthorn. A wonderful view of all the hills, blue to the horizon, with the Wrekin dead in line with the Tanat Valley. Curlews were still calling and a Wheatear scolded me from successive fence-posts. As I closed the hill gate to come away, the west wind brought a great waft of Hawthorn scent down to me – the last I shall smell this year I suppose.

7 July, Saturday

To Hereford to judge at the Rose Show. A perfect summer day, not too hot or too cool, with all the summer flowers blowing in great profusion, Dog Roses arching out from the hedges, creamy masses of Elder blossom, Honeysuckle in lumps, and the later umbelliferous plants threading among them all. I came back by the country route – Mortimer's Cross, Wigmore, Leintwardine, and what a good idea it was. I only met about half a dozen vehicles and the country was wonderful. Stopped and brewed tea, and sat on the hedge-bank on one of the high spots on the Roman Road, about two miles out of Craven Arms. Had hardly moved off again when I saw an owl fly into the hedge. I stopped, and there it was in a tall Elder or thorn just above me, a Little Owl, looking at me very intently with piercing yellow eyes. This was 5.40 p.m. It was mouse-brown, with streaks of lighter colour above and same scheme reversed below.

26 August, Sunday

Evening dashed up to Longmynd with Stella – the sun came out after a wet grey day. We drove up the Burway and down to the gliding station. Walked for about twenty minutes towards Yapsell Bank. The bracken is very short and pale green – I suppose late like everything else.

In the afternoon I saw a Swift flying about, just after we turned into Sutton Road from the bypass. This is the latest I have ever seen a Swift.

2 September, Sunday

Went up on the Longmynd with Stella. We arrived at the tumulus south of the gliding station at 1 p.m., just as it clouded over – there had been lovely sunshine from early morning. We just managed to have lunch out. Then S went off for a walk. I started off later and walked to the end of the hill and back with a small detour to the east. The heather was full of caterpillars and cocoons – there must have been millions and millions. They belong to the Vapourer Moth (*Orgyia antiqua*). The caterpillars had red spots along their sides, and yellow tufts of hair on four segments in the fore-part, on the back, a pair of tufts of black hair on the first segment and one tuft of black on the tail – all quite handsome. The yellow varied from vivid buttercup to soft buff; these duller ones are females, according to the book. The female moths have practically no wings and there are two broods. These must have been the offspring of the first brood. Next lot October – there won't be any heather left!

As we drove away, between Pole Cottage and the Boiling Well, a bird flew very fast and low across the road from the Pole slope down towards Ashes Hollow. It had very pointed wings and a wonderful flight, veering and dashing with the speed and grace of a Swallow. It was warm brown all over the upperparts and not very large. I don't think this can have been anything else but the hen Merlin. What luck. I never thought of bird-watching, there was so much motor traffic!

23 December, Sunday

A flock of Redwings in beautiful plumage has settled in Miss Williams' unkempt Hawthorn hedge which is glowing crimson with berries. The rusty patch is broad and rich, the dark streaks deepest nigger. They have 'cheeks' very well defined by the curved light line above the eye (practically white) and a very dark band below – this one is in fact almost triangular and I suppose a conglomeration of a number of the flank streakings. They were very plump and very busy.

The hedge by the tin shed on the 8-acre on the other hand has been appropriated by Fieldfares. Four or five of these, perhaps more, fly out whenever I go for vegetables, and settle in the oak tree or on the telegraph-wires from which they curse me 'chak-chak' for the interruption. Their beaks are yellow tipped with black. Their heads slatey-blue but their cheeks not so defined as the Redwings. The chestnut of the wing-coverts not so deep or rich as I have seen. All these birds shine a beautiful pale silver below when they take flight.

There is a flock of sixty to one hundred Lapwings on the 14-acre, with several Black-headed Gulls among them. And wagtails in all the plough, with other small birds. There was quite hard frost in the night.

24 December, Monday

Another hard frost. Took lunch and went to the Hem. At Polmere there was nothing but free-range hens (whose eggs I bought), the water being all frozen. Much the same at the Hem – there were a few Wigeon and a Shoveller right away on the far side. Had lunch in the car by the gate. Then went on to the crossroads. From here I soon saw geese out in the middle fields grazing in the rimy grass. One lot got up and circled low, but soon settled again; it was good to see their flight-drill, nearly as precise as Starlings', but more graceful and deliberate. They swept in big curves and the sun caught their white underparts as they turned, their wings long, narrow and sinuous, with the flexibility of a tern's – which one would not expect from a bird so solid-looking on the ground. There must have been nearly a thousand of them altogether. I went down the field to try to get a nearer view but couldn't. In the corner of the hedge was a Sloe bush with sloes still hanging, bloomy and plump like damsons. I ate one; there was no acidity left at all. The branches were thick with tiny flower-buds, in tight brown clusters, each with a pale tip of promise for the spring.

I went back to Marton Pool to look for Siskins etc. The pool was three-quarters covered with ice, and there was very little life. On an oak tree on the far side there was a pair of Treecreepers working busily like little mice. They were almost circular except for the tails, brown with streaks above, with a light inverted V in the wing-quills – a very dark line through the eye – all silvery-white below. Their movements were mouse-like too – a quick dart, then the body still, but the head going like lightning from side to side in the crevices of the bark. They started at ground level and worked up the trunk; when they came to branches they worked the underside, hanging upside-down.

I wonder if they survived?

1963

5 July, Friday

Went in the evening to the Dorrington sandpit with EMR. The first plant we saw was a great clump of white bedstraw, such as I had never set eyes on before. Later we found a similar large plant on the far side of the workings. It is pretty certainly *Galium erectum*, having narrow leaves and swellings above the nodes (as shown in SRC), but I want to see the print before I record it.

There were plants of *Sisymbrium orientale* all over the place, ranging in size with the dryness or otherwise of their position. The roots run horizontally a few inches down – one would have expected them to go straight down, in sand. Smooth round stem, with branches off in spiral arrangement, main stem zig-zagging slightly from one to the other – bracts slender, almost linear, edges with *very* slight waviness of outline. Calyx long and hairy, saccate at base. Flowers yellow, petals turning out flat on long limbs. Style grows fantastically into a long narrow seed-vessel 2½–3 inches long, all hairy at first, shedding the hairs from the tip downwards as it swells. Stigma a small club-like knob on the top. This plant has an air of originality. Basal leaves have spear-shaped end-leaflet and a pair at right angles to the midrib almost separately below.

The next thrill was a splendid plant (the one and solitary) of *Melilotus alba*, 6–7 feet high and generously branched, in all its fresh beauty.

28 September, Saturday

Weather improved so went round to the shingle-beach to see if it was possible to draw the horned-poppy. There was Hilly, back from South Wales, and with news of a phalarope which had been in the harbour an hour before, but had now vanished. We sat in the car while Frank ranged up and down. Soon the Rev. R. S. Thomas, poet, appeared, having been summoned urgently by telephone from Eglwysfach, and joined in the scanning. We got hungry so the Gribbles went off. I settled by the poppy (it was warm behind the concrete wall) and started work on it. But in a quarter of an hour Frank was back; the bird had reappeared in the harbour. It was under the breakwater when I got there, a tiny speck bobbing

Yellow Horned-poppy (*Glaucium flavum*)

white. Then it flew, and showed long pointed wings with conspicuous white bars, and a lovely turn of speed and grace. It was clear it was not a Red-necked Phalarope, but the handbook did not show Wilson's. Coming past in the afternoon to buy a rubber for the drawing, I had a much better view of it; it had come in just below the road and I could see every feather with the glass. The crown of the head was dark nigger-brown, also a narrow band all down the back of the neck. It had a brilliant white forehead, and white 'cheeks', but with quite a large black eye-spot. A tiny line of black joined the back of the eye-spot to the dark brown. The neck and upper flanks were still stained with traces of the summer's copper colour, but otherwise they and all other underparts were white, and as one looked down on the bird from above, made a white outline all round it. The back was all dark brown with each feather beautifully outlined in gold, very clear-cut and elegant. Four feathers in each wing-covert, and a very small patch in the middle just behind the neck, had grown in the winter colouring of pure dove-grey, perfectly smooth without any stripes. The beak was thickish (which indicates *not* Red-necked), and dark all over, not yellow with dark tip as shown in the handbook. The legs were never visible. It darted right and left with great speed, but never spun right round in the best phalarope tradition. Mostly it was on its own but once joined the gulls and got on quite well although so much smaller.

15 December, Sunday

Heavy murk. To the Hem. No sign of geese. But there is water again and Wigeon were there in fair numbers; also saw Shovellers. The usual Mallard and a large flock of Lapwings (a hundred or thereabouts). After eating lunch in the car, went to Marrington Dingle for teasels for Christmas decorations. Remembered after slithering down the steep road (where they had been hauling timber – ruts and mud appalling) that they were on the far side of the river, and as this was in full greeny-grey spate the Himalayan-type bridge, one tree-trunk with notches and a handrail that ceased over mid-stream, did not appeal. Greasy Wellingtons did not seem the ideal footwear for this crossing. I turned left and worked back towards the road and found some beautiful grasses 5–6 feet high. Also Hard Shield-fern and Broad Buckler-fern. †

29 December, Sunday

Showery morning. After lunch went out to Corndon. Spring running well – in a new asbestos pipe! Walked up to gate and then along grass-road running south. Wind increased up on the hill – a bitter northwester; I got ear-ache. Just this side of the bog five brace of grouse got up (I had noticed fresh droppings before this). On the further side a single bird got up scolding; it was too quick for me but I think it was a Snipe by the swerving flight, pointed wings and white underparts, and by the scolding voice.

I came back on a higher curve on to the grass-road. In one of the quarry hollows was a brown clump of dead fern. Picked a piece and although very curled up it seems it must be Parsley Fern. The size and position (on dry shale on the open hillside) also agree – it was about a foot high. The handlist of Shropshire Flora says 'Very rare – no recent record' and gives districts 10 and 12 – the Clee country. This is very exciting; the Corndon district will now have to be scoured.

1964

5 January, Sunday

A heavy grey day. Went afternoon to Corndon to check the *Cryptogramma crispa* (Parsley Fern). The top of the hill was in cloud and there was a hill-mizzle. Found a clump lower down than last week's and then started counting. When I got to sixty well-established clumps of various sizes, I felt it could be called a flourishing colony and stopped, as the rain was getting heavier. But I picked a green piece of infertile frond and pressed it – the stem is much longer than the blade with a few dark scales low down, otherwise green. Leaflets wedge-shaped with spreading veins. The fertile fox-red fronds were of course much more conspicuous – the same colour as the bracken but so much smaller and of an entirely different texture. Also it grows on rocky ground, not in the grass. It was all over the slope where there had been quarrying – in the shallow scoops, in the quarry-slit – it seems to like a *little* shelter. Now all the rest of the rocks in this district will have to be explored. The Atlas of the British Flora does not credit Shropshire with a single record – even a past one.

13 April, Monday

Went in the evening to collect the anemone and corydalis plants which I had left in the pond by the Tanat yesterday. They were still there. On coming out into the main valley road again, I decided to go up the lane opposite and round a sort of loop about a mile long. First came to a delightful cottage, Fron Teg, on the right with a gay garden. Just what I want, on a bank facing south. Trefeiliw is a farm in a hollow on the other side of the lane, tucked under the bank. At the top of the road was a place called Pendomen – with its end built right against a huge mound. What a lot of ancient sites there are in this valley.

6

UNMITIGATED SUPERFLUITY OF H$_2$O

April – May 1964 · Ireland

27 April, Monday

Flew to Cork from Birmingham airport. Left in glorious weather, almost hot. For about twenty minutes looked down on patchwork of green and red, then went into cloud. Climbed until we were out of it, and flew all the rest of the time above the white snowfield. It would have been such fun to see South Wales and the sea. Came down into the murk again at Cork – it was right down on the airfield and the taxi-driver told me it was touch and go whether we landed or were sent off to Shannon!

28 April, Tuesday

Not raining when I looked out of window – and signs of breaks in the clouds. Sun shining by mid-morning. Collected car and left Cork 12.30. Went to Bantry via Bandon and Dunmanway. This is dull. Splendid gorse, but country looked increasingly poverty-stricken the further west. Ardnagashel House proved to be on the edge of better country – Bantry and onwards a scatter of bungalows etc. and as they are of poorer quality than in Wales the effect is even worse. Nor is there the mitigating solid or good-looking cottage that helps in Wales. Was tempted to write off Ireland!

In Ardnagashel grounds there were beautiful slender trees with rich cinnamon bark. I thought they must be *Arbutus* but the leaves were small. These are *Myrtus luma*, which seeds itself here all over the place.

After tea, went up the lane by the Barony River. In the first sheltered corner were handsome plants of *Euphorbia hyberna* (Irish Spurge), just coming into flower. †

At the beginning of this road, in a Silver Birch glade, a dainty animal stepped into the open. I thought it might be a Roe Deer, but it was followed by another and they were half-grown kids. The herd built up to half a dozen in all sizes, followed by an ancient woman in black, bent at right angles, a thing I haven't seen since childhood. She waved her stick frantically like a witch and at last got them into the homeward path.

I went on up the road, which became rough and stony. Branches led off right and left to tiny holdings. Not the tiniest patch that is soil, or can be made into soil, is left – just like Mallorca but for the opposite reason. It is what can be got from the blanketing bog – not from the burning rock.

I found a veronica on top of a grassy wall – then, great excitement, another Irish plant – St Patrick's-cabbage, growing on the top of a bank and several feet up a tree, which branched in two, with the saxifrage all beautifully draped in the fork. *Saxifraga spathularis.* The leaves were large and lush, and the flowers in bud. Just one had rich pink stamens beginning to peep out. All along the banks were violas, which turned out to be *V. reichenbachiana.* In a trickle of stream crossing the path was a small *Ranunculus* which to my disappointment was *R. lenormandii*, not *R. lutarius.* The banks had all kinds of ferns just coming out; *Ceterach officinarum* was one, and *Asplenium obovatum* another. Altogether this was a rich and beautiful spot. Marsh Violets were growing all over the place. A Hooded Crow flew across the road as I went back to Ardnagashel – body all grey.

29 April, Wednesday

10.30 crossed to Garinish Island to see the garden. Conducted round by Mackenzie. *Rhododendron fragrantissimum* flourishing in the open, huge leptospermums which seed themselves and provide leg-cover. Evergreen *Ceanothus* of kinds unknown to me, one with a leaf as large as Gloire de Versailles. *Clianthus puniceus* of a terrific size in full blaze, *Embothrium* – the dark-eyed *Euphorbia*, closely related to *E. wulfenii.* The only rose a large climber spread-eagled over a rock. Bugles as ground-cover. Came away at 1.30 and went along west along the coast-road. Found a grassy hollow just over the wall above Seal Bay and lay in the sun for an hour or so. To find such a hollow is not easy – the land is either gorse or bog, without the nice soft heather bush of home. After this explored on along the coast-road as far as the east tip of Bere Island. Just after the Tim Healy Pass turn, there was a small saltmarsh, which had Scurvygrass and

Thrift in the usual mixture, but by a small stream there was Sea Plantain and *Glaux maritima.* †

Went back to Barony to write up the *Euphorbia* (see Tuesday). At lunch-time found the red female flowers of the Bog Myrtle. The foxy-red male flowers carpet all the flat places.

Beyond Dereeny met a jaunting-car with the owner travelling in lolling ease (I suppose). This was a genuine one and not the dolled-up kind that plies at Killarney. And a few miles further on a man and a boy had a cart-load of seaweed – the long ribbons – I was very interested to see.

30 April, Thursday

Spent the morning in the Barony Valley. Stopped to look at the *Euphorbia* again and found a whole patch of the Kidney Saxifrage in the bank. One or two flowers were out, petals beautifully marked with gold and red. Puzzled over the *Veronica* for some time – it has hairs in single lines up the stem but is not *V. chamaedrys.* Leaves are oblong and hardly have a petiole; the blade runs down to the node.

The weather turned grey after the usual pattern. Had lunch here then set off for Dereeny. Stopped in Killarney and bought a skirt-length in tabby weave of coral-red and gold. The Kenmare Bay is much less populated than Bantry. Dereeny quite wonderful – a beautiful position, with 100-year-old trees, and rhododendrons here and there, but a natural mixture of vegetation which is so pleasing because of the lack of any straining for effect. A glade of tree-ferns, and a wonderful eucalyptus which I went back after tea to photograph. This was not easy owing to surrounding vegetation but I got up on a bank and hope I got enough of it to give an idea. A glade had been cut and half a dozen *Rhododendron sinogrande* planted – what a sight for the future! There was an exquisite glimpse of a distant bridge framed in rhododendrons, opposite the house.

Came back over the Tim Healy Pass. This was fun. Just before getting into Glengariff, spotted a whole row of *Osmunda* ferns on the river-bank, about 3 feet high, bronzy-gold, just uncurling. It was late and there was a hay-field in between but hope to go back.

Lady Mersey told me of two more gardens – and woke me up on the subject of butterworts: there is a *P. grandiflora* with a flower 2½–3 cm – only in Cork and Kerry – not to mention the pale one. She also had flourishing bushes of *Rhododendron fragrantissimum.*

1 May, Friday

Superb early morning – glorious sunshine. No wind. As soon as I stepped out of the door heard a little 'chip-chip' out over the water – the terns had arrived. Got the glass and there was a pair – Common? – with black heads and rather dusky plumage.

Set off for Rossdohan. Photographed the *Embothrium* in Glengariff churchyard and some euphorbias beside the road. One or two of these had the flowers full-blown so I shall be able to settle these problems.

In Kenmare bought a piece of wool-mohair Donegal material of great beauty. Then along the north coast-road – this is dull, for some miles enclosed by the walls of someone's demesne. Blackwater is pretty. At Tahilla, turned down the rough road for Rossdohan. Had lunch by the road and then went in. The Walker family were not there; the very agreeable gardener showed me round. The vegetation here was quite staggering – a profusion of palms, tree-ferns and eucalyptus, in spite of the fact that there had been considerable storm-damage and the shelter was not perfect. A beautiful *Clethra* in flower. Several of the tree-ferns had the rich silver reverse as if they had been dipped in aluminium paint. Here also I had an orgy of photography. There were two prize eucalyptus even for this region, one with an enormous trunk in smooth pure white without a mark, name unknown. The other was a more ordinary variety, but huge, with five or six trunks, all most beautifully marked. I made despairing efforts at photographing these, but it is so difficult to get more than a fraction of these soaring trees into the picture. The acacias were also of a fantastic size; one had solid sickle-shaped leaves and I took it for a gum tree but was corrected. †

Came back over the tunnel pass in thick mist, after a short walk on Knocknagullion. These mountains are *not* attractive – they are one god-dam slime which comes off and me with it. †

2 May, Saturday

Grey weather, but at least not raining. Set off for Killarney, got there in about one-and-three-quarter hours. At Muckross Abbey Gate would have had to leave the car and was so hungry that I didn't feel like doing it. So went on into the town. Here both sides of the street were so thick with cars that I went clean through. Result of all this – I never saw a single

Arbutus or *Osmunda*, nor did I get the wonderful angora rugs I intended to. Turned into a side-road for the Gap of Dunloe and had lunch. Disillusioned with Killarney, decided to go on and see Glenbeigh. The long flats on each side of Killorglin seemed endless and the vegetation here is just ordinary. Normal farming seems possible. Killorglin rather a nice place with a long handsome bridge. As soon as the road approached the mountains again, things became interesting. There were quite a lot of thatched cottages brilliantly whitewashed. At Glenbeigh there is a long sand-bar running right out into Dingle Bay, with Rossbehy Creek behind it. I went down to the dunes and salt-flats (or machair) and had a walk. There was a tiny Mouse-ear Chickweed, *Honkenya*, Thrift (very short and tight), *Geranium molle*, and further out in the dunes thousands of Sea-holly, just pushing through. How I should love to see these all in flower. I came to a dune-slack which was not wet, but smooth like a lawn, and lay down and had a cat-nap. Then back and had tea at the Towers Hotel. Came back via Caragh Lake and then over Ballagh Beama. All the Caragh part was superb. Saw a Dipper on a rock in a river – and up in the hills a Kestrel shot up just by the car – it was on a curve and I had not seen it. There was a high wind from Glenbeigh onwards, and streaming rain set in by the time I came to the tunnel again. In Kenmare the post office door was open at 6.00, so I went in and in spite of the 'closed' notice on the PO counter bought stamps and posted the first film. But I had missed the post and there is no collection on Sundays.

3 May, Sunday

Enquired where *Pinguicula grandiflora* might be, and was told: on the bank above the main road almost outside the gate. Went to look. There were butterworts all right but all in tight bud. The wind howls over this slope. I decided that the Barony Valley, being more sheltered, might be a more productive spot. Started a drawing of the Kidney Saxifrage, then had lunch. Walked up to the end of the road and found a superb butterwort in the mud by the path which is a continuation of the road. Dug it up and put it in the polythene box. Decided that it was indeed *Pinguicula grandiflora*. The leaves are the usual yellowish-green, curled over at the edges. Flower-stem same colour and smooth right at the base, but soon becoming stained with light chocolate colour deepening to purple further up. Also scattered with tiny silvery glands which become thick at the top.

The top ½-inch of stem and the calyx are blackish-purple; indeed parts of the calyx are practically black. There are raised lumps on the top ½-inch of stem. The glands thin out again on the calyx. This has two sepals (lighter) lying straight backwards over the spur and three darker and broader ones tight behind the two upper petals (in the upper lip). The middle one of these has a little notch in it; the division between the three goes practically to the base. The flower is superb, fully the 3 cm from the lower lip to the end of the spur as CTW. Upper lip of two broad overlapping segments. Lower lip of three huge segments, just overlapping. From the base of the sinuses the middle is white, running backwards down the throat, with dark purple-black lines, a heavy one in the centre.

Large-flowered Butterwort (*Pinguicula grandiflora*)

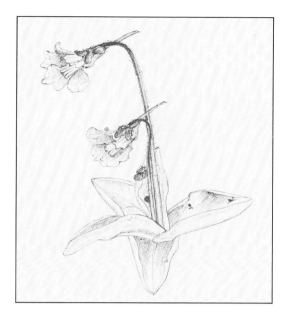

Large-flowered Butterwort (*Pinguicula grandiflora*)

This band is scattered with white bristles, the upper ones pointing inwards. The flower is true deep violet. The spur is lighter and redder in tone; this one was *very* slightly curved, and had a small cleft in the end, viewed from above. A superb flower, the local farmer called it a bluebell. When I remarked on the beauty of his valley, he said they did not look at it like that; he had no money and a terrific lot of hard work.

Before all this, I had spent up to 12.00 taking photographs of the Ardnagashel garden. Two tremendous *Drimys* particularly – some cherries (at last), some azaleas with well-blended colours, view of house etc. After plants, tea, went up the Coomahola Valley to the top of the pass. It is exquisite, with plants and trees all lush, Bluebells lining the river, spurge in great clumps, *Saxifraga* draping the walls. (Drawing of *Pinguicula* about one-and-a-half times natural size.)

Pinguicula grandiflora. On the last day I found a flower fading – the red pigment begins to fade out leaving rich indigo in parts of the flower. Not having been able to see any stamens etc. I opened this flower and found this arrangement against the upper part of the throat: a pair of curved stamens meeting at the top under what appeared to be a vessel full of nectar, pale greenish and with a turned-down rim. Under the lower rim of this the tips of the stamens were breaking into dull gold pollen. There were no anthers as such. So that solved half the sexual arrangements. I must find *P. vulgaris* as soon as possible and discover the rest.

7 May, Thursday

Got the spare parts put together again. Spent the morning shopping in Bantry, collecting the wheel, and reorganising the car. Got away about 1 p.m. (Found *Allium triquetrum* in the hedge just this side of Bantry.)

Went to Lord Glengariff's Lodge and drove through the demesne (as per guidebook). Trees dripping with moss, lichens and ferns, Beeches and birches at their most exquisite, weather awful. Arrived in the upper valley. Fascinating bog-flora, butterworts out etc., couldn't look at them properly.

Evening came back to Glengariff and, after a visit to Houlihan's, went up the road to photograph the *Osmunda*, which I was able to do without invading the hay-field. Got down by a wall draped with saxifrage, ferns, pennywort etc. etc. Too windy to photograph it. Went further up the road to turn, and by good luck this was by a bog purple with butterworts; there was one plant with three great flowers and a bud. If only the wind would stop!! One group would make a lovely photograph. Coming back found some more osmundas lower down the same stream, which would make a better picture.

People in the hotel who had come over the top from Kenmare about 6 said there was a raging hail-storm with the wind blowing the stones upwards, in whirls, and a glorious rainbow and shafts of light, all at the same time.

The sheer unmitigated superfluity of H_2O in this part of the world is something that cannot be described, only experienced. †

8 May, Friday

A grey morning, spent a good deal of it in shopping and photography (at the police station!) in Glengariff. Then up the Barony Valley and did some more to the Kidney Saxifrage drawing. Two gypsy women came down, with a can of milk, etc. They begged 'change'; while I was getting this they were going through the car with eyes like gimlets and a torrent of requests – biscuits, bread, all the left-overs – any old clothes . . .? Gave them the rest of the loaf. Had lunch, then sorted out the surplus plate – few mouthfuls of tongue, arrowroot etc. – and had them ready for the miserable camp at the bottom of the road. Handed them through the car window with 'Here you are – good-*bye*', just as the torrent was starting again.

Set off for the Smith's Peninsula via Castletownbere. Not far beyond Glengariff there were rich purple patches of the butterwort. Took two photographs at what was supposed to be 3½ feet of two of these groups which were quite sensational but will probably not come out like that.

The huge Fuchsia hedges at Adrigole and onwards are coming more and more into flower. One house between here and Castletownbere had banks of geraniums against the walls, also in flower. In Castletownbere there were half a dozen small ships berthed, flying orange, white and green flags (Eire?). From here went over to the north coast. On this side there were some thatched cottages, the one nearest the road very crude, with the roof-ridge sloping and not whitewashed but apparently with electricity laid on!

Then the road approached the sea and a lane led down to it. I went for a walk along the shore, on the edge of the 10-foot-higher fields. The Thrift was out on the rocks, *Cochlearia danica*, a wonderful Primrose-bank where I just came down to the shore, sloping right to the shingle. There was a pair of terns also in this lovely place, and quite a flock of Oystercatchers. I lay on the short turf and watched huge breakers on the end of the Smith's Peninsula.

I put the car into the shelter of the bank and made tea. These are stone walls, 5–6 feet high, overgrown with grass. Then went on west. At the next school-house these walls were topped with massive clumps of what looked like Yucca, half of it dead stuff and not very attractive. Uphill and round the corner, and was in a mountainous rocky bay with heather, very attractive. Over the next headland, and this bay was superb – there was half-sunshine by this time with haze merging into cloud on the tops. The whole mountain-slope on the left was striped with up-ended strata. Below was a turquoise-blue cottage and a golden-brown horse and cart carting golden sand above the blue sea. Got out to photograph this and had a sudden glimpse of a mass of arums over the top of a stone wall by the only other cottage. Got permission to take these too – the wall was like a square stone box and the arums filling it to the brim, 3 feet or more high and lush. Also white Hydrangeas coming into flower. Got this (a) against the stark mountain, and (b) with the bay behind. Had a chat with the woman, and also with the man carting the sand. Then went on a little. Came to three little lazy-beds, made with meticulous care, and protected by perfect little walls on the seaward side. One was just a square box, with the most forward potatoes yet seen. Went down to the smallest; there was a blob of pink which turned out to be St Patrick's-cabbage with very red flower-stems. Plants in this nook had the 'sub-orbicular' leaves of CTW and I thought I had one of the hybrids between this and the Kidney Saxifrage, but no. There was Hemlock Water-dropwort in this runnel. As I came back the owner of the house stopped me: the owner of Arum Cottage wanted to go into Glengariff and hadn't liked to ask me; would I take her? So I called there, but she had decided it was now too late. On the steep slope I had jammed the hand-brake on too hard and had to call the man up before I could get away.

In the morning I had seen a Kestrel stoop on its prey on the heathery headland between Ardnagashel and Glengariff, and then swing out towards the coast. An unlucky mouse or pipit I suppose.

9 May, Saturday

Disappointingly grey. Kept dry long enough for me to finish the *Saxifraga hirsuta* in Barony Valley. Then came down in sheets; I thought the day was doomed, but that I might as well explore by car the rest of the cape beyond Castletownbere as sit in the house. Set off about 2.30. Noticed a streak of pale grey at the bottom of the clouds to the west; by the time I got beyond Adrigole realised this was no longer pale grey but pale blue. Stepped on it. Came out on the northern shore in sunshine, to find the sea nearly post-card blue. Took photographs from the top of this bay and in the next. Arrived at the far end of Arum Bay 4.30 in a comparatively warm corner where Thrift was thick on the walls. Took some photographs although it was nothing like as good as in Anglesey. But the colour ranged from a deep pink through to pure white.

Was actually able to lie in a grassy hollow in the sun listening to the roar of the sea. There was Ling and Cross-leaved Heath and Creeping Willow in this corner.

I was just going for a stroll when a voluble Irishwoman turned up, lamenting bitterly because she had just disposed of a bottle of milk which

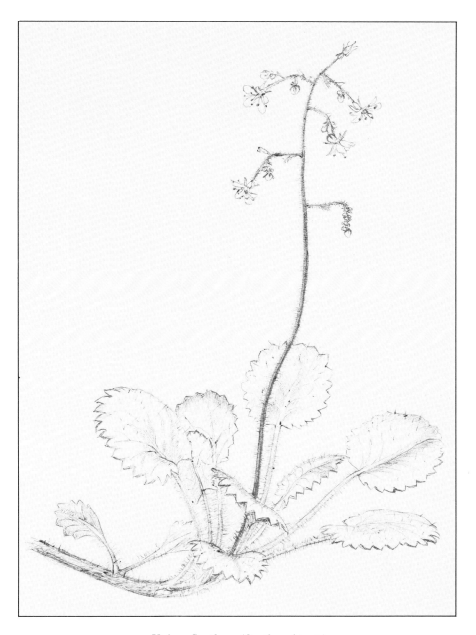

Kidney Saxifrage (*Saxifraga hirsuta*)

she might otherwise have bartered for a headscarf – holding up a filthy beer-bottle. I gave her a lift to the coppermine village, while she more or less rummaged the car for the missing headscarf, which I would gladly have given her and she would even have given me 2s for apparently. All this in bursts of talk like machine-gun fire, mixed with enquiries as to where I came from, was I by myself, was I married? etc. Not long after we parted, the scarf mysteriously appeared in the car-shelf where we had looked several times. I doodled about in this bit of coast half an hour longer, then set off home. There was Lamb's-lettuce growing at the foot of the wall by the road, and Lady's-fingers among the Thrift.

Over the headland towards the coppermines, I saw a pipit (or similar bird) chasing a Kestrel. The Kestrel was flying straight and low and the pipit fast after it and finally above it.

Saxifraga hirsuta (Kidney Saxifrage) has a creeping scaly dark brown stock, rooting at intervals. Then a lower rosette of small wedge-shaped leaves with from three to five teeth on each side. Then a longer or shorter thick red stem, very hairy, from which the main rosette grows. This has roughly eight leaves which are really round rather than kidney-shaped, with seven to nine teeth on each side, with a straight edge running in to the stalk at right angles to it. The leaves are rich green above with paler veins and a few stiff hairs, paler below with shorter hairs. The leaf-stalks are slender and very hairy. (St Patrick's-cabbage has them flat and very broad, and very smooth.)

From the rosette rises a long thin flower-stalk, reddish and very hairy. The hairs stick out at right angles to the stem and look as if they were made of the clearest glass; they have a minute crimson gland on the end. At the top of the stem the flower-stalks branch off at right angles; these and the tiny bracts are also covered with the glands. The tips of the five oval sepals also have them; these sepals are of a fleshy green texture, with scarious edges flushed with red. The pure white oval petals have two strong-yellow spots and above these three minute carmine ones. The conspicuous pear-shaped ovary is pink. There are ten stamens on long white filaments which swell out a little two-thirds of way up and contract again under the large rich pink anthers which have two lobes. These soon burst to give buff-salmon pollen and then drop off. The ovary in my flower had what looked like a waistband of tiny drops of honey-coloured nectar. It divides at the top into a double stigma; the tips of mine were still tight together and tinged with rich carmine, with a gap below.

10 May, Sunday

Lovely sunshine at breakfast, beginning to cloud over by the time I set out, about 10.30. Took three close-ups of *Pinguicula grandiflora* at 3½ feet, carefully measured with the piece of string I had had cut at the tweed-shop yesterday. Seven or eight miles further on encountered the donkey and its very attractive foal which I had met before, so photographed them. Went up the Tim Healy Pass, and climbed up the rocks above to photograph the road. Had to take it in two sections.

Down the other side to Ardgroom, and on to the Smith's Peninsula, round the east end and on to the north side where there is a most attractive rocky bay. The strata give repetitions of the peninsula in miniature, or else long thin offshore islands and reefs: In a pleasant spot overlooking all this I had lunch. It was moorland, and there were little drifts of royal blue milkwort mixed with lousewort, or lousewort and butterwort, but never all three, beside the road. The bogs everywhere are now flaunting the great violets of the *Pinguicula.*

To my great pleasure I saw a green road branching off from the tarmac ahead, and running along the shore. I went for a walk along this. It was reasonably dry and the only straight-forward walk I had. Everywhere else was either tarmac or bog. There was a pool with stitchwort growing in it, and a purple-leaved mint, besides the inevitable spearwort and Yellow Pimpernel. Further along, in the peaty edge of a rut in the road, was a beautiful plant of *Viola lactea* (Pale Heath Violet) in full flower. The curled leaves were almost diamond-shaped, the petals very long and elegant, those of the upper lip very erect; the broad throat was white with many black veins. The colour was the most delicate pale clear lilac. Thought I might pick one flower on the way back to write up further details. Further along an Oystercatcher yelped at me from the top of a wall, its mate having given the alarm. Felt sure it had a nest there but could not find it. The rain increased, so turned back and somehow missed the P H Violet. This was really disastrous. Walked an hour and a half – had some tea and then did a better drawing of the *Pinguicula* which I had brought with me. Was just going to set out on a fresh search for the violet when the heavens opened so had to give up.

Went on round the peninsula. People with raincoats just thrown over their heads were collecting cows and so on in the streaming rain; one woman was going with a bucket for some *water*, apparently. The New Zealand Flax appeared again in its great untidy rusty clumps. A most attractive thatched cottage drew the camera, also a rocky bank above the road draped with St Patrick's-cabbage, Bluebells, Fuchsia, spurge, although the light was now about at the lower limit. All this would have been seventh heaven on a blue day. As I went on home the rain increased, almost nothing was visible, lagoons on the road slapped at the car; it was *just* possible to replant the butterwort more or less in its own home – but *what* a country, how do they endure it?

11 May, Monday

2 p.m. set off for Cork. Of course there was quite a lot of *Euphorbia hyberna* by the road – can only conclude that preoccupation with the strange car kept my gaze firmly on the tarmac on the way out. Photographed a polychrome row of houses in Enniskean, including the blind old-age pensioner's shrine. The cloud varied on the way in – mostly pretty low; it improved towards Cork. Had a brew by the roadside, found I had forgotten the milk, begged some at a small house where they absolutely refused any payment. Arrived at airport an hour before time – luckily as cloud was *right down* on the runway though it was clear a mile away!! Didn't they study the cloud levels before making this airfield? Was just in time to be bundled into a bus for Shannon. It went through very uninteresting country, via Mallow and Limerick, little towns all pleasing; Limerick has some splendid eighteenth-century terrace-houses and a fine view of the cathedral (?) across the very wide river. Fields with Cowslips in were a pleasing sight. Finally hoisted from this soggy land at 9.45 (half an hour later than I had been assured we would take off!). There was Oxford Ragwort on walls near Bandon and also at Limerick. I was surprised it had reached so far west.

7

A CARAVAN IN CAER DIN

May 1964 – May 1971 · Shropshire
& Marches, Anglesey, Mid-Wales

16 May, Saturday

Went out to Bridges afternoon and up the Stiperstones road. Lay down against a grassy bank and fell into a very deep sleep. There were beautiful little clumps of Yellow Pansies in the grass. The southeast wind got colder. Moved round to Black Rhadley and made tea. The gorse on the way compared very unfavourably with the Irish. An elusive bird in the heather gave incessant but short little bursts of song; by no means could I find it.

17 May, Sunday

A glorious day throughout, much warmer than yesterday. Collected Joyce H and went to Edenhope via Rowley, where we looked at the twisted leaves of *Allium* and at the Astrantia and Herb-Paris. We found the Astrantia leaves but not a sign of a flower yet. The Herb-Paris however was in the seed stage – black and shiny – and leaves beginning to look tatty. Both were in fresh flower when DP took me there on 18 May several years ago. Photographed a nice group of Sweet Woodruff at the foot of a tree. This wood is carpeted with an unusual mixture of Woodruff, Blue-bells, Archangel Nettle, Garlic, Meadowsweet, with the two groups of Herb-Paris.

We went on to Edenhope; awful shock – a caravan plus a car and a tent in Caer Din!! We went on to Offa's Dyke, and had a heavenly afternoon lazing in wonderful sunshine. Countryside exquisite with the fresh pale greens, hedges full of stitchwort and parsley (also Sweet Cicely near Bishopsmoat), larks singing ecstatically.

18 May, Monday

The day started cloudy and even seemed to threaten thunder. Set off 12.15 for Llynclys Hill via Alberbury and Four Crosses as A5 was one unbroken stream of traffic. Thought I would have lunch at the house-clearing; what a shock to find a house on it! And quite a piece of the bank fenced in and an Amanogawa Cherry planted just about where I picnicked once in a hollow! The best hellebore is now inaccessible. We ought to have bought this land.

I had lunch in the car by the quarry hollow and then had a stroll round. Cowslips are the feature at the moment; the Heath Spotted-orchids are coming up, very big and lush, and pardalina, just showing the tip of a flower-spike in some cases. On the open slopes there were Early-purple Orchis and Green-winged (a few).

Went round to Jacob's Ladder. This place was rich as usual. The *Daphne laureola* had green berries. The *Sorbus anglica* was in bud, the bushes gleaming silver in the high wind and looking wonderful against the black Yews. Salad Burnet was coming out; found flowers which appeared all female, others all male, others mixed in varying proportions. The filaments are the finest I have yet seen, like spiders' web, drooping under the weight of the buff-yellow anthers. The pistils are five-branched rich crimson hairs.

Cowslips were here also in great plenty. There was only the very occasional flower out on the rock-roses. Could not find any Frog Orchid or Small-flowered Buttercup. In the part where I remembered this, the scrub had been cleared leaving only some very beautiful birches. All kinds of plants had rushed into action here: there was a wonderful flower-bed of Cowslips in a solid mat of Ground-ivy and blue speedwell with some Early-purple Orchis. Here and there were clumps of Three-nerved Sandwort, Lesser Thyme-leaved Sandwort, Hairy Rock-cress and some beautiful plants of a small and slender-looking mullein, leaves whitish all over, narrower than usual? Also Thale Cress with a hairy rosette.

Cleft in the rocks, South Stack, Anglesey. 'There were nests in the cliffs below me . . . I could easily have taken the single egg.' (see p.99)

South Stack. (see p.99)

Dereeny tree-ferns, Ireland. 'A natural mixture of vegetation which is so pleasing because of the lack of any straining for effect.' (see p.115)

Rossdohan, Ireland; circular tree-fern and palm. 'The vegetation here was quite staggering.' (see p.116)

Thatched cottage in Ireland. (see p.121)

Llanberis Pass from Bryn yr Efail. (see p.129)

'Took a photograph from A5 of Menai Bridge with the snow-clad mountains.' (see p. 133)

Cairngorms, Scotland. 'The sweep of the view was tremendous.' (see p. 141)

27 May, Wednesday

Walking back to Crosby Hall from Chelsea Show in the evening, saw a mass of cobwebby material in a bush in the shrubbery along Cheyne Walk. Got in to investigate; found it was a hatch of caterpillars, all hungrily devouring a small Spindle tree. They were a dead putty-brown colour with black shiny heads and spots along the sides. There were dead cast skins in the webs. Tried afterwards to find this creature in the book, but it does not appear to be illustrated.   †

29 September, Tuesday

A superb day, sun really hot. Set off for Anglesey 3 p.m. via Tanat Valley and Bala. From Porthywaen onwards it was all sheer beauty. By 4 p.m. was at Milltir Cerrig; this seemed good going. Stopped and brewed tea. Just round the corner discovered the superb view of Snowdonia, the whole horse-shoe hovering high and misty, and Cnicht through a gap to the west. Down to Bala and over to Cerrigydrudion and so to the lakes at Capel Curig, about 5.45. The sun was sending slanting rays from behind a cloud over Llanberis Pass; the result on the mountains and the lake was magical. If only these photographs show a fraction of it!

Llanberis Pass was a dark gulf. From the bridge at Bryn yr Efail I took a post-card view with lovely lights. Ahead was a wall of cloud over the straits, solid to look at, grey and dank inside. It was clear over Anglesey – arrived at Wern y Wylan in the dusk. I have a lovely room looking out over the bay. In bed can hear the sea and at night an incessant trilling of Curlews on the shore.

2 October, Friday

Brilliant sunshine but strong and keen east wind. Went to the Malltraeth Cob and settled down against the bank which gave protection from it. Heavenly warmth and complete peace, with calls of Curlew and Redshank and a black and white sheep-dog for company. The sun went down in a deep salmon-pink haze.

3 October, Saturday

Arrived at Malltraeth Cob 11.30. Lay till after 4 against the bank, cotton shirt with neck open and sleeves rolled up! Not a sign of a cloud anywhere; a very light easterly breeze.   †

4 October, Sunday

Went headlong for the Cob again. Superb hot sunshine till tea-time, when the first signs of clouds began to gather.

Feeling a little doubtful about previous identification of *Spergularia marginata*, walked along the Cob to check it. Soon found plenty with *pink* flowers. The seeds soon settled it – they have delicious little frills of white tissue all round them – so that was all right.

5 October, Monday

Half cloud and half sun morning (spent in Bangor). Drizzle started at lunch-time, soon turned to relentless rain, and to a wild storm with raging winds by night.

8 October, Thursday

Went to see the Tunnicliffes who very kindly kept me to lunch. Mr T took me in the afternoon to see the *Gentiana pneumonanthe* which I had not been able to find myself. It was in a different 'field' – if the boggy heather ground can be given such a name. They were much more slender than I had expected, with almost grassy leaves. We found a dozen or more, rather more than half with brown withered flowers, but the rest still blue, but furled. One stem had three flowers on it, all the rest were single. They were on both sides of the road; there was a bitter northeast wind and no sunshine and as no flowers were open I did not stop to write notes on it.

After this we went across to Aberffraw and across the sand-dunes. At the gateway we turned left along a grass track and stopped where it divided. Here we soon found tiny plants of *Gentianella campestris*, but as these were all withered and brown I did not record it.

On the way across, Mr Tunnicliffe remarked that there were Fly Orchids on Cors Erddreiniog, and Bee Orchids on a rocky outcrop on the other side of the road not far away. And that the Greater Spearwort grew at Llyn Llywenan not far from the lunch-place.

11 October, Sunday

Weather really terrible – a thunderstorm at breakfast-time and heavy rain and hail as I came down to Menai Bridge. It eased off as I came out at Belan Fort at the end of the sand-dunes opposite Abermenai. What a place to live! It was cosy enough inside. There were towers, moat, cannon, drawbridge, all complete – the earliest part built in 1709, remainder in 1805. It had a sinister look, squatting so low in this desert landscape. After lunch we went up on the rampart and looked out over the straits, here at their narrowest. There was a terrific tide-race running; it looked deadly.

Just outside the fort, the road is a concrete strip across the middle of a marsh. There were gulls and a flock of Redshank on it; the Redshank got up and wheeled as one bird, a geometrical progression of beauty, a unanimity of flashing wings. The saltings were mainly fine grass, Thrift, *Salicornia*, with a sprinkling of *Spergularia salina*.

At Dinas Dinlle I had a walk along the shore and then tea in the car on the shingle-bank. The Lleyn Peninsula gets better weather than we do. However, at this point there was a slight lift in the cloud over one of the passes and a gleam below it – a snow-covered mountainside with black threads of gullies and streams. If only the clouds would lift, what a sight there would be!

Just as I came to Malltraeth Cob, a Barn Owl flew across the road and settled on a fence-post on the right. It had quite a sizeable animal hanging long and limp from its beak, probably a young rat. After turning about and about, it settled to the meal, holding it down on the post in its talons. Unfortunately it had its back to me, but there was a great upward heave of the shoulders as it tore a piece off, and relaxation as it swallowed it. Then another tugging upwards, and down with the next beakful; in five minutes it was finished. It then moved along to the next fence-post from which it started the hunt for more; it spent two or three minutes on each post, watching the grass below for the slightest movement, working steadily along the edge of the forest, always with its back to me. Its broad rounded head was rich gold on top, the back of it and of the neck, and the upper 'shoulders' shaded with dove-grey which had almost a hint of lavender. Then rich gold on the back and more grey shadings on the wing-coverts. The primaries of the folded wings came down far below the tail, which jutted out like a sort of square tab, buff with a dark band about half-way down it. A rather broad and stumpy creature in the rear view presented to me – but magically transformed as the great wings spread and the tail fanned out, the long legs gleaming white. Both wings and tail were buff finely barred with mid-brown; the bars ran round in a huge arc from one fore-wing to the other and added to the sense of power and sweep, breathtaking even in these short flights from post to post. The snowy velvet of the underparts was revealed momentarily.

At last it turned and faced the road and I had a full-front view – the huge white face with the gold of the crown coming down in a fine point in the middle – the long scornful nose, the very dark eyes, the tiny row of deeper-coloured feathers outlining the face (these are actually iridescent as I once learned from a stuffed bird), the shadow of pale grey 'under the chin', then everything else pure white except the dark feet. There was nothing stumpy about the front view – the long powerful legs so tight together, tensed as though straining both down and up, giving it grace and a feeling of lightness and imminent flight.

Once I heard a movement in the grass, and after some minutes of downward peering, with concentration in every feather and feet shifting slightly with excitement, it flopped on it – but missed. The post-to-post reconnaissance then started again, but my going spoilt it. A few slow beats of the huge wings wafted this magnificent bird into the seclusion of the forest.

12 October, Monday

Sunshine and clearance in the clouds came quite early, and there was Snowdonia all capped with white. After various necessary jobs – rushed out with the camera. Went out on Mr Croft's road at Pen-lôn and got one or two but it wasn't really a very good spot. Went back and got picnic lunch and turned down the Llanddwyn road. The northwest wind was very cold, but I found a hollow on the southeast side of the first rocky tump and settled down to eat and read, with the camera at the ready. Whenever the light struck the snow on Snowdon itself, I popped up and took it. Mostly there was a cloud hanging right over it, making it dull.

I had two hours' bliss in full sun here – a thing I had nearly forgotten after a week of bad weather. Wondered whether I would cross to the mainland for photography and laze and enjoy the sun. This was settled by the arrival of two young women, four infants and a transistor. I packed up. Took a photograph from A5 of Menai Bridge with the snow-clad mountains. Another below Deiniolen. Another at Bryn yr Efail. Turned left here and took some more from the little road below the heather brae. Went on up here taking them at intervals, and decided to go up to the slate-quarry by a long slanting road, to get Crib Goch in good effect. Put the car in a parking-space by a locked gate. Took Crib Goch with a foreground of slashed mountainside. Also took the old trucks and a turntable – then went out on a spoil-heap to get more pictures. Found the Creeping Willowherb and Sticky Groundsel. Went down to Llanberis and bought more film and went up as far as Nant Peris and took Crib Goch again – probably too dark for success.

13 October, Tuesday

Glorious sunshine till after breakfast. Mountains nearly clear at first. About 9.00 the bay filled with mist, and also all the other valleys; the ridges of Anglesey stood out in stripes across it, their edges dark and bristling with hedges and trees. After breakfast clouds began to drift in. However the morning was fine. Went down to the village, also to the Cob. There was a solitary pale grey bird, feeding rapidly on the sandy edges. The beak was short and stumpy; looking on the wrong page I took it for a Knot. Corrected by the Tunnicliffes in the evening – it was a Grey Plover. Back and coverts had darkish feathers with light edges, top of head much the same, all underparts white except for front of neck and upper breast which had a smudge of greyishness. Dark beak (short and straight), dark eye and line through with white stripe over eye. Legs long and dark. It fed in a hasty sort of way – two or three quick steps with head down, beak jabbed into sand, then at once up into fully erect position as if it must look round for intruders before getting the next mouthful – and so on without stopping. A gull made a run at it and it flew a few yards, showing a white rump and a slight white wing-bar.

Further along by the forest a female Kestrel was perched on the telegraph-pole wire. Her yellow feet looked huge. She swooped but got nothing and settled again on a telegraph-post. Head rufous-brown as well as body, and transverse bars of dark brown across the back, are marks of the female.

Went to the forest road to check the *Spergularia*, expecting it to be *S. rubra* (Sand Spurrey). It had seeds 'with a raised rim' (CTW) but the leaves were fleshy, the stipules were not conspicuous and the petals were definitely longer than the sepals. Can't be *S. marginata* because of seeds; they are more or less round with a rim of the same colour (darkish brown) as the rest of the coat. Growing in pure sand. Seeds exclude *S. salina*. Stems quite thickly glandular – hairy. Flowers pure white.

To supper with the Tunnicliffes. There were two Little Stints at the Cob lagoon this afternoon about 4.30! They showed me the most beautiful drawings of trees (branches, flowers and fruit), done for a book planned before the war and never completed.

1966

18 July, Monday

In the evening went to Venus Pool. There were a large number of Coots and a pair of Black-headed Gulls immediately apparent. The Purple-loosestrife was in full glory – a solid mass on the far side, and big groups everywhere else. There were three white plants standing in the edge of the water, one at the extreme left, one near the hedge and another in the main pool on the far side. I went to investigate; boots were needed. They turned out to be *Oenanthe aquatica* (Fine-leaved Water-dropwort). I waded ankle-deep to the first one; it stood about 3 feet high, on a stout black stock 1½–2 inches thick. It looked as if the water had gone down recently. From this grew many branches, making a splendidly assured, bushy plant, covered with clear white umbels, 1½–2 inches across.   †

1967

February

To Mr Wood, Lyth Hill Road. He has apple trees with plentiful Mistletoe, and it was all in flower, except for one hanging shoot which had berries. Every joint looks like a ball-and-cup arrangement, with two (at branches) divisions, or *five* (where flower-heads are formed). Single flowers are apt to emerge from the creases at any joint – tightly sessile in them. The flowers are most often in threes, tightly wedged in a thick fleshy calyx. The 'petals' are also compressed, with two longer petals opposite each other and two smaller ones tucked in the ends. The inside of the petals is pitted. The flowers have a decided fruity scent.

†

1968

12 September

A glorious day; walked round the lake with Jane. Went round the east end, and in shallow water found clusters of straight narrow leaves in the bottom. Decided these were the Water Lobelia. Some had thinnish stalks sticking up out of the water, with nothing on the top. Suddenly Jane found one with two fresh buds on it, and there was no longer any doubt. They were delicate lilac. Soon after I found a stem with one open flower, and in the end we had scored about half a dozen. We came back by the rickety bridge at the west end. There was Bogbean, two kinds of mint (one end and one whorled), Sneezewort, Bog Asphodel, water-lilies (suppose White), and the western bog was full of Myrtle (smelling divinely).

The Paishes arrived for lunch. While Jane rested afterwards, the rest of us went down to the lake again. We did not find the *S. repens* (Creeping Willow). The thick rush in the water is the *true* Bulrush. I found Marsh Cinquefoil.

Eventually set off in the two cars, Dorothy with me. Showed me place for Stonewort near Cregennen Lake. Greater Spearwort is in bog near Fairbourne. We had tea on the wall high above the sea with all the sweep of the Lleyn Peninsula and a wonderful light. There was a family of young Stonechats flitting from telegraph-wires to walls to bracken and back again – smooth rosy breasts, white at neck and on primaries, chestnut upperparts – brownish heads. The well-defined black had not developed. The odd Cormorant flew by.

We went on to Broadwater, and crossed the railway on to the dune-slacks and shingle. David soon found the Autumn Lady's-tresses – so much smaller than I had imagined – a careless glance could pass it over with the euphrasias of which there were plenty. The glass showed up its exquisite detail: all parts covered with silvery hairs or glands, the tight spiral of the flower-stems, bringing each individual flower nearly, but not quite, over the next below – flowers tiny, wiry, white, the lip with frilled edges and a bar of apple-green with veins in it, so exquisite and so exotic-looking when magnified. They were quite plentiful. There was also a good colony of Yellow Horned-poppy – but not a single flower! It was much later than this when I tried to draw it at Aberystwyth in 1963.

1969

30 September

Went back to the nature reserve of Sunday to write up *Gentiana pneumonan-the* (Marsh Gentian). Most of them were single stems and short. I chose the prize specimen which was nearly a foot high, with three flowers on it.

The stem is slender and tinged with reddish-brown on the side towards the sun. The leaves are in sessile pairs clasping the stem about 1½ cm apart, not exactly above each other, nor at right angles. There are two fine redder ribs running from the centre of one of the leaves of a lower pair, to the sinus between the pair above, the stem twisting slightly counter-clockwise – say 22½ degrees. The upper pair must be placed 22½ degrees clockwise, to meet this?

The leaves are smooth and about 2 cm long, and the narrower the further up the stem. There is a well-marked crease for the centre vein broadening at the bottom and becoming pale green.

There were three flowers, one at the tip of the shoot and one springing from each of the two next leaf-axils below, both on the same side of the plant. The flower-stems were about ½ cm long, with a pair of bracts just like the leaves but much smaller, 2–3 mm below the calyx. Above the bracts, the flower-stem thickens and becomes corrugated and redder than any other part of the plant. The calyx is a gradually-expanding tube, dividing into two longer and three shorter points, thin and fine, with rounded sinuses between them.

The flower is like a loosely-furled umbrella, the folds turned counter-clockwise. Except that there are five ribs with bands of lime-green tissue, and hyacinth-blue folded in between them. The tips are expanded into oval 'petals' but these were tightly wrapped in a hyacinth point in the lowest flower which was not much beyond the bud stage, and still not spread in the middle flower which needed sunshine to make it expand. The top one was fading and over. The ovary is long and narrow with a short two-branched stigma at the tip. Five stamens with long filaments are attached to green patches at the base of the tube.

When fresh, the flowers lean out at a slight angle from the stem. Nearby was a brown spike which had had four flowers. The seed-vessels of this were fully erect and tight to the stem. The stalk, flower-stems and calyces had reddened considerably and were browny-beetroot colour. The buff ovaries were protruding above the silvery-brown tissue of the dead flowers, having grown a stalk inside them, and had split in two at the top. The seeds were cylindrical, ribbed, attached to a central column. The lower leaves of this plant were still green.

1970

28 August, Friday

Packed up picnic lunch and took David and Dorothy up Llangefenni Valley. Conifers solid, 15–20 feet high on the slopes above the slate-workings. They look really awful and I am glad I joined the protest movement. What a relief to look at an open hillside with its varied vegetation even if only in shades of dull green. The longer grasses whitened by wind and rain give it a gleam, the contours show in detail, and soon it will be warmed by the autumn bracken. The Sitkas are dull and reflect no light at all.

A farmer was turning a tiny field of hay and the scent filled the air. After lunch we walked on up and soon came to the open hill beside the road (Sarn Helen) where banks of sphagnum were threaded with the tiny plants of *Wahlenbergia hederacea* (Ivy-leaved Campanula). It has a branched white root down in the base of the sphagnum and works its way to the surface, bearing leaves alternately, and more frequently as it comes to the light. There are three points on each side of the central one, and occasionally one extra; the divisions are shallow. There are a few scattered hairs. The flowers are borne singly at the tips. Calyx has a cup-shaped base with five long points; a fine vein runs up each from the stem. The corolla is a tube, white for two-thirds of its length, then lavender-blue with five rounded petals at the crown. An exquisite tiny gem.   †

1971

28 April, Wednesday

A glorious day of unbroken sunshine. Went out in the evening looking for somewhere to walk and arrived at the Mitchell's Fold area. In the last of the tall Hawthorns before coming out in the open, saw a large nest, near the top, and a Carrion Crow flew out. Decided this tree was climbable and got up it. The nest was more than a foot across. The main construction of sticks. Inside this was a grass nest, and this in turn was thickly lined with wool, nearly an inch thick and almost felted. The whole cup felt hot when I put my hand in. There were three eggs, greeny-blue with splashes and spots of dead-leaf brown.

There was quite a good population of Peewits on Stapeley Hill, and I picked up an eggshell which could only have been one of theirs, although the background colour was rather light, almost biscuit colour. There were huge splodges of near-black on the larger end.

The sun was behind the only cloud of the day, from which pale copper rays shone in front of the dim forms of the Welsh mountains. Aran Fawddwy looked splendid. Cadair Idris was only just discernible. The only sounds came from the lambs, the Peewits and the pipits. It was like being bathed in clear spring water.

29 April, Thursday

The day started with glorious sunshine, but clouds soon came over and the rest of it was hodden-grey. I had made for Fron Goch in hope of a sun-soak but was disappointed. Told Charlie about Aston Munslow and asked him if he knew of any hay-wagons etc. lying about the countryside. He said there was one at Carreghofa – the last time he saw it, it was being used to fill a gap in the hedge, to stop the cattle falling down the river-bank. After tea, I went down to investigate this, and found what was left of the wagon. It had fallen down the bank itself, and disintegrated. The front and back axles were complete with their wheels, the rest hopeless. And the wood was wormy and softening.

I worked down the riverside path, mainly by using a small stream as a staircase. Fresh fern-fronds were coming up. I came to the weir, and having the tiny field-glass on approval, decided to watch for a Dipper. Found some farm polythene, and was hardly settled on it when the bird appeared on a fair-sized rock in mid-stream. Most of the stones had droppings on. This bird's underwater virtuosity is beyond anything I had ever imagined. It took a header into the very turbulent water between the two steps of the weir, where there must have been a pretty strong current as there was quite a spate. It was under for a surprising length of time – then the black head would appear among the waves as it came up for a breather. This would be repeated about three times, after which it flew out looking as dry and unconcerned as if it had just taken off from terra firma! It settled on stones on the far side of the river, and after a pause flew up to a hole in the wall on the other side and popped in, but was out again almost immediately. I concluded it was a cock bird feeding his hen. This place was very well chosen – quite inaccessible, with a fast race below. The bird was very smart, in his black suit with gleaming white shirt-front. The interest of all this made up for the greyness of the day and the fact that the polythene contained a hidden pool of water, which gradually worked upwards.

1 May, Saturday

To Fron Goch. Had the Cartwrights to tea to see about the house. Went to the tap in the wood to get water and started counting the *Orchis fuchsii* – there are three below the path where they have flowered pale and thin every year – but I began to find them on the upper side as well, and counted nine. Then I found a Twayblade, with leaves nicely spread and flower-spike short and tight. This was a pleasing discovery.

After tea I took the Cartwrights to see it, and we went on past the spring and up the bank to the top fence. Miss Cartwright found two patches of Herb-Paris; both were small growths and looked unlikely to flower. The Archangel Nettle with silver-splashed leaves will soon be in flower. There is a good Bluebell patch by the Herb Paris.   †

8

ALONE WITH ALL THIS SPLENDOUR

September 1971 – June 1973 · Scotland, South Wales

18 September, Saturday

I set out from Inverness for Aviemore. The run got steadily more exciting as more and more mountains became visible. Boat of Garten, the Osprey place, is only a few miles off this main road. After booking for Sunday and Monday nights at Aviemore, I went on to the Cairngorm ski-lift, passing Loch Morlich and a tract of old Caledonian Forest, where splendid Scots Pines grew in deep heather and bilberry with a scattering of Junipers of all sizes from shrubs to moderate trees. The ski-centre is at 2000 feet, with a fine swirling tarmac road to it. I had a short walk, and lunch on the edge of the car park sitting out in warm sunshine, and then went up in the chair-lift. There is a circular restaurant at the top of it, tucked right under a crag to prevent it being blown away. The track on up to the summit was worn to the width of a two-lane road and was heavily populated. Never have I been on a mountain with such a mass of people. There were two Army landrovers by the cairn. The wind was terrific; I held on to my spectacles in sheer terror of their being snatched off and smashed on the rocks. The sweep of the view was tremendous and I took photographs, although the even pale sunshine left very little shadow anywhere. The rock was of a warm pinkish colour, with quartz all over the place, mostly broken to a fine gravel.

I walked to an outlying ridge crowned by a castle-formation of the pink rock in horizontal strata, then down a little to another outcrop, where I found the Alpine Alchemilla, tucked flat in a scoop, six inches below the general level. On the way back, I found two cushions of *Silene acaulis*, close-packed in the lee of rounded stones. This tundra-flora is most interesting. I had tea in the car park. Just by it was a small herd of

141

Reindeer, one, a white one, with a superb head. The others were white with patches of mole colour.

Alchemilla alpina. The base of the plant is a foxy-brown scaly root-stock and each rounded pale green stem rising from it has this papery silver-edged wrapping. The leaves emerge tightly folded at first, like fingers held close together, covered in silky hairs. They have five, or occasionally seven, leaflets, rich green above, and silver-silky below, where the pale midrib shows strongly. There are up to four teeth on each side, pointing forward and all in the upper third of the leaflet. From above, the silky lower coat shows as a glistening fringe.

The flower-stems spring from just above the root-stock, and are silky and tinged on one side with brown. The several branches each grow from a sheath in the angle of a three-leaflet bract, with many minute greenish flowers in each head, opening in succession. Four pointed green petals spread flat above a hemispherical ovary. Between them are four minute silky scales which may represent the calyx? Stamens four, dark. Stigma pale green. This plant grows quite flat in exposed positions, but holds its head up where there is shelter.

19 September, Sunday

On the way to Aviemore, I made a detour to see Culloden. The site belongs to the National Trust in Scotland, and is beautifully cared for. A cottage of pre-1746 survived the battle and is now a small museum. The gables are built of peat-blocks and the roof is thatched with heather, held down by heather-ropes tied to poles at the eaves, and pegged into the peat across the gables. Inside, among other exhibits, was a spinning-wheel with three bobbins.

Soon after leaving Culloden there was a notice: 'Stones of Clava', so I decided to go and look at them. I was very glad I did, for this was a numinous place. The 'stones' were three megalithic tombs of 1800–1500 BC in a line down the centre of a glade enclosed by Beech trees, rather gnarled and stunted, and with the lower branches sweeping the ground, making a high wall of seclusion round the whole site. Footsteps were muted by deep soft moss, and the only sound was a slight sighing of the wind in the leaves. The great stones imposed their presence even more forcefully in the strange setting than others seen in vast spaces of open moor, or in the flat lands of Anglesey under huge skies.

The first and third were passage-graves. All had piles of smooth rounded rubble, like giant sea-washed shingle, between the inner megaliths and their encasing circular walls, and were attended by outer rings of standing stones. The middle tomb had three narrow ribs of rock set in the ground, equidistant radii from grave to circle. Near the last and grandest grave a noble menhir, a slender solitary watcher, not rough-hewn like the others, but beautifully dressed and squared at the top, brooded in its aloof significance, now known only to itself. I was alone with all this splendour, in gentle sunshine and total peace.

How I would love to roll back the film of time, and see these mighty chieftains in their prowess and their state, and then at the end of their days to be a witness of the funeral rites which must have been as splendid as their tombs. These were no mere savage tribes; the grandeur of the geometry and the size of the stones speak for their powers of conception and construction, the nobility of their imagination. Who were these people?

I came out on the main road again at Daviot and stopped at the Landmark Centre at Carrbridge where I had lunch at one of the picnic tables. These, and places for car-parking, are scattered in an open pinewood in a very pleasant way. Moved into my room at Aviemore, and then went up to the small car park at Coire na Ciste. I walked down to the stream and took to the path beside it on the opposite bank. There was plenty of fresh-looking *Alchemilla alpina*, and I also found Dwarf Cornel. I walked up on to the ridge where at about 2500 feet I found *Loiseleuria procumbens* (the Alpine Azalea) growing tight under a boulder. The vivid pink flowers caught my eye. This was a great thrill. It was not the first time that I have found a May-flowering rarity with flowers out in late September or even early October – the White Rock-rose on Brean Down was another.

Loiseleuria procumbens (Alpine Azalea). The stems are dark grey-brown with peeling skin and well-marked nodes. The leaves are alternate, very tightly packed, averaging about 4 mm in length, yellowish-green flushed

Alpine Azalea
(*Loiseleuria procumbens*)

with brown and red. They are oval and blunt-tipped, shiny above, with the edges very much rolled under. Between these and the very thick midrib, not much of the glaucous undersurface is visible.

The flowers are in twos and threes on the ends of the shoots, on 2–3-mm rich red stalks, and the calyx is also red, campanulate, dividing to five points. The flowers are about 4 mm across, the five petals alternate with the sepals and twice as long, rich pink, deeper in the centre and at the tip. Five stamens with black anthers, stigma pale on a green ovary. The old seed-vessels of the normal May-June flowers had turned dark brown and black, and new shoots had grown beyond them and produced these late flowers on the tips.

I went back to Landmark for supper. This is a first-rate establishment. The building itself is pleasing, built of wood and painted dark. A long low gallery in the middle, where there are books, maps and crafts for sale, has a higher circular wing at each end, and the whole structure is on a curve. One wing contains the restaurant, and the other a lecture- and film-amphitheatre, with a wide passage encircling it in which is a museum of Scottish life, from the last Ice Age onwards. Entry is through a 'cave' made of swathes of polythene dimly lit blue from behind, while a sepulchral voice chants on and on: 'Twenty thousand (?) feet under the ice' *e da capo*. We gradually reach something warmer with the interior of a croft, and all the apparatus of life in the Highlands through the ages, ending in about the eighteenth century.

The meals were good and reasonably priced, and there was a film-show every night after supper. On this particular night they had two RSPB films on Sea Eagles and The Birds of Strathspey.

20 September, Monday · Caledonian Forest

Found a beautiful footpath, and went along it in the hope of getting photographs of the huge Scots Pines with undergrowth of heather and Juniper. On a bank saw white flowers and realised that they were *Vaccinium vitis-idaea*. Stem rounded, leaves thick, smooth and slightly shiny above, with the edges rolled over. The lower sides are much paler and glandular. From below, the tiny teeth are more clearly visible. It is an evergreen, but many of the leaves were bright red. Their 2–3-mm stalks are held parallel to the main stem; the blade then leans outwards. The flowers hang in a cluster of four at the end of the shoot, with six tiny red oval bracts edged with green enfolding the stems. There are four triangular sepals. The flower is an exquisite white bell, dividing at the edge into four outward-curving points, a double rib running up the centre of each one. The stamens are in four groups, rich golden-brown and deep within the bell. The stigma is very pale green and protrudes beyond it. Red berries were mixed with plentiful flowers on these beautiful plants.

This was a very beautiful and unusual place. The pines were splendid, with all the individuality of trees in their prime. The Junipers were in every conceivable shape, some upright and symmetrical, others sprawling at all angles. The ericaceous undergrowth was lush and deep, and so was the vivid green moss.

Later on this day, and on the next, I looked in more detail at the plants in Coire na Ciste and on the ridge above it. On the opposite bank of the stream, lower down, found several plants of prostrate broom (see 21 Sept.). There was a curved-leaved bluish sedge which defeated me. These *Carex* specialists have surely solved the problem of what to do with their spare time!

I became fascinated by the flora in this corrie. It was remarkable how many plants were still to be found in bloom so late in the year in this high and more or less north-facing place. Their lushness in the sheltered bottom of the corrie contrasted very strikingly with the sparse habit adopted by the same plants, or where these could not survive by different ones, in the windswept upper regions. It seemed sensible to put these observations together in one account. (See below.)

I had dinner at Landmark again. The films were on Loch Lomond and Rhum, showing the Bullough Castle, and explaining the habitats and the Nature Conservancy's plans for them.

A Cairngorm corrie in late September

The lower parts of the corrie are a fascinating contrast with the tundra on the ridge above. The stream runs in a deep cleft where there is shelter from the wind, and the vegetation is positively lush. The main plants are Ling and Bilberry, with a groundwork of Heath Bedstraw and other trimmings. Clumps of Hard Fern are particularly handsome. The dark chocolate stems and fine primrose of the fertile fronds, standing stiffly, surrounded by the broader, shorter sterile ones, which spread out like emerald shuttlecocks against the Heather.

Cowberry makes a patch of richer green, with white bells here and there, and a few leaves turning red. It grows in a mound of moss, fine heath-like Crowberry threading through it, with its minute and lustrous leaves, white-lined below, crowded on red-brown stems.

Weak-stalked Tormentil scrambles through the Ling, still flaunting a few golden flowers, and the Bilberries give shelter to colonies of Dwarf Cornel, whose five-veined leaves catch the eye by their larger size and four-square pattern. The three uppermost pairs are crowded close to the top of the stem, and begin to be stained at the tips with dark red-purple.

The path leaves the stream and comes out in the upper basin of the corrie. The Bilberry ceases; only the Ling now clothes the banks. In any available bare spot where competition is less – the edge of the path is a favourite – the Alpine Lady's-mantle spreads its five-fingered leaves, silver-silky below, and its dim panicles of greenish-yellow flowers. Here and there among the Ling are the larger bells of the true Heather, mostly turned to bright sienna, but with vivid magenta spots among them. Less frequent still, the greyer and more elegant stems of Cross-leaved Heath are tipped with balls of faded flowers, now a luminous pinky-brown.

The path turns steeply up among tumbled rocks. From a crack in a huge slab the Bearberry hangs down, a lustrous leafy triangle studded with scarlet berries, on the black and silver stone.

In the bottom of the corrie there are bog-holes filled solid with sphagnum in brilliant emerald and glaring mustard-yellow.

The path leads higher still, among huge boulders which have been prised by frost from an outcrop of rock above. Deep hollows among them give shelter, and a particularly favoured one is brimful of lush Cowberry, gay with scarlet berries and cluster after cluster of buds and flowers like pearl-drops in rose-red calyx-settings.

Nature as well as man makes bonsai trees. Just here and there a seed of pine or Juniper has contrived to germinate, but without companions to stand shoulder to shoulder with them the little trees are condemned to a dwarf existence. Gravel and rock confine the roots, and wind and frost prune the branches, so that about a foot in height is the limit of their growth.

On the upper slopes existence becomes harder still. Here are clumps of a fine hair-like sedge, gold as ripening corn. They spring from a carpet of crimson moss, packed tight and hard and laced with silver lichen.

On the top of the ridge, exposure is total and nourishment scanty. There are flats of gleaming white gravel, and even the rocks seem sheared off by the tearing wind, and lie flat and smooth. On this barren ground the few surviving plants lie close as ivy. Bearberry is still lustrous, and when it meets a gravel patch puts out a long shoot, bare of leaves except at the tip, a skeleton arm reaching desperately for a softer soil, some chance of rooting beyond the hard and shining quartz. The sedge-tufts here are half gold, half bleached white by the blast.

But suddenly there is a patch of different texture and heightened colour, a tangled mat of closely-interwoven Crowberry, Bearberry and Mountain Azalea, all silver-threaded with lichen. On grey-brown and foxy-red stems an inch from the ground, these tiny plants mix their shades of evergreen-apple, avocado and russet — all with lower leaves turning tangerine, blood-orange and pepper-scarlet. The azalea has rich sienna seed-heads from its summer bloom, but also, even in late September, an all-over spangle of rose-pink flowers and deeper buds, a miracle of life and colour most moving and wonderful in this high and desolate place.

21 September, Tuesday

Spent a good deal of the morning hunting for a Nature Conservancy botanist to enlighten me about a completely prostrate broom which I found in the lower part of Coire na Ciste the previous day. There were a number of plants which all grew, not only flat, but downhill. There were two disintegrating flowers. CTW says this grows only in Cornwall and the Channel Isles. The botanist was out. Then to Jack Drake's nursery at Inshriach, where I spent the middle of the day. It is set by a stream with good shelter of trees, so that there is opportunity for a beautiful woodland and bog garden, with *Meconopsis* and primulas etc. The most memorable sight was the sheets of Autumn Gentians which were in full blow. Outstanding among them was the variety Kingfisher, both for its freedom of flower and purity of blue, a lighter shade than most of the *sino-ornata*.

To Landmark for dinner, and a film of Culloden afterwards.

22 September, Wednesday

This day was spent in travelling from Aviemore to Craignure in Mull. I left at 10.30 and stopped at Kingussie to look at the Folk Museum. There was a black house completely equipped. The door led into the cowhouse and the living-room was entered from that, a good idea for warmth. The cowhouse was much the lighter; the room was nearly dark. The bedroom was beyond that, again. There was a big shed with a collection of farm and other implements, including a tripod 6–7 feet high with a chain and an iron cauldron for dying the wool, very elegant in shape.

Fort William and Oban very disappointing; tweeds such as I bought seventeen to eighteen years ago have vanished. The trip between these two places was very nostalgic. Took a photograph of Garbh Bheinn across the water. The railway is closed and Kentallen station ghostly. The boat was late and we arrived at Craignure in dusk and drizzle.

23 September, Thursday

Started with the same drizzle. I went to look at Duart Castle which is right on the end of an isthmus, and has been held by the Macleans since the thirteenth century. I was struck by their courage in tackling the restoration job. There was some fine furniture including Wordsworth's bureau-bookcase, wonderful Breton cupboards in a bedroom, and good oriental rugs everywhere that visitors were allowed to walk on. There was a mighty kitchen-range just like the one at Eton Cottage only larger.

I went on to Carsaig, passing Ardura on the way. After this the road (to Iona) had been improved and tarmaced and could be taken in 50-mph swoops. In the intermittent drizzle this stretch looked dreary, and the road to Carsaig off it even more so. However, after the steep drop to the pier, where I had lunch, the sun came out, and there was a wider prospect. In the afternoon I set off along the shore eastwards, struggling over huge boulders until I found a path above the cottage. Here a little stream came down, edged with marigolds, and there was a marsh with Asphodel and Grass-of-Parnassus. The path then led out on to the rocky shore between the cliffs and the sea, with a view to Jura and Colonsay. With the sunshine, as always, came the colour – pinkish rocks and deep blue sea – and a sense of bliss.

There was a cave, a waterfall and a stack made up of hexagonal columns as on Staffa – basalt – so the plants were Carrot, Purging Flax and Carline Thistle.

As I came past Ardura on the return journey, the mainland and its mountains were suddenly revealed, glowing in reflected pink and lilac from the sunset, with rosy clouds above. I tore along the Duart road to get photographs but it was fading and they would have been better a quarter of an hour sooner.

24 September, Friday

There was glorious sunshine first thing as I set off at 9.45 for Iona, hoping to get photographs of that peacock sea. Three-quarters of an hour later thin cloud began to gather and peacock-hopes to dissipate. A dull and ordinary sea was only the first of several disillusionments which made this the least satisfactory day of the whole holiday. I had just missed a boat. Having at last arrived on the island, I found that the tiny chapel was the only thing that really appealed. It has a fine late-Norman doorway and a superb decorated tomb-recess inside. Outside the Abbey was a cast of a Celtic cross in concrete, cold in colour, dead in texture. The church itself was empty, but filled with the sound of canned Bach. My outraged feelings at all this were slightly assuaged by a loud and emphatic 'Hell!' coming from the cloister. I told the student-type who had just had a rubbish-bag explode under him that he had expressed my sentiments exactly – and why did they have to have a concrete Celtic cross? He said the original was being eroded by the weather . . . I tore away down the road and at the end of it came to the machair and the famous silver sands – and a monumental pile of tins and a dead car . . .

I found a hollow where I had lunch in shelter from the wind, and then walked over the high point of the island [332 feet]. There was an enormous-seeming length of land on the western horizon, which I supposed must be Coll and Tiree, as there was a double-pointed hill just visible far beyond it, which could only be something in the Outer Hebrides.

On the way back I came upon a scene from the pre-industrial age. In a field sloping down between the road and the sea the oats were being harvested, cut with sickles and tied in sheaves with bands of straw. Other workers followed, setting up the stooks as we did that evening in Skye in 1957. Perhaps this was worth it, but on the whole I never want to go to Iona again.

25 September, Saturday

Woke at 7 a.m. and realised that there was a wonderful sunrise coming up over Ben Cruachan – luckily my room faced that way. Camera of course was in the car. Rushed out in dressing-gown to get it, and took a series of photographs of the increasing rosy glow, and then of the first spark of the sun's edge as it came up over the mountain.

During the morning I walked up to the first ridge above the hotel in perfect conditions. The sea was really blue, the mountains ethereal, streaked with shadowed gullies. I sorted out all the mainland heights from Ben Nevis to Cruachan, with Ben Starav's big mass in the middle, a splendid panorama of the western end of Scotland's roof.

On the way up to Tobermory in the afternoon I had a fine view of a Buzzard hovering below the road between me and the sea – so much easier to see if the background is land instead of sky. Tobermory luckily can't be spoilt, its quayside houses so full of character and gaily painted. Stocked up with supplies, and set off for Calgary. Had tea by a little loch. The flora thereabouts was mainly ragwort. The road went on and on, with terrific hairpin bends the last few miles into Dervaig, all wild, lonely and varied, and very beautiful. Calgary is at the very end of the earth. Here I settled into Mrs Elizabeth Mackenzie's cottage, spotlessly clean and well equipped.

26 September, Sunday

Drizzle most of morning, which was spent in domesticities. Afternoon reconnoitred the area, found the beautiful little bay.

27 September, Monday

This was a superb day; the same wind was blowing, but it was warmer. About the middle of the morning I went down to the shore to try to find the *Mertensia*, but couldn't see a trace of it. Meanwhile the day warmed up. I went round to the other side of the bay, and on the way saw a hen Linnet. Her upperparts were mid-brown, upper breast rose-tinged, lower parts near white with vertical streaks.

Met a charming young man with wavy locks flowing from a bobble-topped knitted cap, and luckily got into conversation with him over a bird that was hopping about the rocks. He said the poverty-stricken islands were being bought up by the Germans for the shooting. He had wanted a cottage in Islay but found that the whole estate was owned by a Japanese consortium. He mentioned the Mull theatre at Dervaig. Next performance Thursday, urgent to book, only 35 seats!

I went along the roadway to the pier. There were duck in the sea below. They came in closer and finally settled on a seaweed-covered reef where I was able to have a good look at them – twelve ducks and two drakes. The ducks were coppery-brown all over, looking dusky in some lights. One drake had clear-cut white wing-coverts with black quills, and a very conspicuous white circle on the side of the tail. The top of its head was nearly black and the back of its neck grey. There was a circular greyish bib on upper breast, dark below. The other drake had the same white circle, and white wing-coverts, but not so clear-cut and there was some broken grey at the shoulder. The back of this one's head was no paler than the top; the whole head was dark. Underparts same as the other. They were Eider, the two drakes either this year's young, or in eclipse.

I went back in the afternoon, and watched two of the ducks diving just under me, quite near to the shore. They half-spread their wings just as they dive, so that the last you see of them is the three points of wings and tail. One duck watched me carefully between dives, and I her. She shone with a dark coppery lustre. A lighter band, almost grey, ran up from the base of her bill in an arc over her eye. The triangular shape of the head was very clear. Suddenly, instead of diving, she set off swimming, as hard as she could go. She had spotted another duck with something large in her bill and she meant to get it. Whatever it was looked black and round and the duck was holding it in the end of her bill and trying to swallow it, while swimming away at top speed. It reminded me of the hens at home, when one of them gets a choice morsel and can't swallow it because hotly pursued by all the others. Several times the duck had to dip it in the water and get a fresh grip. The pursuer turned herself into a torpedo by stretching out her neck at water level, but to no avail; the other gave one almighty gulp and at last got it down. She eased the passage, or perhaps celebrated the victory, by standing up on her tail and flapping her wings in triumph. All the birds were noticeably big and heavy. One of the ducks was preening on a seaweed-covered rock. The curves were massive, shining, almost reptilian. Their quacks were a deep croaking, almost a grunt. Two herons were flapping along the shore as I came away, and I saw a hen Stonechat, mid-brown all over the upperparts, underparts warm pink.

28 September, Tuesday

It appears there is a chance of seeing an eagle by Loch Frisa. On the way into Dervaig there was a small tree in the hedge whose leaves were solid scarlet, round, and toothed at the outer end. This was my first acquaintance with an Aspen, and a memorable one. It is the third tree seen in this glorious intensity of autumn colour in Scotland, and not achieved further south, the other two being the Mountain Ash by the waterfall above Kentallan and the Sycamore at Appin in 1952. What is it in the northern climate that brings them to this glory?

I parked by a bridge and set off along a spine of hill from which there was a view down the length of Loch Frisa. Ne'er an eagle, and the going was rough in deep heather. I nearly fell into a hole hidden by it, but the hole contained *Antennaria dioica* which was new to me. I worked down to the stream, near which were the leaves of Melancholy Thistle.

Just outside Dervaig I gave a lift to three students with enormous packs, and on arriving at Calgary had them in to lunch.

In the afternoon I went to see Mrs Mackenzie's garden at the castle.

3 October, Sunday · Glencoe

One of the really superb days of unclouded sunshine all through. Garbh Bheinn was a pale-grey-blue silhouette. It was very cold at 9 a.m. but warmed up steadily. This was the day when I was booked (I thought, and according to my tickets) for the night train from Inverness. I was all packed up and in the queue for the car-ferry when I was struck by sudden and total revolt. Back to the hotel and telephoned BR at Inverness who could find no booking for me anyway. Booked for the next night. Took the luggage out and set out for Glencoe. In the village bought a length of real handwoven tweed and a beautiful bean-pot with a lid, then went on up the glen. Opposite Clachaig picked up an American youth looking for the scene of the massacre. Assured him they all murdered each other everywhere all the time and gave him a lift – he was making for Crianlarich. Couldn't think how I ever got up Dinner-time Buttress etc. – the sight of these old stamping-grounds set me talking about the glories of mountain-climbing, and the totally different world to be found on the tops. He suggested that a plane-view might be equally good, but I said NO – you haven't worked for it, and anyway the heights and the interest are all flattened out from up above them. He got out just above Queenshouse. I decided to try the Glen Etive road, and just as I drew level with him again, he took off into the heather on the left, raising an arm hopefully towards the summit. I had not realised that I had spoken such winged words.

The Glen Etive road was now tarmaced, with very generous passing-places. Buachaille Etive Mhor was looking superb in the brilliant light, so I took photographs, also of a small Rowan which was leaning over the burn, its leaves all scarlet. I had hoped to try the slopes of Clachlet but the burn was here a river. I worked a little way up towards Buachaille until I was near its grassy sloping foundations, and then realised that nowhere on this side was I likely to be able to see across Rannoch Moor to the mountains beyond. At this point I heard sounds in the sky – and high above me was a skein of about fifty geese heading southeast. They were flying in a long arc rather than a chevron, and were too high for naming, but were a splendid sight as they caught the sun.

I decided to try the Black Corries road. It was extremely rough and after about a mile a notice said 'Footpath only. No cars.' There was nowhere to turn so I went on, and in half a mile found hard ground I could back into. It was also a suitable lunch-place. I settled by the bank of the burn in real heat – sleeves rolled up, no woollies. It seemed a miracle at this date and so far north.

A car came along and I sprang up to warn the driver that cars were not allowed and couldn't turn anyway beyond this point (as I had been told by some walkers coming down). He disclosed himself as the owner of Black Corries Lodge, intensely amused at being warned off his own land. He did not retaliate against me but asked me to put any other invader in the river. He returned to his Lodge and I to my sunny bank, where I dozed in the heat.

About 3 p.m. I brewed a cup of tea, and at 3.25 started up the road to get a better view of the moor, and the mountains whose tips were beckoning over the line of the intervening brae. Thoughts of the innocent American starting on his mountaineering career with no instruction, no knowledge of the local geography, no equipment – what sort of footgear did he have? – clouded slightly an otherwise perfect day.

A stream came down in a gully on my left. It was quite a deep gully and in it was a tree – a rare phenomenon hereabouts – of which only the crown could be seen, but that very conspicuously, for its leaves were clear golden-yellow fluttering in the sunshine where all else was grey stone and faded heather. I took a slanting stalker's road but soon left it and struck a course straight uphill. There were now good views of Rannoch Moor and its pools, and Cruachan appeared round the corner. I took photographs. I reached a little spur and sat down. Patches of open gravel had *Antennaria dioica* growing on them, very neat with its little circles of leaves, white-felted below. More geese came over, only nine of them this time. It was remarkable how little life there was; the two lots of geese, and a Buzzard at the start of the Black Corries road both going and coming, were all I saw.

I went across to the gully to investigate the golden trees, and found they were Aspens. They looked wonderful against the sun and I tried photographs, but even if successful they will not begin to express the shining flutter of the leaves against the silver stems, and their lushness in this barren place. There were seedlings 6–9 inches high trying to start life in the heather on the open hill above them, several dozen of them. These have pointed leaves. What with wind and sheep, I wouldn't give much for their chances.

Came down to the car and had another brew and sat till the sun disappeared behind Buachaille Etive Mhor in a wonderful glow (photograph). On the way down the glen I picked up a boy who had done

Crowberry Ridge and left him at his camp by the seven Sycamore trees. Took the old road by the Clachaig Hotel. The door was locked. I looked in at the windows; it all looked exactly the same as the night Tim and Ursula sat on each side of the fire and I in the middle drinking in their adventures. At Glencoe village found Garbh Bheinn against the sunset sky reflected in the loch, a picture of peace and tranquil colour that made a fitting end to a halcyon day.

1973

20 June, Wednesday

Set off just after 12 for Cilycwm. Very cold; had to go back and change into jumper and tweed skirt. Slight drip of rain till early afternoon. Had lunch in roadside quarry beyond Knighton. Arrived Cilycwm 4.15 (actual driving time two-and-a-half hours). House delightful. A most impressive collection of Camellias, magnolias etc. in tubs, pots and boxes. After tea we went up the valley of the Towy, all exquisite country, past Twm Siôn Catti's Crag. After calling at a farm we explored a hillside bog above a very beautiful wood. The bog was plentifully besprinkled with sundew, and some Butterwort in flower. There were also plants of Whorled Caraway here and there, and one or two had flower-spikes but all in tight bud (*Carum verticillatum*). There was Bog Pimpernel also in bud. In the wood were exquisite ferns unfolding, one with very soft fronds and a lemon scent.

In another place we went down to the river across a small field which was liberally besprinkled with *Orchis ericetorum* (broad lip with central lobe shorter than side ones – a mere little point) in a delicate pink. In the river-bed below the bank was *Trollius europaeus*; one very handsome plant made an effective pattern against a rock and the ripples of the water behind it. All the plants were on our, the shadier, side of the river. I remembered the solitary plant I found on Llynclys Hill in deep, deep shade. In the ditch running up the hedge at right angles to the river were plants of wintergreen, and the leaves of Great Burnet, neither of course with flowers so could not record them. Also in the bog had been quite a lot of Marsh St John's-wort, in the short woolly rosette stage. During this expedition a number of roses were pointed out to me, in particular one which is not in CTW, with bluish undulate leaves and sharp-pointed twisted tips whose name I did not catch, *Rosa villosa* etc. Specimens were taken home, but unfortunately I did not record them. Ended the day with a strong impression of the beauty and interest of this country.

21 June, Thursday

We set out at 10.15 for Llanstephan, leaving a notice for a farm-reserve on the way. We followed the Towy which grew from a modest stream to a broad estuary. Small hills frequently crowned with castle-ruins bounded the flat floor of the valley. Just before Llanstephan, we left the car and went down on the salt-flats. Here were a lot of old friends, *Glaux maritima, Honkenya,* Thrift of course, Sea-purslane, Sea Beet, Sea-blite, and in damp places on the land side luxuriant groups of Hemlock Water-dropwort. In a thick growth of grass and rushes was a mat of Marsh Bedstraw solid with flowers which emitted a rich honey scent. In the saltings was *Spergularia marginata* and Sea Plantain, also *Triglochin maritima* (Sea Arrowgrass). This had spikes of varying sizes up to 2 feet, stem ribbed, flattened on one side, leaves linear, fleshy, flowers minute, greenish (I lost the flowering spike). Seed-vessels oval, about 120 on my spike, on 3-mm stalks. Pistils had been six or seven per ovary: each one topped a strongly-marked section and alternated with its neighbour; a pistil which was slightly lower than the next crowned a section of the seed-vessel which swelled out more widely in the middle. We spent an hour here.

We then went through Llanstephan and by rough tracks to Lacques Farm and got Mr John's permission to go down his field to the shore. The bull was in the field and was quite harmless; it had cows and calves with it, but nevertheless he would not guarantee anything. The bull was right by the gate and let us by peaceably. We went down the field and over a stile into the jungle. The 'path' was steep and if it had been wet I do not think it would have been possible to adhere to it. I promptly went headlong (literally); however there was no damage. The jungle consisted of 6–7-foot Nettles, Brambles, Dropwort and occasional trees. Half-way down was a small stream; we followed the bed to the bottom. We settled on the shingle and had lunch – and a brew, with a flat stone instead of the kettle-lid which had fallen out. There were about a dozen Shelduck, two Curlew and Black-headed Gulls out on the flats, which were extensive. This was the Taf, not the Towy. After lunch we walked to the left. This area is a mixture of purplish-red sandstone and greyish limestone. *Asplenium marinum* (Sea Spleenwort) was growing in a crack of this as at Benllech. There was lush fresh growth of *Crithmum maritimum* (Rock Samphire) not yet in flower. There is going to be a splendid picture when it does, as it is mostly growing in the cracks of huge rocks heavily splashed with the mustard-yellow lichen. There were large bushy plants of *Raphanus* which I ignored at first thinking it was Rape spilled over from the farm, but gradually realised its decorative quality and its character.   †

9

HOW LONG CAN WALES STAND IT?

August 1978 – July 1982 · Anglesey

8 August

We went to Cemlyn Bay and parked at the end of the shingle-beach. The Sea-kale was in two solid drifts of blue wavy leaves among the stones – fresh and beautifully undamaged.

B fed the gulls. They circled round with the usual screams and yells, but suddenly I heard the queer grunt of a tern – and there was a pair of them soaring far above us, distinct from the gulls by their longer narrower wings and infinitely superior grace and skill. They never came close at this point, but we moved around to the lagoon, near the house, and had a front-stall view of the whole colony out on the island, where they were mixed with gulls and about a dozen Oystercatchers. They flew round, hunted and settled again with snowy angel-wings upraised before they folded them – a moment of supreme beauty.

Then several of them came over to our side and did all the aerobatics one could wish – the slow-motion flight, in which one could watch the flex of the wing flow along its whole graceful length, the near dead-stop in mid-air, the hover exactly like a Kestrel's with white forked tail full-spread, and finally the plunge for the prey, in the last two or three feet flying vertically down like a Gannet with wings only closed in the last split second, but without the Gannet's dive; the beak just skimmed the water and the bird was aloft again in a flash. The limitations of gravity, resistance, weight do not appear to exist for it. The dazzling white of the underparts also outlines the fore-edge of the wing, making it a clear-cut curve of effortless power against the pale grey mantle. This bird is one of Nature's moments of sheer perfection.

159

9 *August*

The dune-slacks at Aberffraw were an almost continuous flower-bed, as I had never seen them. The wet season could have contributed to this; the two dominant plants were Thyme and Lady's-fingers which between them made a sheet of colour. The Thyme was at its freshest and most brilliant, with flowers packed close together and varying considerably in intensity of pink. The Lady's-fingers did not flaunt its usual yellow, but a soft brownish-rose shading down to silver at the base of the flowers, and here and there a plant in brilliant carmine. Through and among these was a sprinkling of *Viola tricolor*, very small and mostly white, a tiny white *Euphrasia*, Lady's Bedstraw about an inch high, and clumps of pink Centaury, some of them quite wide, more in bud than in flower. Here and there was a tiny white flax, and silver-furry sprays of Hare's-foot Clover.

We went on to the Bird Hospital near Valley. At a road junction near Rhosneigr were large-flowered Knapweed and Woad. At the Bird Sanctuary an enormous parrot greeted visitors just inside the gate, brilliant peacock-blue with a tail as long as the rest of him (S American).

An Eagle Owl was the most interesting patient, a massive bird at least a foot high and broad in proportion. It had long ears and large dark eyes. Its copper-brown breast had heavy dark vertical streaks on the upper part and very fine horizontal bars on the lower. In the pools were several Ruddy Shelduck.

Iona. 'I came across a scene from the pre-industrial age.' (see p. 150)

Mull. 'Tobermory luckily can't be spoilt, its quayside houses so full of character.' (see p. 151)

Scotland: Buachaille Etive Mhor from Black Corries Road. (see pp.154–5)

Scotland: Rannoch Moor, Ben Starav and Black Mount. (see p.155)

'At Glencoe village found Garbh Bheinn against the sunset sky reflected in the loch, a picture of peace and tranquil colour that made a fitting end to a halcyon day.' (see p.156)

Barclodiad y Gawres from across the bay with gorse.

Dune Slack and Snowdonia.

Snowdonia from Pen-lôn.

1980

13 April, Sunday

Robert and I decided to go to Anglesey. It took one hour from Portmeirion to Menai Bridge. We tried Malltraeth but there was nothing of any interest. We called on the warden at Serai. He was not in a forthcoming mood, and on the whole seemed to think that naturalists, and especially bird-watchers, should be classed with the ecological dangers, with which I am inclined to agree.

Anglesey was looking its very dreariest. The cloud level was down to a few hundred feet and everything without exception was grey. We moved up to Cemlyn and stopped by the wall alongside the lagoon. Robert scanned the water first; there were three birds, wading not far away, and it wasn't long before he said in unbelieving tones: 'Flamingoes.' Now this is an unmistakable bird, and they undoubtedly were flamingoes, but the next thing that dawned was that they were not the Mediterranean/African species because they were flame-coloured all over, with no white. One was larger and more intense in colour than the other two, and had six inches of pale shank above water level whereas the smaller birds' legs were completely submerged. The big one was a really startling colour, verging flame except for the wings which were a few shades lighter but tipped with the flame. The straight part of the beak next to the head was whitish, and the fluffy underparts of the body from the legs backwards.

The two smaller birds were in exactly the same scheme but paler. The body-colour was a beautiful shade of salmon, with more vivid heads and tails. We thought they might be females or immatures, but learned afterwards that they were probably different varieties. They were feeding non-stop and only occasionally lifted their heads right up – mostly they brought them only just above the water and then in again – but when they did, the silhouette was glorious, with the perfect S-curves of the immensely long neck ending in the decisive black of the ferocious point of the beak. The contrast of these brilliant birds with the unrelieved cold grey of sky, land and water was more striking, we decided, than it would have been against a more colourful background or in better weather.

We searched for the warden to enlighten us. After trying everywhere else, Robert boldly attacked the fortress. This was not quite as formidable as it would have been in the old days, because a new front door was visible, where before a maze of wall would have had to be penetrated. It was a massive oak one however. A man appeared in answer to the ring, clearly the Hewitt's man-servant who had inherited the property. He had found the Welsh farmers too difficult and had therefore given the land to the National Trust. He didn't really know anything about the flamingoes except that they had been around for some time, and that there had originally been four of them. The warden lived on the southwest coast at Church Bay. I found this episode enthralling as it was the first time over twenty years that I had seen anything human emerge from these high and hideous walls.

We went to look for the warden but could find nothing but holiday cottages. The wind was blowing hard and cold, and Robert did marvels in balancing the Gaz stove across a ditch where a high stone and earth bank beside the road provided the only shelter.

After supper I telephoned Bill Condry as a last resort. Of course the flamingoes were escapes; they had been living wild up and down the coast for several years. They were South American birds. The implication behind his remarks was that escapes were of no real interest to the serious ornithologist, and they had become stale news anyway. We didn't mind; they had made our day.

1981

Anglesey, 24 June – 2 July
25 June, Thursday

I stopped at the Beaumaris boatyard to identify the tall plant with clouds of yellow flowers noticed on the way in the previous night. It turned out to be *Brassica napa* var. *campestris* which had been a problem when found at Llanystumdwy twenty-one years ago: 'Bargeman's Cabbage'. It makes a voluminous bush, many-branched and purple-stained at every joint, the colour running down the stem below. The large rough leaves are rounded-triangular with two detached leaflets at the base. The whole bank just above the tideline from the gate to the end of the peninsula was foaming with a 6-foot band of these showy plants.

I went to South Stack and parked at the first RSPB place, and from there walked out to the cliff which as usual was bright with tiny plants, of which *Sedum anglicum* was the most conspicuously beautiful, the flowers crowding each other in solid mats wherever the soil was too thin for anything else to grow. Out on the dryest cliff-ledges its leaves were bright crimson – the perfect background for the starry white flowers with their slight glow of rose. It spread itself in summer snowdrifts on the stone and earth banks which marked old field-boundaries; on one of these, Sheep's-bit Scabious was growing through and poised its vivid blue knobs a few inches above it, with brilliant Thyme nearby and yellow hawkbits scattered round. On one of these banks were four or five rosettes which could have been first-year plants of *Senecio spathulifolius*; the leaves were paddle-shaped and shiny above, paler and with strands of white cotton still clinging below.

In the afternoon I walked up the slope in the opposite side of the road to look at the Cytiau'r Gwyddelod, the hut-circles, and a little stone bowl, about a foot across at ground level (or present ground level), possibly for crushing or grinding corn. A long narrow round-ended structure like a giant's bath was sunk deeper in the ground than most, its walls gay with stonecrop and other flowers, and Foxgloves standing stately over. The dominant plant on this slope was gorse, with bracken and some Ling. The strangest discovery was a 2-foot high extensive thicket of *Pernettya* under the bracken, nowhere near any garden. The tiny flowers were exquisite seed-pearls and the young shoots above them red-tinged. A bird dropped a berry? – but it must have been years ago to have made such a colony.

I moved up to the other car park only to be met by a thick sea-mist which put an end to looking at anything in this area. Back to Valley and via Bodedern to Llyn Llywenan: the rain ceased at Bodedern. At the north end of the lake there were three cars and ornithologists in action. The focus of attention was a family of Ruddy Duck beautifully placed near a long drift of white water-lilies. From this point I couldn't see them clearly enough to record them: it was 5.30 so I brewed. Afterwards I went nearer to the lily-patch but the birds had gone; a wretch of a man in waders was splashing about in the water.

The outstanding umbellifers of the hedgerow are Alexanders and Hemlock Water-dropwort. Great drifts of these are intermingled with Foxgloves and Red Campion, with Yellow Rattle turning up everywhere.

26 June, Friday

There was quite a lot of sunshine but a very cold and rough northeast wind. I went to the Council offices at Llangefni to see if it would be possible to get a copy of the Tunnicliffe drawing. I was very kindly received. The Chief Executive Officer came out of a meeting at which they were actually discussing a building to put the collection in. He said that as far as Anglesey County Council were concerned I could certainly have a copy, but the family held the copyright and I would need their permission as well. I should apply to the executors at the Midland Bank in Bangor.

I tried to get to the Cors Erddreiniog Nature Reserve but couldn't find a way in. The NWNT carelessly omitted to make sure of a right of way across the intervening field, I learnt afterwards, and the farmer is now unyielding. So I went to the Cors Goch Reserve and drove along the road to the north of it, where I had lunch in the car in good sunshine. I was on the wrong side of the bog – a man came along in a huge lorry and told me so, politely. There is clearly some quarry or similar enterprise at the end of this road, and over the wall and one field away was a caravan-camp. There had been no such intrusions into this unspoilt part of rural Anglesey the last time I was there.

I moved round to the south side of the swamp and went into the reserve along the lower path, where *Orchis fuchsii* was plentiful, with one Fragrant Orchid among them. On the slope of the hill were rock-roses, but not as good nor as many as on Llanymynech Hill. I turned at the end of the little hill and came back over the top of it, in gusts of cold wind. At the end of the hill, at Nature Trail Mark (1), I turned right along a rough cart-track instead of left as I should have done and found myself in a grass- and heather-covered 'field' in which were quantities of orchids, most of which turned out to be *Gymnadenia conopsea* – Fragrant Orchid. I counted two hundred, of which one was a splendid spike with 5 inches of flowers. The plants had on average three basal leaves, and four or five of decreasing size up the stem, all unspotted. The flowers were pure unmarked rose-pink with pronounced glitter, even to the naked eye. The side-petals are dead horizontal, and the lip is barely divided into three; it looks more frilled than cut. There is a very long narrow spur. The scent is terrific, and rather sickly, like an over-sweet talcum-powder.

On the way out to the road I found the Gromwell in flower, which I had last found at Wigmore in October 1959 with shiny white seed-vessels like china. This was a well-developed plant with about a dozen stems from the base. Both leaves and flower-stems are alternate on rounded light green stalks which are rough with very short hairs. The leaves are lanceolate without teeth, darkish green above, paler below. There had been single flowers in the axils of the leaves on the secondary stems, on the lowest of which were sitting two rounded green seed-vessels in each calyx, already showing the glaze of the developed fruit. The shoots ended in clusters of four buds usually; the open flowers are minute forget-me-not type, greenish-cream. There were two plants; the second was smaller and paler.

I went up to Llaneilian, and parked outside the lighthouse enclosure. Walked on the cliff-top on the southern side of the point; the wind from the northeast was wicked. In the flower-decked rock-ledges and earth-banks, the Sheep's-bit was vivid. Contemplated one of the really splendid Carrot plants which was growing in the shelter of the wall, altogether more massive than any seen before. The central umbel was about 10 inches high and in full bloom, a solid flattened dome, snowy-white except for the one very dark purple-maroon flower in the middle. Round this were half a dozen thick pink stems reaching twice as high and outwards at an angle, their umbels not yet spread, lacy with fine-branched bracts, the flower-heads dusky-rose. With its dainty fern-like leaves, this plant was a satisfying picture of sturdy structure embellished with exquisite detail. There were others like it near South Stack. This short-thick-stemmed and markedly rosy form I had not seen before; it seems to be a maritime type.

There was no sign whatever of terns, only Herring Gulls and crows. I brewed by the churchyard wall, the only effective shelter. The church was locked.

27 June, Saturday

I went to Llyn Llywenan by the upper road. The hedge-banks were massed with Hemlock Water-dropwort, Foxgloves and Red Campion, these two noticeably darker and richer in colour here on the limestone than in other parts of the island. The same ornithologists were at the lake which they visit daily, but no Ruddy Duck. They told me that terns no longer go to Llaneilian because RTZ is tipping on their favourite haunt. Death to RTZ – another crime added to their horrible doings.

I went on to Cemlyn. The terns were on their nesting-site but much too distant for me to distinguish small detail. I moved on to the car park and had lunch. It was a lovely sunny day but the cold wind was still blowing though not as strongly as yesterday. Afterwards I walked along the shore. There were plenty of Sea-kale just at the foot of the earth-bank where it joined the shingle, in all stages from young curly plants through the flowering stage to green seed. They don't set many of the fairly large round capsules. Parallel with them on the bank above was a solid line of Sea Beet, shining strong green in marked contrast with the glaucous kale, and with long green spikes of flower. Our kitchen-garden plants seem to have had a native preference for the shore of the sea.

Finding a nook under a rock giving shelter from the icy wind, I got down in it. I realised that there was a steady movement of terns going and coming across the headland, those going outwards loping along in a slightly undulating flight, each wing-beat taking them many yards. The returning birds had a much more purposeful action; they flew straighter and faster. Their tails are folded into one fine point when they are on the move like this. I went across the headland and found they were fishing in the open sea on the far side, a few near the shore, but most of them much further out. Every now and then one would pass low right over my head: its speed was such that it was all over in a one-second flick; still it was an experience to have had one within a few feet. Later I went round the rock by the river and the weir. There was an occasional lazier tern fishing in this pool, which was otherwise the preserve of several pairs of Black-headed Gulls. The tern hovered, not motionless as a Kestrel often is, but with a slight steady beat of the wings most of the time, giving the visual impression of a very shallow V. The head cranes downwards and the tail is full-spread in a splendid curve from one long outer feather to the other, and snow-white.

In the car park was a *Spergularia* with petals white at the base, the outer half lavender, and with very fine narrow leaves. Under the rocks by the shore was the fleshy-leaved one; the flowers of this were lilac all over. I had tea in the shelter of the wall in glorious warmth, terns still coming and going. A great deal more detail needed to settle the identity of the Spergularias – see October 1964 when I did them properly.

28 June, Sunday

I went to Malltraeth, and saw the warden, Tony Bennett. I explained what I wanted to do at Llanddwyn Island. In spite of my having not got a permit for any of the reserves, he said I could tell his deputy warden there to take me to whatever I wanted to see, which was nice of him. He is rabid about the destruction of wildlife habitat. In the old days the wildfowlers used to line up all along the Cob and shoot hundreds of birds every weekend in the winter without making any real impression on their numbers. Now he issues only sixty licences, but the birds are a mere fraction of what they used to be. In the last minutes of this conversation he told me that the Llanddwyn car park had been moved, and it is now one-and-a-quarter miles' walk from it to the island. I decided however to go and see what I could do.

At the entrance to the forest was a man collecting 50p from every car. The road through the forest is now tarmaced but with bumps, reducing the pace to a crawl. There is a broad sandy strip kept clear on each side between the road and the forest which is now grown up into a solid black wall 25–30 feet high. In this strip was a fine drift of Viper's-bugloss, like dwarf delphiniums in the size and the brilliance of the spikes. I took photographs in spite of the fact that no parking is allowed anywhere along this road. The car park was a horrifying sight, 150 cars at least nearly filling it and more arriving all the time, although it was not yet 12 a.m.

The sense of claustrophobia and total regimentation (no doubt necessary in view of the numbers) was quite too much for me and I came away as fast as the bumps would allow.

Where to take refuge? I decided to try Pen-lôn. Blessed relief. There were only three cars in a very small car park, and an open sky, a place from which one could revel in the wonderful panorama of all the Snowdonia peaks, the Elephant Mountain, the Rivals and all the rest. I went for a walk, and took off from the main track on a footpath to the left. The warren, apart from dunes and slacks, is one big hay-field, and even a few trees are growing here and there, mostly birch and Hawthorn. Lush deep fuchsia-purple orchids were everywhere (*O. purpurella*). Then near a birch tree I found one which looked to me like *O. incarnata.* In a big dune-slack there were small white flowers which were a complete puzzle as there was no illustration in Collins like them.

I went back and settled down for lunch in glorious sunshine behind the warden's shed where there was shelter from the wind. The warden found me there, and we were soon in deep conversation on all sorts of topics. The little white flower is Wintergreen. There are Dune Helleborines which he will take me to see this afternoon – pointing to a dark line of forest on the horizon. How far? About a mile and a quarter. Doubts seized me. However, after lunch I got into the boots and we set off. Conversation did not flag. Of course he knew Charles Tunnicliffe. Occasionally they would go on an expedition. There was total silence. After quite some time CT would suddenly stop and ask: 'Are you all right?' remembering that he had in fact set out with a companion. They then continued as before. Another sudden stop – out would come a notebook and pencil and in a matter of minutes there was a bird, all but alive, in some posture or movement not recorded before. The warden was Welsh (Richards). He had married a Cockney wife but she got on all right with the locals; she could more or less understand but could not speak the language.

Helped by all this chat to forget my feet, I kept up reasonably well, and we came at last to the forest. In the usual sandy strip beside it were more Viper's-bugloss, also the common one, and a drift of the Dune Helleborine, not yet in flower, with their tips inclined. What chance of their being out by Wednesday? On the way back the warden pointed out a shorter route – down a lane near Newborough Church, at the bottom of which I could park by a white gate. It looked not much more than half the distance we had come.

On the way back we passed a fenced-in piece of ground with four Soay rams in it. They all had splendid horns, and one a dark fleece, a very beautiful warm brown, which I coveted. One of the others was dripping with loose wool; they needed rooing urgently. The ITE also keeps some ewes, in another part; this is an experiment to find out what effect they have on the vegetation since rabbits no longer keep it down. The ewes are also horned. They were all to be dipped the next day.

On the track we found a dark *Orchis purpurella* and a paler one which had been picked and thrown down. There was also a white one. Another albino was Ragged-Robin, of which there were five spikes. It was 4 p.m. when we got back to base; I set off at once to write up the *Orchis incarnata*.

I couldn't find any basal leaves. There were three stem-leaves, of which the upper two reached level with the top of the spike. They are plain lightish green folded on the midrib so that the two halves of the blade are nearly parallel. The bracts are conspicuous, broad at the base and tapering to the point which is level with the top of the flower. Two petals from the sides arch up and towards the centre, and fold over each other to form the hood; these are pale pink. A third deeper pink central one closes over these to roof in the structure. Under this hood are two dark pollinia; two still darker and narrower petals stand erect behind these with outward-turned tips. The lip's two side-lobes are very broad, with dark lines making semi-circles parallel with their edges and enclosing a scatter of dark spots. The central lobe is only a point at the end of a strong central rib of deeper colour, along which the lip folds back more and more as the flower ages, till the side-lobes are back to back. The spur is very broad viewed from the side and curves down to a blunt point. The whole flower gives an impression of flesh-to-salmon or rose-pink. I had tea behind the warden's shed. The sunshine, the peace and the beauty made this place perfection.

spur viewed from the side

29 June, Monday

I went down to Pen-lôn to write up the *Pyrola*. On the way to the dune-slack I found more *Orchis incarnata*, to a total of four. The third one was in a much fresher condition; none of it had yet turned brown. It had four stem-leaves. The colour of the lowest flowers was a rather dirty pinkish-white, and the lip of one near the top was almost crimson, but this was the only one with this colouring. The lips of several flowers were bent back till they touched. The top of the spike was blunt. I took a photograph. The lip of *Orchis purpurella* is concave and shows no sign of folding back. Quite the contrary, the edges curve upwards.   †

The Creeping Willow was in seed, with lumps and strands and cobwebs of white silk, and the *Pyrola* tends very much to grow near or even through it, so that the whitish flowers don't show up as much as they would on their own.

I moved round to the Braint car park for lunch. This is not nearly as nice: bungalows near, litter, view not so good. At the Pen-lôn roundabout were two ambulances (I had heard the siren), two police cars and I think a fire-engine, all in baffled pursuit of a car which was supposed to have gone through a wall at Pen-lôn.

In the afternoon, I went to look for the Narrow-leaved Helleborine but failed, miserably, to find it. However this part of the warren had interesting variations on the other. There was a drift of fourteen *Orchis incarnata*, and in another place a patch of almost as many white orchids. The Wintergreen was there, and Viper's-bugloss. I moved back to Pen-lôn for tea. Mr Richards was just leaving. I told him I couldn't find the helleborine; he said my sight must be poor.

30 June, Tuesday

The day started with low heavy cloud and Scotch mist. Got the keys of Barclodiad y Gawres and a leaflet about it from the custodian at Beaumaris Castle. The circular piece of glass let into the top of the monument has been broken by vandals although 3 inches thick, so I had to get an electric torch. Stopped at Malltraeth. There were six Lapwings and two Oystercatchers on the lagoon, and two Cormorants and a pair of Shelduck in the estuary. To Aberffraw. The road across the dunes is now walled in, with generous pulling-in places. Had lunch in one of those. The flats were all just grassy, with no sign of the sheet of colour we saw in August three years ago.

Went on to Barclodiad y Gawres. Here the car park is also now walled across, and 20p charged to go in. No scurvygrass was visible beside the path – it had covered the banks in April last year; a good example of Nature's double-cropping.

Arrived at the monument; there was the usual key fun. The gate has a really massive padlock, so placed that one of the bars of the gate prevents the full application of such powers as one has on the keyhole. Tried both keys and as usual couldn't open it with either. In this crisis, perceived a MAN sitting on the top of the mound with his wife. I soon persuaded him to come down, and explained the matter in hand. They were quite unaware of the existence of the monument, thinking it was just a rather good viewpoint. Another couple appeared. Neither man found it easy, but at last we got inside. The flashlight came into action and we found the stones with the zig-zags and the spirals. It was fascinating to see by the doorway, standing between two massive stones, the menhir watchman as at Clava – but this one was a miniature, only 18 inches high and of a different stone from the megaliths I think. He seems important. This must be looked into.

By this time eight to nine people had arrived from nowhere, including two girls of about eight and ten who were greatly thrilled, father having keyed them up with: 'Hi, you know them cave-men, this is where they lived.' – a few million years here or there . . . The girls posed one at each end of the spiral-marked stone leaving only two of them visible in the middle and a flash photograph was taken. One of them stroked the top of the stone which her quickened imagination saw as a recumbent figure: 'What was his name?' – just like the child shown the Bronze Age skull at Clun. So to a child, as to tribal man, the name is vitally important. And she saw true – the line of the stone was just that of a medieval effigy.

HM's lecture on Bronze Age (or earlier?) Megalithic graves was well received. With mutual gratitude the iron gate was locked. The strong man and his wife were on a trip from Wolverhampton, and acclaimed me almost as a neighbour when I said I came from Shrewsbury. Here we were in a foreign land . . .

Next to Trearddur Bay to find Porth Diana. Overshot it apparently. Only one woman had ever heard of it, and when I went on as directed, the only likely-looking headland was cleft from the mainland and surrounded by steep rocks and a deep band of slimy seaweed. No time left to tackle this obstacle. The furthest headland I found was a strange mixture of gorse, Bell Heather and Tormentil with drifts of lush orchids, mostly rich purple. I never identified these satisfactorily.

1 July, Wednesday

Went down the lane by Newborough Church as indicated by Mr Richards. It was very narrow, and deep between high hedges, in which there was a huge Fuchsia worthy of southwest Ireland. Parked by the white gate; after this the track comes out on the open warren. Up to this moment it had been raining, a fine Scotch mist, but by the time I had got the boots on it had stopped. It was quite a pleasant walk, and only about a third of the distance to the helleborines that it was from Pen-lôn. The sun came out. A man from Kettering on holiday somewhere up the lane said it was about another half mile on from the helleborine place to Llanddwyn beach. The Viper's-bugloss looked splendid, with five or six branches in brilliant flower.   †

I came to the helleborines. They were not in flower and only a few ever will be, as they are smitten by a sort of black scorch which starts in the flower-buds and works backwards down the spike. One plant was totally discoloured. I think some of the Twayblades were suffering too; I saw quite a number with aborted flower-spikes all over the warren. I wrote up all I could, and took photographs of the best plant I could find, which had three stems, but the black was appearing in the flower-spike of even this vigorous one.

Epipactis dunensis (Dune Helleborine). The plants were up to a foot high. Fairly stout round stem, slightly brown-stained at the base, and with sparse very short white hairs. There were no basal leaves. The lowest two leaves (or bracts) were much smaller than those above, stiff and fairly tight round the stem. Above these were four stem-leaves, about 3 inches long and $1\frac{3}{4}$ inches wide, meeting round the stem at the base, oval-pointed, with nine main veins running longitudinally. The upper side was bright apple-green, inclining to yellowish, the underside lighter with the veins very prominent. The bracts like the leaves but narrow and not wavy as they are, looking as if they will always be longer than the flowers. These were in tight green bud. Most of the plants were single-stemmed; several stronger ones had three stems each. I counted twenty-eight plants in all.

Note: Catriona Paskell was in Anglesey a week later, and found better and healthier colonies in the forest where she penetrated and plenty of them.

Back to Pen-lôn. Walked in the usual direction and found a shelf on a dune where there was shelter from the strong west wind, where I lay for an hour or so and got slightly sunburnt! Then clouds came over. On the way back to the car came upon a sandy circle 6–8 feet across, in which there were clumps of *Sedum acre* at its freshest and most brilliant, a strong yellow with a hint of green in it. The stems were nearly all an inch or less, with the fleshy pink-stained leaves overlapping. This plant is next-door to a cactus; the five-pointed stars were jostling each other in solid masses. There are ten longish stamens, and in the centre are five upstanding fleshy segments which presumably are a multiple pistil. Some of these were quite vertical and nearly touching, others were beginning to spread outwards.

2 July, Thursday

Packed and loaded. 11.30 set off for Pen-lôn. It was raining on the way with piled-up dark clouds over Snowdonia and the northern end of the island, but as I got near, the usual break of blue sky appeared over Newborough, and at Pen-lôn the sun was shining. The rest of the day was lovely. Only the ITE van was there. Had lunch sitting out in warmth in the lee of the shed; the wind was fairly strong west. In the afternoon made for the usual dune-slack, looking at the willows on the way. In all these years I have not recorded *Salix repens*, though I have photographs of them in sheets of golden catkins.

Willows are of course dioecious – a fact which I ought never to have forgotten, and was stupidly puzzled by the two types, one clotted with lumps of silk and the other not. The females on the whole are smaller and flatter and occupy the slacks and lower ground. Their leaves are tiny and green on the upper side. The males grow on tumps and other lusher and more prominent positions, and, having sent their pollen on the wind, can concentrate on growth. Hence the taller and more upright shoots and larger leaves with the silky undersides more visible, a wonderful white-silver, shining brilliantly where the leaf is rippled, as it is between the veins. The floss on the females is smoother than satin to the touch; if it could be spun, it would make the most exquisite gossamer textile ever invented, but it wouldn't hold for two minutes. I found the open seed-vessels deep inside it, a two-celled follicle, now brown and with outward-curving points, a minute silk-factory a few millimetres long. It did not occur to me to count the fibres attached to each tiny dark speck of seed, nor to measure their length. This must be done. In the dune-slacks the small creeping plants carried great blobs of it, some clotted with moisture, others poised loose and misty, ready to float away. An earth-hugger, this plant, it both shuns and courts the wind, cunningly using it when it suits its purpose. And what a wind . . .

I found a spike of the Wintergreen with one unopened bud at the top. It had the ericaceous look mentioned for all the rest of the tribe. One petal was stained with rose.

There was an hour of bliss before I had to leave – the warmth of the sun, the *silence*. The sough of the wind in the dune-grass, the small hum of a bee, the quicker whizz of a fly, do not break the silence; they add to it the throb of life and the sense of its miraculous power.

1982

16 July

This was a lovely day of warmth and sunshine. With the help this year of the new check-list, 'The Flowering Plants and Ferns of Anglesey', I started the botanising in a triangular patch of rough grass at Fryars, about a mile from Beaumaris, which I entered by a ditch which ran across it to the shore. It was thick with Curled Dock and Grass-leaved Orache. I was surprised to learn that this dock is the commonest of the tribe; it isn't the one which frequents my gardens, which is the Broad Dock. I couldn't find any of the three plants that I was particularly looking for, but did find one stem of Bristly Ox-tongue, and a fine clump of Lucerne, which drew attention by its rich lavender-blue, the same colour as Bush Vetch, which was also there. The air was full of the Lucerne's honey-scent. Its trifoliate leaves are large compared with those of the vetch. Luckily I found one very underdeveloped but coiled seed-pod, otherwise it wasn't setting seed. There was a magnificent group of *Sonchus arvensis* on the bank of the small stream which comes down at the end of this lush little meadow.   †

I moved on to Trwyn y Penrhyn where there was just a mass of rough grass on the shore side of the road, and no sign of the brackish water which should contain *Ranunculus baudotii*. In the field on the opposite side is a beautiful pool, but the field-glass revealed no sign of the crowfoot and it was inaccessible anyway. I had lunch here. I then went on to Penmon to look for *Erodium maritimum*, said to grow by the church. The churchyard was a mown lawn. The church was shut. A parked coach was playing pop music. I took photographs of the splendid romanesque doorway with the dragon tympanum and then got out as quickly as possible.

I went up to Mariandyrys and drove all round the northern end of it without seeing any possible access; it was thick with gorse and scrub. I came around a corner to the western side, and by a gate were two cars, and in a quarry were four women painting. I asked if there was any access that way (a rough cart-track led on) but the answer was not encouraging. One of them said there were lovely flowers and came with me to learn their names. The steep bank on the left was quite rewarding – there were: Basil, Marjoram, Purging Flax, *Hypericum pulchrum*, Saw-wort, Greater Knapweed as well as the common one, Burnet Rose, Little Spurge. The women were very friendly; one of them had had a boy at Prestfelde. They were going to the Plas Newydd coffee-morning the next day and leaving afterwards.

I went on down the road and had tea at a junction at the top of a very steep lane, where there was a sweeping view of the splendid curve of Red Wharf Bay. So ended Day One, in which I scored three new plants but not the ones intended.

17 July

This was a dull and cloudy day. Snowdonia was swallowed in murk. I went to the Plas Newydd coffee-morning, where I acquired the May 13th number of *Country Life* which turned out to be the summer gardens number; what luck. Here I got an introduction to botanist Mrs Rees, who took me home with her, and showed me on the modern map how to get in to Mariandyrys, and told me of a Mrs Cragg in Beaumaris who has a Broad-leaved Helleborine growing just behind her garden.

I had lunch by the shore just beyond Plas Newydd, and then went on to Aberffraw. I walked about on the common, but didn't find any of the things I was looking for. However I found great pleasure in the minute beauties of Restharrow, Common Centaury and Hare's-foot Clover, all exquisite in detail, and in writing them up. Brewed tea by one of the walls. The murk came lower and lower and turned to a fine Scotch mist. I decided Anglesey was the depth of gloom and I should have to go home if it went on like this.   †

18 July

To the top northeast corner of Mariandyrys as directed by Mrs Rees and went up the rough lane. I had hardly parked by the top-most house and got my boots on, when a woman emerged and invited me to go through the garden and up a path she had made to get on to the hill. This was a blessing as there were the usual gorse defences. Also very refreshing to be met by 'Do come in' instead of 'Keep Out'. I walked all over the hill for an hour but couldn't find Lesser Butterfly-orchid, Moonwort or Petty Whin which I wanted to see. I went down for the lunch-bag and met the good lady's son who invited me to eat in the garden, but I preferred the hill-top. It has a splendid view of everything – out to Puffin Island and Great Orme, a huge spread of sea to the north, Snowdonia to the south, and below in the foreground a particularly fertile and sheltered shallow bowl of land between two arms of hill, totally unspoilt and owned by the farmers, as the son told me. He himself holds twenty acres, and gave Mariandyrys to the Trust. I spent a lazy afternoon in the sun in this splendid place. Wandering round the lane later, I was picked up by Margaret Williams and friends, and taken back to tea with them. Then to Artists' Corner and wrote up the Saw-wort. †

19 July

To Porth Diana and parked in the boatyard. A path and a stile led to the reserve, and almost at once I found a beautiful little plant of *Tuberaria guttata* (Spotted Rock-rose) with a fresh flower looking up at me, a most satisfying moment. Apart from the flower, it was quite different from what I expected. There are very broad basal leaves which lie flat on the ground, varying from one-and-a-half times to twice as long as broad, with three lengthwise veins. They are hairy all over, each hair growing from a bump in the surface so that the leaf has a corrugated look.

The whole plant is not more than 4 inches high, more often 1–2 inches. The flower-stems are erect, their leaves much more like ordinary rock-rose leaves, long and narrow, and also hairy. There are two very small outer sepals, narrow and pointed, and within them three much larger ones, broadly triangular. The half of the outer surface of these, which is exposed when in the bud stage, is tinged with red and covered with black spots, each of which carries a hair. They are also thickly edged with hairs. There are five petals, roughly triangular with an inward curve in the middle of the outer edge, clear yellow deeper at the centre, and spotted with red near the base. There were a few plants which carried only tiny flowers with toothed ends to the petals and no red mark.

It is difficult to believe that this is always a true annual. There were numbers of small rosettes which clearly had not reached flowering stage and weren't going to this season, but which probably would next year. Or is this plant not hardy enough to survive a British winter except in seed form? Also CTW say that the basal leaves die away by flowering time. This is not so. The height of the flowering season according to R. H.

Roberts is in May, and here we were two months later and they were perfectly good and fresh.

There were plants scattered all over the top and middle of the reserve, nearly always appropriately where a flat slab of rock showed through the thin vegetation. None of them had more than one flower out. Considering that this is near the end of their season, and that it was now 12.30, perhaps I was lucky to see that much. Dorothy Paish had always told me that I must be on site by 9.30, otherwise the flowers would all have dropped! I photographed the best one.

Six or seven Soay sheep were in the next field, their fleeces varying from near-black through a perfect mid-brown to paler shades. I took several photographs.

I went on up to the RSPB reserve car park at South Stack and had lunch. Last year's flower-beds at the cliff-edge were all over. Then to the upper car park, calling on the way at the restaurant for news of the excavations at the hut-circles. They all finished weeks ago. The dominant plant at this time of year all over the South Stack area is the Carrot. There was a superb plant 3–4 feet high and wide in the bank of the lower car park which I photographed, and they ranged downwards in size from this to miserable single-stemmed heads pushing up through the heather on the rocky slopes above the lighthouse steps. Here the *Spergularia rupicola* (Rock-spurrey) was conspicuous and very beautiful with masses of lilac flowers against the hard bare background.

20 July

With Margaret to Aberffraw instead of Red Wharf Bay as planned, because the north wind was blowing straight into that one. We parked on the small piece of common just across the river from the village; it was not unduly crowded. The wind blew quite freshly here too; however we had lunch sitting out. We then set off through the dunes and I got my shoes full of sand; boots are required. Arrived at the beach and we encamped like all the others. Luckily I had the anorak and took possession of a large piece of sail which had been cast up most conveniently. In due course Margaret went for a swim. The population increased slightly. I felt this was a day that was more or less of a write-off, but on the way back through the dunes Margaret led me to the finest colony of Sea-holly I had ever set eyes on, and in full freshness too and just starting to flower, a state in which I had never seen them. They were scattered about on the very steep slopes of a deep hole between dunes, very sheltered. I would love to know how deep the roots go.

On the way back to Llangoed we passed Cors Bodeilio, with an acre or so of Meadowsweet which filled the air with scent. Opposite, up a rough road is a weaving-school and shop, and a vegetarian restaurant.

21 July

After yesterday, I felt I must get back to the botany in earnest, so made for Pen-lôn. There was a new warden, one Hughie, a scraggy but nice individual, who explained that nobody must leave the paths. He didn't himself by way of example. The warren is covered with deep grass; they are trying sheep to get it under control (they would need a flock of 1000 for that, I should think). Richards is transferred to Llanddwyn; both he and Tony Bennett are there today. With both the botany and peaceful picnic-site abolished thus abruptly, I became desperate and decided to face the horrors of the Llanddwyn car park and the effort of the walk to Llanddwyn Island. The entrance fee was now 70p. The Viper's-bugloss was over; instead there was Evening-primrose in the sandy strip beside the road. The car park was only slightly less jam-packed than on that dreadful Sunday last year. I had lunch at one of the picnic tables. I had this corner more or less to myself, but the wind blew straight in and made it rather uncomfortable. Got into the boots and set off. The dunes were lined on the shoreward side by sunbathers and their brilliant plastic gear, spreading along on each side of the arrival point, but Llanddwyn is so vast that they did not dominate. The sand was slightly soft and Llanddwyn Island was hazy in the distance . . . about half-way along, the Marram grass at the edge of the dunes was varied by a splendid patch of Silver Orache and Saw-wort growing together. The orache was really silver with stems deeply pink-dyed, and the group had a modest and original beauty. I didn't see any *Cakile maritima* which I found here years ago.

From this point on, I began to hear various little clicking and croaking noises and felt sure there were terns about, but couldn't see them. However when I got near the island, there they were, a pair of them, just like the first time I was here. (Was it at Llanddwyn or Four Mile Bridge that I saw my first terns?) I then spotted the warden's shelter, and sure enough there was dear old Richards in his beret, tanned and just the same as ever. I explained the objectives. He went out and scanned the area with his glasses, and having made sure that TB in his landrover was at a safe distance, he set off with me to show me the Adder's-tongue patch. This was a small field in the middle of the island with a rudimentary fence round it. Right on the edge by the path had been a splendid drift of the Common Adder's-tongue – it had been completely flattened by persons who had sat on it, pretty heavily by the look of it. R went further in and picked two stems for me. I explained about the Moonwort (wrongly as I found afterwards – it is the Dwarf one that is listed as at Llanddwyn). He went back to base, and I went on to the lighthouse to record the Sea-lavender. It was growing in plenty on the rocks on the left side of the steps, in full flower this time, and making a fine contrast with the mustard-coloured lichen on the rocks around it.   †

There was good plenty of *Geranium sanguineum* all over the landward end of the island, also of *Rosa pimpinellifolia*, and Heath Groundsel all over the place.

Back at the shelter, I had another chat with Richards. There was a good clump of Sea Rush growing nearby. He told me to walk back near the waterline; the sand is harder there. I took his advice; it also shortened the distance as I cut across the arc of the bay, but it meant that I missed getting the detail of saltwort and Frosted Orache. However, there were other interests. The tide was right out. About half-way along was a stranded jelly-fish, its arms all flattened out to one side and looking partly melted. The body had very dark blobs of purplish-brown all round the rim and the centre was opalescent, quite unlike the pale lumps I remember in childhood at Borth. There were the usual worm-casts, and thousands upon thousands of queer things like caddis-fly cases, planted upright in the sand, averaging about an inch and a half above the level of it, and with four or five arms on the end. The upright pipe (as I suppose it is) was encrusted with minute bits of stone about the size of a pin-head, a quite effective mosaic. The arms were quite rigid and made no response when touched. The whole structure was pale sand colour.

Then there were shallow saucer-size depressions in the sand, perfect circles with a hole in the centre. I wonder if this was the work of a creature, or just the effect of swirling sucking water as it pulled down through patches of particularly soft sand? There were bits of seaweed in brilliant emerald-green, both ribbons and threads.

Belan Fort boomed its three guns at 3 p.m.; I heard it another day also.

The vast openness of this beach is exhilarating to mind and body. The space is mostly sky and one is enveloped by it, floating in wind and sun as if ready to take off like a bird.

22 July

I went to Pen-lôn, Hughie not being on duty today. To car park II, with the idea of finding Narrow-leaved Helleborine, which Richards says is just by the path when you swerve away right at the corner of the fence – the same directions as last year. I did just this, but couldn't see a sign of it. RHR says it only exists in one place, in 'a conifer plantation, Newborough Forest'. I don't think Richards knows his plants very well; this was clear yesterday.

There were quantities of splendid *Dactylorhiza fuchsii*, many of them 18 inches high. In a fairly lush dune-slack there was the best colony of Round-leaved Wintergreen yet; it whitened the floor of it in two places, growing in thin *Salix repens* which makes a very good ground work for it.

There were also very flourishing and deeply-coloured Sheep's-bit. They have basal tufts of narrow leaves averaging ¾ inch in length, with a glandular surface and a scatter of fairly large white hairs. The flower-stem lies out at an angle, slender and smooth. They have clusters of smaller leaves alternately on the lower part of the stem, and occasionally half-way up. The flowers are in a round head, each one deeply divided into long narrow-strip petals, the outermost opening first and containing the pistils, the inner ones two cleft stamens.

Near the car park I found Red Bartsia in flower – first seen beside the Ridgeway near Avebury.

I had lunch here, then went to Aberffraw to get photographs of the Sea-holly.   †

23 July

To Llyn Padrig to look for *Ranunculus lingua* (Greater Spearwort). I took the upper road from Beaumaris. In a garden on the outskirts of Llandegfan there were three bushes 6 feet high and 4 feet wide, smothered in white flowers. I thought they must be some sort of *Olearia*, but the leaves were those of an evergreen *Euonymus*, bright and shiny on both surfaces, oval and toothed. I sneaked four cuttings, and hope they will survive, if only to satisfy my curiosity.

The Llyn Padrig area turned out to be very satisfying. On the opposite side of the road is the small medieval church in its circular churchyard wall, locked and deserted but still giving focus and atmosphere to an unspoilt stretch of Anglesey countryside. The little lake was framed on its further shore by willows and on the left by a reed-bed, leaving the near side open (luckily) to the cow-pasture which sloped down to it. Beyond, after a grassy field, was a large farm, its grey stone buildings snuggling in a group of really good trees, altogether a timeless scene.

There was a convenient gate nearby, and I hadn't gone far towards the water when I realised that there was quite a flock of Canada Geese grazing on the right, and more of them on Llyn Padrig. There must have been fifty or sixty of them altogether. They soon got up and circled round making a terrific noise, and after some minutes departed for other shores.

At the waterside were rushes, with conspicuous clumps of Marsh Ragwort, a good deal of Lesser Spearwort and a scatter of Sneezewort and Ragged-Robin. But no Greater Spearwort till I moved left to the reed-bed where at last I found it, by dint of balancing on the more solid lumps of vegetation in the oozy black bog. †

There was a good colony of the plants towards the reed-mace on the left, and they thinned out from here towards the open side of the lake. There were quantities of the Lesser Spearwort; it was almost the dominant plant apart from the rushes. Here also were Bogbean (not of course in flower), Marsh Pennywort, and Marsh Cinquefoil, also over. When I emerged from the ooze, I found the rosettes of Meadow Thistle on the firmer ground. †

I went back to the church where banks on each side of the path to the west door gave shelter from the wind, and was deep in writing up the spearwort when a nice young couple arrived on bicycles. They had a guidebook which said the church was medieval. We got on to the subject of megaliths, and they told me about the Scottish peninsula opposite

Gigha which they say is full of them, and where there is a local character who has written a book about them. It sounds as if this combined with Gigha would make a good holiday.

At 3 p.m. I decided I must try to find the Rhosneigr saltmarshes. I tried both ends of the town and failed dismally, with a desperate loss of time and the usual horror of massed cars, plastic beach apparatus and far too many humans, also roaring planes over RAF Valley where the flare-paths were all twinkling in different colours. Decided that Llyn Coron was now the only hope so shot back to Aberffraw and took the road to the left immediately after the bridge. From this point to Llyn Coron it was all peace and beauty again. The road divides Aberffraw Common from the farmland and is not frequented as it is right away from the beach. There was rough ground between the road and Llyn Coron with any amount of plants including Sneezewort, Greater Skullcap, Red Bartsia in plenty, Marsh Cinquefoil in seed with very silvery leaves, Marsh Cudweed on the stony flat shore and Common Water-plantain among the rushes. But no sign of *Ranunculus circinatus* which I had hoped to find. I went back along the road and had tea in the angle of a stone wall which gave shelter from the wind.

24 July

I went to Mrs Cragg's to see the Broad-leaved Helleborine. We went round the garden. There was a yellow *Sedum* about a foot high which runs all over the place and the pearly *Polygonum campanulatum* likewise. She sticks *Crinodendron* cuttings in an open frame as if they were lavender, and they grow. The soil is heavy boulder-clay. The house and garden are at the end of the road (on the new estate at the entrance to Beaumaris) with a piece of rough ground and the Baron Hill Woods beyond. Only a strand of barbed wire marks the boundary. The trees are splendid, including a very big Scots Pine, in which Red Squirrels are quite often seen. We stepped over the wire and went to look at the Broad-leaved Helleborine, of which there was one handsome stem at the edge of the wood. †

From the end of Mrs Cragg's garden we looked down into Mill Dingle, and she indicated the buildings where the Bulkeleys had once had a private gas-works, which they subsequently extended and supplied the town as well. All this fell into disuse and disrepair when the public supply came, but as far as her new road was concerned, they would have been better off with the Bulkeleys, as British Gas now wants an exorbitant sum to lay a main up the road, and a still more unreasonable one to connect each house.

Having surveyed all this from above, we went round to the Dingle to see the *Senecio tanguticus* (identified as such by Kew) which she discovered growing in boggy ground by the stream, in the heavy shade of the trees. It is 4–5 feet high, with cut leaves, and flowers in large sprays. The buds were just colouring. Its origin and how it got there are unknown; it is not in the floras.

The Dingle has been given to the town by the Bulkeleys and the Council is improving the paths and generally making it a pleasant place to stroll in.

I then made for Fedw Fawr where it was possible to drive just on to the open hill. There were several cars parked on the only possible places beside the road but there was nobody about. I discovered that what they come for is the fishing; they all drive down the concrete steps to the shore. Fedw Fawr is a good spot, a big stretch of open moor sloping up gently, and a sweep of blue sea northwards with Penmon and Puffin Island to the right. I had lunch in sunshine, and wrote up the helleborine. I then set off to explore. The dominant plant appeared to be Bog Asphodel, partly in flower but more in fruit, with the brilliant orange colour beginning to flush them – this although there was no sign of bog.   †

Working up the slope I soon found that the dominant plant was really the gorse, which had been cut very low indeed and was just grown enough to be very painful to the ankles. The further I went the narrower the path and the worse the prickles, which precluded exploration away from the track, and hardly left room for other plants anyway. Boots are required. There was a splendid plant of Common Cat's-ear. I was renewing my acquaintance with more ordinary plants as well as seeking rare ones.   †

I had a delicious siesta in a grassy hollow where there was less gorse than average. The evening calm in this peaceful spot was heavenly. The vast blue spaces of sea and sky had their perfect counterpart in a field of Rape nearby.

25 July

Overcast and dull nearly all day. I set off for Penmynydd to find the Giant Bellflower, and soon discovered it in a grove of trees on the right after going through the churchyard gate. The cover was thick and gloomy, and the ground almost solid with this coarse 5-foot plant.   †

To Cemlyn, where a tern which perched on a wire (or rather on a cork on the wire, its webbed feet being unable to manage bare wire?) was identified as a Common one by the black tip of the beak only running to one third of its length. Ampelopsis is growing up the Great Wall. Sea-purslane, with its grey spathulate leaves and rather squalid appearance, was growing in the mud-flats beyond the house. I had lunch by the end of the shingle-bank, and photographed a fine Sea-kale plant 2 feet across, growing tight down in the stones, its stiff glaucous leaves pale-edged and convoluted. I then left for Porth Swtan. About a couple of miles along the road there was a splendid standing stone which I photographed. It had a groove round the edge like the one at Clava.

At Porth Swtan the lane was jammed with cars and the tiny horse-shoe bay of rocky cliffs with narrow sands was lined solid with Red-Indian-skinned bodies and royal blue and scarlet plastic. I fled. Mad to go anywhere near the coast on a Sunday. The rest of the afternoon went in a desperate search for peace and beauty. At the second attempt Llyn Llywenan filled the bill. I settled at Ruddy-duck corner: the only sounds were the occasional lap of a miniature wave and the trill of a Curlew. While having tea I noticed that somebody had trodden a gap in the reeds, so I went to investigate. It led straight to black ooze and a group of Greater Spearwort and a fine stand of Yellow Loosestrife which was in perfection and very showy.   †

26 July

To Red Wharf Bay via the telephone-box lane. On arriving at the shore, the first plant I met was the *Atriplex hastata* (Hastate Orache). The strongly-ribbed stem is stained carmine and slightly mealy. The leaves are mealy below and very slightly speckled above; they are fairly long-stalked and hastate right up to the flower-spike.

I walked along to the right under the low earth-cliff, picking my way painfully over a jumble of large stones and boulders. There was very little of interest botanically. I did find one plant of *Samolus valerandi*, growing right on the surface of a rock over which there was a steady trickle of water. It was good to see this elegant little flower again, last encountered at Cors Goch in 1960. I returned to the car, walking out on the shore which was only partly sandy. The low rocks disappeared entirely under a thick coating of mussels, which in their turn were almost hidden by an incrustation of the small limpets which have holes in their tops. I have never seen such dense colonisation by either of them, still less both together.

I moved round to the Wern y Wylan approach to the shore, a much nicer route leading to a deeply-treed lane at the bottom with a broad verge for the car. Coming out on the shore, I found the saltmarsh stretching away to the left, and I renewed my acquaintance with the sea-tolerant plants. The area was a jig-saw of pools and inlets filling half the space or more, unlike the marsh at Newborough which is all solid vegetation.   †

I went to Bodeilio for a vegetarian lunch. There are fine Tudor buildings, exhibitions of weaving and pottery and an attractive shop. I spent the afternoon and evening at Fedw Fawr.

27 July

After shopping and packing, I set off for Aberffraw Common to make a last effort to find the Moonwort, but stopped a few miles from Beaumaris to pick a piece of the *Hypericum hircinum* which grows in a broad band on top of the wall bounding the Baron Hill Woods. It has also hopped across the road in various places and is steadily colonising all the way to Menai Bridge. †

The sun was shining; it was a glorious morning with Snowdonia looking its loveliest most ethereal blue. I turned along the Bodorgan road which is much pleasanter than the main one across Aberffraw Common, with no concrete verges (yet) or walled parking-spaces. I set off on the hunt. Not a Moonwort did I find, on either side. What I did find were splendid Carline Thistles in perfection; all I had ever come upon before were very short-stemmed single-flowered specimens, withered and silvery. These were a foot high with four or five heads on each and in their prime. †

A pair of Ravens were croaking round. I had lunch in peace and warmth by the car. Other vehicles were appearing, but not too many and not too near. I curled up in the sun and the breeze – it was quite hot – for a final rest before the journey home. A flat cloud with a straight edge was gradually approaching from the northeast, and by 2.30 it had arrived. So had a mass of traffic and seasiders; the cars were now right up to mine and the place was intolerable. I left with all speed; it made departure from Anglesey easier but was an unfortunate note on which to end. Llanberis Pass was the same: every nook that would hold a car had one, and at Penypass they were jam-packed on both sides of the road as well as in the car park. Betws y Coed was a seething mass. And August still to come. How long can Wales stand it?

ONE OF THE GOLDEN DAYS

August 1982 – September 1983 · Shropshire & Marches, Anglesey

22 August

To Hanwood with Kim, to botanise along the Rea Brook, which was quickly reached by a footpath opposite the garage. Immediately there were unspoilt views both up and down stream, of tree-hung meanders and miniature gravel-spits. Hedge Mustard was growing with great luxuriance, 4-foot bushes of it (*Sisymbrium officinale*), great plumes of it, eventually bending over in the pale brown seed stage. Another dominant plant was *Angelica* in green seed, the pinkish-purple stems conspicuous. *Chrysanthemum vulgare* (Tansy) was widespread, not in large colonies like these, but mostly single plants, apparently taking the place of Ragwort which was totally absent.

The dearth of birds was marked. The only ones we saw in over an hour were a flight of small finches which came across in a series of little swoops, and which Kim thought were Goldfinches. Before last winter a Kingfisher, sandpipers and Sand Martins could be seen. The holes in the occasional earth-cliffs, about 8 feet high, were unoccupied, this summer. Even Moorhens have gone.

Thistles were the next preoccupation; the occasional clumps had at least three varieties in them – a few *Cirsium vulgare* (Spear Thistle), but mostly smaller-flowered *C. palustre* (Marsh) and *Carduus crispus* (Welted Thistle). In the latter the stem is white with close tomentum, and has three rows of green undulating wing, narrow and spiny. Only one of these ribs stopped short of the flower-head in my specimen. The oval calyx is made up of numerous scales, ending in very long, narrow green points which are bristly but not hard and spiny. These are shorter the higher up they are, and the row of scales immediately beneath the flower are quite short and are tipped with the same deep fuchsia-purple as the florets.

They do not bend outwards at any stage as the others do. The long conspicuous anthers protrude beyond the petals, and are several shades darker in colour.

Another plant that was new to me was *Sonchus asper* (Spiny Sow-thistle). This has its leaves much more thistle-like than the usual weed (*S. oleraceus*), narrowing from base to tip, with the edges strongly undulating and the lobes ending in spines. They have a wide central vein, broadening considerably to the base, where the auricles are tightly folded together, their faces sometimes touching. The upper surface is shiny deep green, the lower matt and greyer. The smooth sepals have minute transparent thorns sparsely scattered on the midribs. The achenes are pale brown, flattened and ribbed, and the pappus is unbrached.

Helped by Kim, I learnt to spot some fish, which otherwise I should have missed. These were Chub. There used to be Trout but the Minsterley creamery has put an end to that. They are still in the Yockleton Brook which joins the Rea, just above the bridge, where we came out on to the road. Kim says that Clive Tanner told him that, in pre-creamery days, Mr Brodie-Hoare of Meole Hall, who owned the land a good way up the stream, used to give him permission to fish in the Rea, and he would catch more Trout of whopping size in an hour than he could carry away. What impoverishment.

1983

18 June

To Porth Diana with Trina and Malcolm. There seemed to be less *Tuberaria* than last year when I saw them a month later. However, there were two little groups, one with eight flowers and the other with sixteen plus four more within about 9 inches. These flowers almost touching, ideal for photography which went ahead. There were no Soay sheep. We went on towards South Stack and took a side-road when just past Porth Dafarch and were able to drive further out on the heath than I would have thought possible in these restricted days. Lunch. We set off down the track but had eventually to take to the heather; luckily it and the gorse were very short. More than half the gorse was dead (not burnt) which must have been the result of the bad winter. Just as I was getting desperate, T and M, who were ahead, found a splendid colony of the *Senecio spathulifolius*, several hundred of them in a grassy slope where the gorse and heather had given out, quite near to the cliff-edge. They were past their best, with on average three faded flowers and two fresh ones in each head. The white cobwebs had all disappeared, apart from a few strands here and there washed down by wind and rain on to the shiny surface of the leaf and stuck there, but even this was not frequent. It was heartening to see such a flourishing colony. It is clearly in no danger of extinction at present.

We curved up towards South Stack, passing another lane which appeared to lead to a point within about five minutes' walk of the *Senecio*! The RSPB car park was jam-packed; we went on to the upper one and had tea. T and M went to the lighthouse steps, and reported glorious rock-gardens, more *Senecio* and Puffins.

We made a dash for Cemlyn and pulled up at the end of the shingle. The *Crambe* were in full perfect bloom and the terns were fishing in the sea. T and M found a splendid group of the vegetable and photographed it, and we watched the terns with delight, in the perfect evening calm that was coming on. We drove round to the further car park before leaving. Ivy and Ampelopsis are steadily clothing the Great Wall. We saw with disgust four people walking on the shingle-bank right by the tern colony on the inner side. The terns did not seem as numerous as in other years. I drove along the lane by the pool but saw no sign of *Ranunculus baudotii*.

19 June

To Pen-lôn for the BSBI meeting. Soon linked up with RHR and Nigel Brown who is a charmer. He runs the Bangor U. Botanical Garden which is just by Menai Bridge. We set off along the public track and it all seemed rather dull to me at first (and far too many people). However, the *Dactylorhiza purpurella* clan were sorted out, and we began to see increasing numbers of *D. p. incarnata*, which I had identified correctly last year. We came to a splendid group of fourteen good plants and the photographs got into action, including T and M.

D. purpurella itself (*D. maialis p.*) is characterised by the diamond-shaped lip and rich dark colour. The head of flowers is very dense.

D. p. var. *incarnata* has more yellowish leaves, markedly hooded at the tip, and the lip of the flower folded right back as I observed last year. And of course the colour which is quite different.

D. p. var. *incarnata*, subspecies *coccinea*, has its leaves broader in proportion to length and more crowded at the base, and the really deep *red* not purple colour, a gorgeous creature.

RHR showed us *Equisetum* × *littorale* (*E. fluviatile* × *arvense*) which has five sharp teeth at the node with scarious edges. Also a clump of *Polypodium vulgare*. And a hybrid between *Dactylorhiza fuchsii* and *D. purpurella*. This has darker flowers than *D. p.* and lip tending to *D. p.*'s three lobes.

Centaurium minus with rounder basal leaves and flower with longer tube was contrasted with *C. littorale* whose leaves are smaller and have parallel sides, and whose flower-tube is not longer than the calyx. There is also a hybrid between these two, which is sterile, and therefore goes on flowering in August when the other two are over. The flower of *C. littorale* tends to be larger and deeper in colour.

Equisetum variegatum is tiny compared with most of them, very slender.

Grass *Vulpia fasciculata* has the lowest glume only ½ mm long. Mr R showed me this in an effort to get me 'hooked on grasses'. It hybridises sometimes with Red Fescue.

Newborough Warren and Aberffraw Common are both rich in mosses. The northern and southern mosses meet here. *Selaginella selaginoides* (Clubmoss) is here at its southern limit. It produces better specimens on damp ledges in Cwm Idwal than it does at Aberffraw. There was one spore-bearing shoot about 2–3 cm high, with round spore-bracts in axils of pointed leaves, all the yellow-brown colour of common seaweeds.

The most BSBI-ish episode of all came over *Mibora minima*, a rare grass. This flowers in April and was now reduced to two or three desiccated pale grey threads lying flat on the ground. This did not deter the members who formed a bottoms-up circle, eye-plus-glass practically down on it. This was followed by an orgy of photographing. How Nigel Brown found it in the first place, and relocated it in the second, was a miracle. The same rituals only more so were performed when we came to Moonwort, with rather more reason. I did my utmost to get Trina to take this performance, it would have been an invaluable record of BSBI in action, but she didn't. The other lamentable omission was mine not to write it up on the spot, which I regretted later. I noted some obvious landmarks – the gate, two large rocks etc. – and asked Mr B how to reach them from the road.

Rosa pimpinellifolia was scattered about at this end, with very large and beautiful white flowers. There was also a scatter of Bee Orchids just in perfection. RHR remarked that a bee had never been observed to visit one, in spite of the marvellous mimicry, and that they are self-pollinated. What a fascinating revelation.

The *Salix repens* was in its usual fluff. It was leaving dumpy catkin-shaped seed-vessels bare in places, some of which had turned a beautiful tawny-red. I asked NB about this and the minute specks embedded in the fluff. He confirmed that these are the seeds; the relevant seed-heads that he investigated were empty. So all the fluff must have been packed in as well? And how much to each capsule?

A *Rubus* with very fine large white flowers was met occasionally and was thought by a member to be *R. caesius* (Dewberry).

Somewhere around 4 p.m. we retreated to the car and then to my tea corner on the other side of Afon Ffraw with relief. We had walked roughly four miles in the heat . . . Afterwards we went to last year's access to Llyn Coron. The vegetation was very lush and far less interesting than last year. Yellow Flags were very handsome and were photographed, and Malcolm caught a damselfly. These are smaller than dragonflies and when at rest fold their wings back in line with their bodies whereas the dragonflies keep them out at right angles. This damselfly had two black spots under the end of its wings; its body was black, with a sky-blue segment near the tail. It is a very beautiful but incredibly fragile-looking construction.

Trina registered water-crowfoot by the tiny bridge over Afon Ffraw on the way back.

*View from Lynclys Hill looking
southwest from near 'Jacob's ladder'.
The view is very similar from Maes
Uchaf. (see pp.21, 128)*

*Hilda and Malcolm Leel on Hilda's last stay in Anglesey, loading Hilda's car with picnic gear
outside the Bulkeley Arms, Beaumaris. Taken by Trina Paskell. (see pp.189–97)*

Hilda's 'shack', Maes Uchaf at Fron Goch ('the upper field of the red hill-breast') on the Welsh end of Llanymynech Hill.

20 June

To Trwyn y Penrhyn to search for the *Ranunculus baudotii*. I didn't have to. I came round the curve to be absolutely hit by slabs of it in two very small pools flanked by gorse bushes. Only a wire fence and a few yards of meadow intervened. There was such a mass of it that I did not feel guilty in taking a piece. I put it in a bowl in some of its own water (the colour of pale tea) and wrote it up later.

Then to Penmon. Walked to the well. Was considering the remains of the round cell-walls beside it, and there on top was a small plant of the *Erodium maritimum* (Sea Stork's-bill) which I failed to find last year. I went on up the path too and there were lots more. I wrote up one which had two developed seed-heads, ne'er a petal did I see. All these plants averaged just over 2 inches diameter. Back at the cell again, I found four plants which must have got thin roots deep between the stones and had developed to their full potential, with 8-inch shoots still spreading flat. Wrote up both sizes with care.

Then went on down towards the point.

Penmon is ruined by the constant going and coming of very heavy lorries carrying stone from the quarry. Not beautiful squared stones, but aggregate . . .

I stopped by a rocky tump, which was golden with rock-rose in full beauty. It was almost cold today, a complete change from yesterday. In the afternoon, I got down to the shore by the coastguard station, and found a gorgeous display of Tree-mallows just in fresh beauty. These flowers to my mind are at the head of the league of the dark-centred, rayed-petal types. The size of the flower, the richness of its red-mahogany depths, and the firm definition of the lines drawn from them, add up to total glamour, and remove it altogether from the washy-magenta of the rest of the family. The petals are also more clear-cut. The big velvet leaves seem to have a rigid framework running to the sinuses, so that the lobes droop between them like a half-opened umbrella. I ought to have looked into this but didn't. I was lost in admiration of these splendid bushes, some of them huge – 10 or 12 feet high, all growing right against the earth-cliff with their roots under the shingle which came up to it. There were two dozen at least. This lovely sight was one of the highlights of the week.

I moved up to Artists' Corner which was heavily contaminated by cows, and then to the stile-corner by Bwrdd Arthur for tea. There were masses of rock-roses all along the road here, but few on the hill itself which was grazed right down by sheep. The first plateau was just a smooth grassy lawn and the hill-top was little better. I saw no sign of *Geranium sanguineum* but there were handsome plants of Slender Thistle with big rosettes of basal leaves and 12–18-inch spikes, several of which had the central flower just pushing out its small rather pale head. The leaves had noticeably broad lobes, with pale edges.

I hadn't the time that this splendid place deserved, and must go back to it.

21 June

To Aberffraw Common to write up the Moonwort. Parked at the Bodorgan end and walked along the track to the black gate. Soon found the two rocks I had noted. I searched the grassy place near them, quite a lot of it on hands and knees, but not a sign could I see of that good little group of five spikes photographed by everybody on Sunday. Nor any other plant of it at all. After a good deal of this, I gave up in disgust. I hadn't gone far on the way back, when a head appeared above a bank, so I asked it if it was a botanist. It said, 'Well . . . er', and turned out to belong to a botanical photographer. He had just taken a fine colony of Bee Orchids, and Moonwort was next on the programme. I led him to where we were on Sunday. He thought he should look higher up; he had been told it prefers thin dry soil. I left him at it and turned my attention to a fine spike of Bee Orchid which had three flowers in various stages of development, showing clearly the whole process of self-pollination as mentioned by RHR. The top petal and two side ones are soft rosy-mauve. The swollen lip is dark brown velvet with clear yellow markings and ends underneath in a tuft of fur. It has two tiny lobes at the side well furred, altogether as good an imitation of a bumble-bee's well-clad body and legs as could be wished. Standing up behind all this mimicry is a pale green column with two knobs at the base. From these knobs spring the stems of the two pollinia (or filaments); they lie tight against the column, and their round heads are enclosed on each side of it at the top behind a semi-circular membrane, which shows their golden colour through. As they mature, they break free from this and bend forward and down and almost inevitably, as the filaments are mere threads, and the anthers great golden clubs, leaving the membrane in which they were hidden a white film. In the flower I was investigating, one of these anthers was just resting on the floor where it had landed, but the other by some means unknown had its filament in a backward curve so that the anther was right in the throat of the flower.

I then went for lunch. Was still eating when the photographer returned, having found the Moonwort and marked two groups near a rock with a stone pointing towards the track where it divided, and another by tying some grass together. I thanked him warmly, and set off full of hope. I found the parting of the ways, and on the right there was a rock . . . there was a smallish stone . . . I got down on hands and knees and searched eagerly 10 inches on one side of it, 18 inches on the other, but not a Moonwort presented itself to my longing gaze . . .

No tied grass could I see anywhere . . . No other Moonwort, which after all there must have been . . . appeared either. The bitterness became extreme. Why can't I see Moonworts – I can see other minute plants . . . I retired to a grassy shelf by a big rock and rested. There was an absolutely miniscule *Euphrasia* where I lay and I found my grievances assuaged by the marvels of this tapestry of tiny plants which covers the barren sand. As soon as it is fixed, all woven so tightly together in beauty and fitness and carrying on their small lives from year to year with such persistence. Also the Bee Orchid sequence was worth a lot to have worked out so soon after being told.

I went back to Llangadwaladr and took what I thought was the road to Llyn Coron. Parked and walked down a lane nearly choked with vegetation and came to an impassable ford – the footbridge was made inaccessible by 5-foot high nettles. Went back. I was on the wrong road (not very clever today); took the right one and arrived in a farmyard. Was given leave willingly to go through a field to the lake-edge. It failed to produce *Ranunculus circinatus*, *Polygonum minus*, or *Elatine hydropiper*. In a boggy patch just above the lake was a fine colony of *Ranunculus hederaceus*, but I didn't want that one.

I went back to the Aberffraw tea place. Afterwards I went to the little stone bridge. The stream was white with water-crowfoot above and below it. The job was to get a piece to identify; the banks were vertical, and the water 3 feet down. In the end I used Charlie's ash-stick and hooked it up. It is *Ranunculus fluitans*, with no floating leaves and long strands of submerged growths held downstream by the strong current. Not at their full potential length because the river is a small one – but deep and strong enough in that flat country. It spreads out into a respectable river by the village. This is the only place in Anglesey where *R. fluitans* occurs. It makes an exquisite miniature landscape with the rushes and the little bridge.

22 June

To Cors Goch. Went to look at the Fragrant Orchid place and counted about ten flowers. It is nearly five weeks earlier than when I saw it last year. I walked over the top of the hill but couldn't find any *Viola lactea*; for this one I am too late.

I went down to the swamp. There were very handsome plants 18 inches high growing in the edge and also right in the water, as I found when I went along one of the board-walks. This undulated slightly so that I was in the water several times; I was pleased to find that the Joe Brown boots still don't let in a drop. The plant was Red Rattle, said to be common on waste ground etc. with no mention of water. Here it was right *in* it. By the board-walk it must have been a foot deep. The plants were deeply purple-tinged, with strongly-squared stems, leaves toothed. The flowers were large and conspicuous, pink with a hint of mauve, the lower lip in three lobes. CTW says this plant is 'hemiparasitic'. There was nothing much but reeds for it to be parasitic on in this place, so if its normal habitat is waste ground, there is a problem here.

I had lunch on the verge of the road which luckily had little traffic on it. Then went to Cors Bodeilio. Got over the stile but soon encountered such a tangle of thistles and brambles as to make me reflect that after all I was on holiday . . . I retired to the weaving place which had an exhibition of Moslem craft superbly displayed. Had a huge cup of tea. It was hot in the restaurant right up under the roof. Went to the Bwrdd Arthur stile-corner – to discover I had no water so could not brew.

I set off to look for the Penhwnllys disused quarry and *Potentilla tabernaemontani*. After miles and miles of lane there was a crossroads and a signpost. I landed in a farmyard. The farmer and his wife appeared and I explained the objective. There are two disused quarries on his land. He directed me to one of them, through two fields and three gates. When I got there, the quarry was not visible because it was filled cram-jam with the densest thicket-wood I have ever seen, quite impenetrable and very sinister. The second quarry *was* visible away to the right, also with some woodland but normal-looking. There was now no time for this. So this year's botanising in Anglesey ended with the only-too-typical frustration.

26 September · Llanymynech

There was solid fog early, yellowish at first in the low light, but soon turning paler and sinking in solid white bars along the valleys, leaving just the tips of the foothills visible. Berwyn was hidden in higher and denser cloud. I went up on the hill, but earlier would have been better; by the time I got to the crag, the white cotton-wool was dissolving into low grey wisps, which were driven along the river-valleys towards England by a steady southwest breeze. The really wonderful sight was not this, but the cobwebs, not the usual kind but three-dimensional ones, nearer fabric than thread, so close-woven was the gossamer. The dew had been heavy, and they were spangled with droplets so small that I counted twenty of them on a bare inch of thread, but though minute they were brilliant reflectors of pure celestial light. Miraculously I had the sun behind me when I bent to look at one of them, to find an inverted rainbow lying across it, very softly orange and green and blue, living specks of opal. The fineness of the filigree was breathtaking. These super-cocoons were everywhere in hundreds. I only saw one of the more usual cartwheels but it was a superb structure.

[Undated]

This was one of the golden days from the start. I made sandwiches and set off for Maengwynedd. There was just a movement of air from the east, but it was so warm that I shed the cardigan on getting out of the car at the sheepfold. I had lunch just inside the near end of the sheepfold with my back to the wall, studying with delight the detail of the mountain. The strata slope gently downwards from left to right across the face. They must also tip gently upwards from the west in parallel with the general slope of the plateau up from Llandrillo; the tougher layers can be traced as slightly protruding lines across the escarpment particularly just below Craig Berwyn. This formation must provide the goat-track by which I came down from that point on the great day of the Army exercises in the snow.

Just before 2 p.m. I set off, to climb as far as I could towards the Bwlch. The only signs of life were one or two Meadow Pipits, and a pair of very vociferous and apparently angry Ravens, which kept up their clamour most of the afternoon. I worked slowly and steadily up on a fairly clear track. In the old days it gave out about half-way up the slope, and one had to make one's own way over the roughnesses and round the rushy tussocks. About three-quarters of the way up, I began to think of what could possibly be seen from the top on such a day – and *could* it. First, the stone had been put up again, what joy this was. Then sure enough, the first glimpse over the col was met by the rough little lump of Tryfan, with solid masses of mountain to right and left of it. Two or three hundred yards along the fence to the right, and the Snowdon horse-shoe came into sight and completed the group, blue, clear-cut and superbly framed by the slope of Berwyn and the curling paths leading round the head of the next cwm to Cadair Bronwen. It was sheer bliss to have got here again on such a day and be greeted by perfection – to be able to look *over* some hill-tops – north to the Horseshoe Pass, out to the south and east as well. The stone is 9 feet high, slim and elegant, lichen-patched with pale apple-green. It was warm from the sun.

NOTES

48   Caer Din Ring: a hill-fort near Mainstone in the Clun Forest upland, one
of HM's favourite places in Shropshire.
'Had a blissful afternoon lying under the western side of the earthwork out
of the wind.' First of many references to the 'basking' habit (see Introduction).

49   'when I turned the glass on it': see p.27 above, and Introduction. This
passage is a good example of HM's patience as a bird-watcher.
'a day for seeing Snowdonia from the Bwlch.': Bwlch Maengwynedd in the
Berwyn Mountains; Bwlch (Welsh): pass (see also p.198, and
Introduction).
'swan-census': a county census organised in 1961 by the Shropshire
Ornithological Society.
SRC: Stella Ross-Craig (see References).
CTW: Clapham, Tutin & Warburg (see References).
'I moved up to the Holy of Holies.' This was a small meadow or pasture
on the limestone slopes of Llynclys Hill, above Pant (see Introduction).

51   'The house has been abandoned and the site is already beginning to be
grown over.' This has nothing to do with HM's property, Maes Uchaf, at
Fron Goch on the Welsh end of Llanymynech Hill. It refers to a site at the
upper edge of a particularly interesting scrubby pasture on Crickheath
Hill (Grid Ref. SJ 273230) where the foundations of a house were laid and
then abandoned for some years before their eventual and unexpected
completion (see p.128).
'Jacob's Ladder': a flight of wooden steps, near Pen-y-coed, where the
footpath leaves Llynclys Common and goes southward along the top of
Blodwel Rock. [Still, in 1985, one of the best botanical localities in
Shropshire.]
'the thicket' becomes 'the same wood' in the next paragraph.

52   'Lucy': Lucy Lunt, an old friend of HM.
'Cowslip Hill (Boreton).' Also known as Boreton Bank: a very interesting site
on a dry sandy slope above the Cound Brook, first studied and described
by Edward Rutter (see Introduction) both before and after the onset of
myxomatosis in the mid-1950s. [The subsequent changes in the vegetation
were rapid, and ultimately led to a much reduced diversity of species.]
'I found . . . Hare's-foot Clover . . . Realised . . . that it could not be. . . .
Seems it must be a hybrid. C. Sinker thinks *T.arvense* × *T.striatum*
possibly.' [C. Sinker no longer thinks so: no such hybrid is known, and the
Boreton plant remains a puzzle. A specimen was sent to Cambridge for
determination, but I have no record of any reply.]

53   'Mr Rutter': Edward M. Rutter, outstanding amateur ornithologist and
botanist.

54   'I remarked on a large and lush plant of Water Betony, not yet in flower.':
See entry for 19 July.
Joyce Haseler: a friend and neighbour in Meole Brace.
'the house-site': see p.51 above.
'the tram-cut.' The old extraction route from a [now] virtually inaccessible
limestone quarry on Llynclys Hill crossed by a rough lane, running
northwards past 'the house-site', at a point known locally as the 'Black
Bridge'.
'Had news . . . on the telephone from Mr Rutter.' This was a new and
exciting record for the area. [The 1970–83 Survey for the new Shropshire
Flora (see References) showed *Scrophularia umbrosa* to be locally frequent
in the southeast quarter of the county.]

56 Weekend trip via Snowdonia to Anglesey.
'Found I had left the glass at home': presumably her hand-lens rather than her field-glass – see p.27 above and Introduction.
Solidago virgaurea var. *cambrica*: cf. 'typical' Goldenrod, pp.65–67.

57 Not the first time HM had visited Anglesey, although the first in the Diaries.
'The first new plant to me was *Gentianella amarella*': rather surprising she had not met it on Llynclys Hill or Wenlock Edge, where it is not uncommon.

59 Reg Arthur: Assistant Warden for the Nature Conservancy on Newborough Warren National Nature Reserve, of which the dunes at Pen-lôn are part.
'I left with desperate feelings about 7 p.m.': see Introduction; the whole passage is quite characteristic of HM and her feelings when a brief spell of 'freedom' was over.
Twayblade: it is usually apparent when a plant was drawn *in situ*, not picked.

60 A Tuesday visit to Broniarth Hall near Guilsfield, just across the Welsh border. 'This is wonderful country' and 'The perfect house to my mind' may be first hints of active house-hunting: see pp.70, 112 and Introduction.
'Suddenly I saw a tern; that wonderful flight': a subject to which HM returns often and in great detail – see pp.99, 159, 166, 179, 185, 190 and Introduction.

61 Purple-loosestrife: another recurrent subject (see pp.68, 69, 70).

62 *Mentha niliaca*: now regarded as a form of *M.villosa*, the Large Apple-mint, of hybrid – and garden – origin.
'The Shropshire Handbook': see References, under Lloyd & Rutter.

64 Rhialgwm: a hill near Hirnant, between Llanfyllin and the Tanat Valley; another Sunday afternoon spent 'basking' and botanising in HM's beloved Welsh border country: see p.48 and Introduction.
'Telephoned Mr Sinker, who disclaimed any knowledge of mints.' True, alas. [Mr S's second, and final, failure in these annals.]
Hilly and Frank Gribble again: see p.46.
Goldenrod: see p.56.

66 Mr Harrison: well-known Shropshire artist and naturalist, Reg Harrison.
'Witherby': *Handbook of British Birds*: see References.

67 Polemere or Polmere: a small, intermittently dry pool near Great Hanwood.
The Hem (Moor): a large area of winter-flooded grasslands beside R Camlad near Forden, Monts. – much frequented by wildfowl.

70 'To Wellington to see Mabel': not traced.
'Beet-factory flood-water': the settling lagoons of the British Sugar Corporation works at Allscott.
Ellen May Hughes (nee Morris): see p.90 and Introduction.
Cefn Glaniwrch is in the Tanat Valley near Llanrhaeadr ym Mochnant.
Tynyfedwen is a farm at the head of the beautiful and secluded valley of the R Iwrch, Cwm Maengwynedd.

71 'went up on the Downton end of Haughmond.' The only reference to walking in this area, which was clearly not one of her favourite places.

72 The start of a botanical fortnight in Anglesey.
The 'yellow filter' indicates black-and-white photography, but there are no monochrome prints in the Diaries: perhaps HM was not satisfied with the results.

72–74 Bristly Oxtongue. Perhaps the liveliest botanical description and drawing in the Diaries; HM had a fondness for prickly or shaggy Compositae.

Penmon near Beaumaris, not to be confused with Pen-lôn near Newborough.

75 Rutter joined HM at Beaumaris for Monday to Saturday of the first week. Cors (Welsh): (peat) bog or fen.

76 Cob: a stone pier or breakwater, as at Lyme Regis; the word is used locally for the embankment impounding the lagoon at Malltraeth.

77 Reg Arthur: see p.59.
'with glass and telescope': HM's field-glass, EMR's telescope (see p.27).

78 CTW: see References.
Dai Morgan at Cemlyn: not traced.

79 Penmynydd: the ancestral home of the royal Tudor family was an unmarked farm.
'Tufties': Tufted Duck.

80 & 81 Records of conversations are rare in the Diaries; this long passage of indirect speech and the interpolated afterthought about the briar-pipe are clear evidence that HM was writing for others to read.

82 & 83 Sea Rocket: already seen (and drawn) at Paguera, Mallorca: (see p.36).

84 'yellow filter': see p.72 above.
SRC: see References.
Reg Arthur: see pp.59, 77.

85 Grass-of-Parnassus: another drawing done *in situ* (see p.59 above).

86 'the Oxtongue absorbed all the time and energy there was.': see pp.72, 73, 74 and Introduction.

87 The visit to Widcombe Hall, Bath, was on Nursery business.
Monksfields: farm on Long Mountain, near Welshpool, home of Mr and Mrs Paish until autumn 1961 – they had left by November (see p.46). HM had their permission to take blackberry plants from the garden, but new owners arrived while she was doing so. After a debate, they helped [personal diaries, checked by RG]. She later had a walk ['on the top road'] 'west of the pub': she must mean the Welsh Harp, now a farm, though it had been a pub and then a Youth Hostel in the 1940s.
Spectre of the Brocken (after a peak in the Harz Mts) is an uncommon optical-meteorological effect in which the observer's shadow, projected on to a distant cloud, appears magnified and ringed by a halo of light or a rainbow.

89 Maengwynedd; 'Walked half-way up to the Bwlch' (see p.198). Bwlch: pass (see pp.49, 70, 90, 198 and Introduction).
The Hem goose-fields again, in which EMR was very interested (see p.67).
The Leighton redwoods are among the biggest in Britain.
Snowdrops are perhaps truly wild in a few of their Shropshire localities.
'cruddled' (Shropshire dialect): curdled.

90 'the Holly forest': The Hollies near Snailbeach, not The Hollies farm near Gatten (see p.39 above).
Magpies on the backs of sheep: unusual, but by no means rare; tick-feeding?
The late Mrs W. E. Morris of Tynyfedwen, mother of Ellen May (Hughes) and of Maengwyn (see pp.70, 198 and Introduction).
'the Llanrhaeadr fall': Pistyll Rhaeadr, highest waterfall in Wales.

91 'Men stock-planting, the soil is just wonderful.' A rare reference to work at the new Nursery site, by then about a year old.

'Stopped on Knockin Heath for lunch . . . Removed self and effects with all speed.' The only recorded occasion when her habitual 'basking' was interrupted.
CTW: see References.

92   Two successive April Sundays in southwest Shropshire; one with EMR, one alone.
Caer Din again, with Joyce Haseler: see pp.48, 54.

93   Mr Downes of Grinshill: a retired gardener and keen alpine plantsman.
Concerning HM and bird-song, see Introduction.

94   Mansells: 'Peter' (I.G.) and Barbara Mansell of South Mytton House; he and HM were friends from school-days. [Damson blossom is still a sight locally.]
'the house-site on Llynclys Hill': see pp.51, 54.
'the swooping lines of the hills ("the train of the prophet")': I have been unable to trace this quotation, though I suspect Freya Stark, whom HM greatly admired.

95   Frank Gribble: see pp.46, 64.
The start of a ten-day visit to Anglesey, recording no less than four halts on a drive of less than 100 miles.
Geoffrey Winthrop Young was well known to several generations of Cambridge climbers, as was 'old Owen'.
The 'Pyg track' up Snowdon takes its name from Penygwryd (Hotel).

96   'I sent the wings to Stella': her niece, Stella Chick (née Green).

97   These notes on her trip to Bodnant show her keen professional interest in exotic shrubs and trees other than roses.
Sagina subulata (not *subularia*).

98   Mrs Crichton and Mr Owen: not traced.
First record of a visit to South Stack on Holyhead Island – a fruitless search for Annual Rock-rose.

99–102   Return to South Stack: a detailed account of her exploration of the area and the unexpected discovery (for her) of an unknown composite, which she correctly identifies as *Senecio spathulifolius* [now treated as subspecies *maritimus* of *S.integrifolius*]; description and drawing of this 'Field Fleawort' follow. Her decision to 'come back tomorrow instead of going home' is characteristic.

103   Chelsea: HM was a regular exhibitor and medal winner at the Chelsea Flower Show.
Susan Rogers, who worked in the office at Murrell's Nursery.
Plaish Hall, between Church Stretton and Much Wenlock.
Claytonia alsinoides (now called *Montia sibirica*), Pink Purslane, has greatly increased since 1938: the map in the new Flora – see References – shows over 40 localities, mostly in the Plaish area.

104   'The Holy of Holies' and 'the house-site' on Llynclys Hill: see pp.49, 54, 94 and Introduction.
Glanhafon: near Llangynog, at the head of the Tanat Valley.

105   Stella Chick (née Green), her niece.
The Vapourer moth (*Orgyia antiqua*), feeds on various trees and shrubs.

106   Bird observations at the nursery.

107   Polmere and The Hem: see pp.67, 89.
Marton Pool: near Chirbury (not Baschurch).

108   Dorrington sandpit, south of Shrewsbury, was another of Rutter's good sites.
SRC: see References.
'the harbour' is Aberystwyth: see p.136.
Hilly and Frank Gribble: see pp.46, 64.
R.S.Thomas, poet and vicar of Eglwysfach [later of Aberdaron].
Yellow Horned-poppy (*Glaucium flavum*), drawing on p.109.
[?]Wilson's Phalarope.

111   The Hem again – see pp.67, 89, 107 – and Marrington Dingle.

Volume I of the Diaries ends here, on 15 Dec, 1963.
Volume II starts on 29 Dec, 1963.

HM was understandably excited to find Parsley Fern on Corndon Hill, but makes an untypical geographical mistake: Corndon is in Montgomeryshire [now Powys], not Shropshire. The *Handlist* (see References) understandably, therefore, has no record for this area. Hilda was an excellent geographer, and generally took meticulous care over correct locations and the spelling of place-names. The only non-trivial errors I have spotted are this one; her use of 'peninsular' as a noun (p.121 etc., now corrected); and the odd hybrid coinage 'Llangefenni' when she means Aberllefenni (p.137) – a momentary confusion with Llangefni in Anglesey? She expected the same high standard of others: there is, among her loose papers, an interesting letter, dated 5 November 1980, from the author John Llewelyn Jones; it reads, in part:

    'Dear Miss Murrell,
               Pistyll Rhaeadr
    Thank you so much for writing to me. You are of course absolutely right about Afon Disgynfa feeding the falls and I am honestly at a loss to know how the mistake occurred . . .
    You write evocatively and with vivid detail about your beloved Berwyns and your letter was a delight to read. Thank you too for the shot of the falls encased in ice . . . Marvellous sight.'

                                     [cf.p.90]

112   HM revisits the Corndon Parsley Fern colony. She is right that the *Atlas of the British Flora* shows no records, recent or past, for this region [even in the 1976 edition].
13 April 1964: cottage-hunting again in the upper Tanat valley: see pp.60, 70.

113   Start of a fortnight in southwest Ireland, one of HM's less happy holidays. The weather, the slippery wetness and the signs of poverty depressed her.
Myrtus luma, etc: throughout this visit, HM's professional interest is stimulated by the magnificent specimens of exotic shrubs and trees not hardy in most other parts of the British Isles.

114   Garinish Island Gardens – see preceding note.

115   'bought a skirt-length in tabby weave of coral-red and gold.': see p.44 and Introduction.

116   'bought a piece of wool – mohair Donegal material of great beauty.'
'had an orgy of photography': see Introduction.
'These mountains are *not* attractive – they are one god-dam slime which comes off and me with it.' See p.113 above.

117   Machair (Gaelic): calcareous coastal grassland on shell-sand (Hebrides, etc.).

118–119   Mostly description and drawings of *Pinguicula grandiflora.*

120   'The sheer unmitigated superfluity of H_2O in this part of the world is something that cannot be described, only experienced.'

121   'the Smith's peninsula': I cannot make out why HM used this name, which I have not seen elsewhere, for the Beara Peninsula. What map was she using?

122   'a voluble Irishwoman turned up': another typical encounter with a 'character', HM playing the reluctant listener's part (see Introduction, and p.80).

123   Kidney Saxifrage: HM's drawings from Ireland are more loving than her narrative.

125   'The strata give repetitions of the peninsula in miniature': HM had an unusually good eye for the relationship between geological structures and landforms (see p.198 and Introduction).

126   'it was *just* possible to replant [!] the butterwort more or less in its own home – but *what* a country, how do they endure it?'
Oxford Ragwort actually reached the south of Ireland before 1900, but is rare.

127   Back in the Shropshire hill-country. 'The gorse on the way compared very unfavourably with the Irish.' [! Distance lends enchantment?]
'An elusive bird in the heather gave incessant but short little bursts of song.': see p.93 above, and Introduction.
To Edenhope again with Joyce Haseler: see pp.49, 54, 92.
'DP': Dorothy Paish (see pp.46, 87) had shown HM *Astrantia major* in Hampton Beach.
'awful shock – a caravan plus a car and tent in Caer Din!!': i.e. within the ring-work of the hill-fort; an understandable if somewhat proprietorial reaction.

128   'the house-clearing; what a shock to find a house on it!': see pp.51, 54, 94, 104 and Introduction. The Japanese 'Amanogawa' Cherry, with its cramped fastigiate habit and suburban profusion of pink blossom, would have offended HM's sense of what was 'proper' in that wild corner of the landscape.
'We ought to have bought this land.' Who? The Shropshire Conservation Trust? HM herself?

129   Chelsea again.
'caterpillars . . . hungrily devouring a small Spindle tree . . . black shiny heads . . .': probably a species of sawfly.
Start of another Anglesey fortnight.

130   HM's first meeting with Charles and Winifred Tunnicliffe was the result of her leaving, on their doorstep at Malltraeth, a dead male Guillemot which she had found on the shore of the Menai Straits [Clive Tate]. The Guillemot drawing in the Tunnicliffe Collection (see Introduction and p.164) credits HM for the find and bears the date 29 Sept., but no year. It was presumably 1964, but it is curious that the incident is not mentioned in the Diaries.

131–132 A trip to the mainland, then back to Malltraeth; the Barn Owl description is the longest entry of its kind in the Diaries.
Early snow on the mountains (12 Oct): into Snowdonia for photographs.

134 *Spergularia* is a difficult genus. 'To supper with Tunnicliffes' who lived at Malltraeth.
The last of four brief entries for 1966.

135 The first of two entries for 1967. The only page in the Diary for 1968, but it reads as though in mid-narrative.
'the lake': Llyn Gwernan near Dolgellau.
'Jane': untraced; said by Mrs Paish to have been an artist-friend of HM's.
Dorothy and David Paish: see pp.46, 87, 127.
Yellow Horned-poppy: see pp.108, 109.

136 The only page for 1969, though again clearly part of a longer record.
Five years after Charles Tunnicliffe first showed her the Marsh Gentian on Anglesey (p.130), HM returns to the site to describe the plant.

137 The only written-up entry for 1970, the year HM sold the Nursery and retired.
David and Dorothy Paish: see p.135 above, etc.
'Llangefenni': a rare slip of the pen; it should be Aberllefenni (Llangefni is in Anglesey).
'Conifers solid . . . They look really awful and I am glad I joined the protest movement.' The Council for the Protection of Rural England? See Introduction.

138 'Sarn Helen': the made-up track which goes over the head of the Llefenni Valley, towards Dolgellau, is thought by some to be part of that great north-south routeway through Wales.
[Deleted from this published version are some rough and very incomplete botanical notes on a visit to Provence, 26 Sept – 5 Oct 1970.]
Mitchell's Fold is a stone circle on Stapeley Hill.

139 Fron Goch: the first mention of the 'shack' which HM had bought on the southwest end of Llanymynech Hill (in August 1962 – but see also p.112 and Introduction).
'Charlie': Charlie Haycocks of Carreghofa, who looked after the garden at Fron Goch; not to be confused with Charles Warren, Murrells' foreman.
Aston Munslow: Miss Con Purser's remarkable White House Museum of rural crafts and farm equipment.
'having the tiny field-glass on approval': see Introduction.

140 Cartwrights: J.M.Cartwright, builder, of Meifod; not to be confused with Rex C., forester, of Knockin.

141 Start of a joyful fortnight in the Scottish Highlands and Islands, recorded in HM's style of 'lyrical realism' at its best and most sustained. She took her own car by 'Motorail' from Crewe to Inverness.
The pinkish colour of the Cairngorm granite is in the feldspar crystals.
Reindeer inhabited the northern Highlands well into the historic period (Fraser Darling 1947), but this herd is the result of a recent experiment.

142 & 143 These paragraphs on the 'Stones of Clava', and the next day's description of 'A Cairngorm Corrie in late September' (pp.146, 147), illustrate the range of HM's interests and knowledge as well as the flexibility of her style: 'this was a numinous place.'

144 'Landmark. . . . This is a first-rate establishment.' As an experienced exhibitor – and traveller – HM appreciated good organisation and presentation; cf. Iona, p.150.

145   'Sedge which defeated me. These *Carex* specialists. . . .' Sedges are not *that* difficult, just different[!].

146 &   'A Cairngorm Corrie. . . .': quintessential Hilda Murrell, as I am sure she
147   would have liked to be read and remembered.

148   'prostrate Broom': *Cytisus scoparius* subsp. *maritimus* is supposedly confined to coastal cliff-tops in south and west Britain and Ireland; HM's plants may be a similar but independent genetical 'sport'.
Inshriach Alpine Plant Nursery, established by Jack Drake, is one of the outstanding British nurseries.
'a black house': stone-built crofter's cottage, abandoned and burnt in their thousands during the 'Clearances'.

149   'basalt – so the plants were Carrot, Purging Flax and Carline Thistle.': basalt is a *basic* igneous rock, and gives rise to fairly lime-rich soils.

150   Environmental bad taste was epitomised, for HM, by the concrete Celtic cross and the canned Bach at Iona Abbey.
Machair (Gaelic): calcareous coastal grassland on shell-sand (see p.117).
'the high point of the island': 332 feet. The double peaks visible beyond Coll and Tiree must have been Beinn Mhor (2034 feet) and Hecla (1988 feet) on South Uist.

152 &   *Mertensia maritima*, Oysterplant, a rare northern coastal species.
153   The Mull Theatre at Dervaig became quite famous.
Graphic description of Eider duck behaviour.
'my first acquaintance with an Aspen': very surprising – they are quite common on the Marches.
'I gave a lift to three students . . . and . . . had them in to lunch.' Typical of HM's spontaneous friendliness and generosity: see Introduction.

154 &   Glencoe: one of the best narrative passages in the Diaries. Hilda was a
155   hill-walker all her life – her father was very keen, and took the family with him. She may possibly have climbed Dinner-time Buttress in the 1950s when she visited Glencoe a lot. She certainly did the traverse on the Three Sisters in Glencoe then, with the aid of three young rock-climbers who took her over the bits that required ropes [Ursula Betts *per* Trina Paskell]. The impulsive delay in her departure from Scotland is as characteristic (see p.100) as picking up 'an American youth' and introducing him to the joys of mountaineering.
'bought a length of real handwoven tweed': see pp.44, 115, 116 and Introduction.

156   Clachaig Hotel: visit in the 1950s (see above).
Old friends of HM, Tim and Ursula Betts; she is honorary 'Queen' of the Nagas in northeast India, about whom she made a remarkable film. Catriona (Trina) Paskell is one of their daughters (see pp.173, 189).

[There are no Diary pages for 1972, 1974, 1976, 1977, or 1979; one Shropshire entry and some species lists from Savoy in 1975 have been omitted.]

Two days botanising in South Wales, presumably with Mrs I.M.Vaughan: 'during this expedition a number of roses were pointed out to me.' Cilycwm near Llandovery, where Mrs Vaughan and her husband then lived; she was the (wild) *Rosa* Referee for the Botanical Society of the British Isles. HM was not an expert on native rose species. She had joined the BSBI in

1969 (see Introduction) and may have met Mrs Vaughan at a field meeting.
Twm Siôn Catti: legendary Welsh 'Robin Hood' figure.

157   'We': HM and IMV?
Llanstephan is on the Tywi (Towy) estuary, south of Carmarthen.
Lacques Fawr Farm.

159   Two days in Anglesey – the only entry for 1978.
'B fed the gulls.' Barbara Keen, a friend from Valeswood, near Shrewsbury.
Superb description of tern in flight (see pp.60, 99, etc. and Introduction).

161   A day in Anglesey – the only entry for 1980.
Robert Green, HM's nephew.
Interesting description of (South American) Flamingoes.

162   I am not familiar with the Hewitt 'fortress' at Cemlyn and its 'high and hideous walls.'
Bill (W.M.) Condry of Ynys Edwin, well-known Welsh naturalist.

163   Another week in Anglesey, once again seeming to start in mid-story.
'a 2-foot-high extensive thicket of *Pernettya*': *P.mucronata* is a common South American shrublet, grown in gardens for ground-cover.

164   'a copy of the Tunnicliffe drawing' (see pp.130, 136); presumably the one of two male Guillemots, one of which HM had provided on 29 Sept 1964.
NWNT: North Wales Naturalists' Trust.

166   'Death to RTZ': (Rio Tinto Zinc) HM's low opinion of the sense of environmental responsibility displayed by certain industrial giants is surprisingly rarely seen in the Diaries.

167   Spergularias: see p.134.
Tony Bennett: Nature Reserve Warden.
'the forest': Newborough Forest.

168   'The car-park was a horrifying sight': see Introduction.
'Collins': probably McClintock & Fitter (1956); Fitter, Fitter & Blamey (1974) has excellent coloured illustrations of the Wintergreens – see References.

169   'Soay rams . . . they needed rooing urgently': to roo (Shetland and Orkney dialects, Norse root): to strip (sheep) by hand, to pluck (the wool of) sheep. *OED*.
ITE: Institute of Terrestrial Ecology.

171 &   Barclodiad y Gawres: chambered cairn near Rhosneigr.
172   HM's impromptu lecture on Megalithic graves reflects her well-informed enthusiasm (see p.142).

173   Catriona (Trina) Paskell: plant ecologist and daughter of Tim and Ursula Betts (see p.156).
ITE: see p.169 above.

175   Ten days in Anglesey, a year later – though the break is not apparent.
Prestfelde: a preparatory school in Shrewsbury.

177   'gave Mariandyrys to the Trust.' The North Wales Naturalists' Trust (see p.164).
Spotted Rock-rose: HM finds this rare plant on Holyhead Island at last.
R.H.Roberts: a leading Welsh amateur botanist, BSBI Recorder for Anglesey, and an authority on the marsh-orchids (see pp.181, 191.)

178   Dorothy Paish: see pp.46, 87, 127, 135.
Soay sheep: see p.169.

RSPB reserve: the Royal Society for the Protection of Birds is one of several organisations with Nature Reserves on Anglesey.
'With Margaret to Aberffraw': Margaret Williams, mentioned on p.177.

179 &
180

The change in wardens at Pen-lôn upsets HM's botanical plans.
'TB': Tony Bennett, the previous warden. 'R' is 'dear old' Richards.
'queer things like caddis-fly cases, planted upright in the sand': tubes made by a bristle-worm, probably *Lanice conchilega*.
'shallow saucer-size depressions . . . perfect circles with a hole in the centre': feeding-burrows of lugworm, *Arenicola*.

181

'RHR says': R.H.Roberts (see pp.177, 153 and References).

182

'rosettes of Meadow Thistle': HM probably means Marsh Thistle, *Cirsium palustre*; Meadow Thistle, *C.dissectum*, is not recorded from Anglesey.
'We got on to the subject of megaliths': see pp.142, 171, 172.

183 &
184

Red Squirrels: 'quite often seen' on the edge of Beaumaris.
Senecio tanguticus (*Ligularia tangutica*): an occasional garden escape in England, but this is the only Welsh record.

185

'narrow sands . . . lined solid with Red-Indian-skinned bodies and royal blue and scarlet plastic. I fled.': see Introduction.

186

Page incorrectly headed 'Anglesey 1983': obviously a slip of the pen, but was it because HM wrote up the 'fair copy' of her diary a year later? She also headed the second and third days of this trip 'Sept. 17th' and 'Sept. 18th' respectively, though she corrected the latter herself to 'July'.
'an incrustation of the small limpets which have holes in their tops.': almost certainly barnacles (HM was not very strong on marine biology).
'I went to Bodeilio for a vegetarian lunch.': an experience – HM was not a vegetarian.

187

'a last effort to find the Moonwort.': this became an obsession – see p.194.
'Llanberis Pass . . . every nook that would hold a car had one . . . Betws y Coed was a seething mass. And August still to come. How long can Wales stand it?'

188

Back in Shropshire.
Kim Dodwell: a friend and arboricultural expert who helped HM with her gardens. HM gets to know her thistles (see p.182) and hears some fishy tales from Kim.

189

HM's last stay in Anglesey. Her Anglesey notes always seem to start on the *second* page, even before they have been transcribed. These were loose.
Trina Paskell (see pp.156, 173) and Malcolm Leel.

190

'the bad winter': 1981/82.

191

A field meeting of the Botanical Society of the British Isles.
R.H. Roberts: see pp.177, 181 above.
Nigel Brown: Director of the University College of North Wales Botanic Gardens.
'*D.p.incarnata*' etc: HM still seems a little unclear about marsh-orchids.

192

HM, not yet 'hooked on grasses', takes a disrespectful view of BSBI ritual behaviour.
'around 4 p.m. we retreated . . . to my tea corner': HM's own ritual preferred.

193   *Ranunculus baudotii* found at last.
The word 'Description' is written in the margin with an insert sign here:
HM presumably kept her botanical descriptions separately, for later
incorporation in the written-up Diaries.
'Wrote up both sizes with care.' Interesting confirmation of her concern for
the individual plant rather than the species as a collective entity – see
Introduction.
The open discrimination which HM shows in favour of Tree-mallows
(and against 'the rest of the family') is a good example of the plantswoman's
aesthetic eye over-ruling her scientific detachment (see Introduction).

194   The saga of the fruitless Moonwort-quest continues.
The floral anatomy of the Bee Orchid is particularly finely observed.

195   'Why can't I see Moonworts – I can see other minute plants. . . .'
'Charlie's ash-stick': presumably cut for her by Charlie Haycocks (see
p.139).

196   'the Joe Brown boots': named after the famous climber.
CTW – see References.

197   '*1983 26 September. Llanymynech.*' If the year at the head of the page is
correct (see p.186) this is the penultimate written entry in the Diaries,
and one of the most peaceful, shot through with transcendental joy: It is
located in Volume II between entries for 27 July, 1982 and 22 August, 1982,
but this is clearly a mistake.

198   The final extract is on a loose, undated page. Handwriting and style suggest
a recent date, but I was puzzled by an apparent anachronism: HM states '. . . the
stone had been put up again', implying that it had not been so on her last
previous visit. In response to an enquiry by Joan Tate in April 1985,
however, Mr W. E. Morris (the farmer at Tynyfedwen) wrote 'The stone
post was put straight up in April [19]53, first time I took tractor to Bwlch
Maengwynedd.' Had the stone fallen again subsequently, and, if so, who had
re-erected it? Or was the entry a recent transcription of a very old note?

    The problem resolved itself when I was given the chance to read the last
letter which Robert Green, her nephew, ever received from Hilda. It is dated
15 October, 1983, and [in part] describes what is unmistakably the same
expedition as having taken place 'three weeks ago next Tuesday', i.e. 27
September. It is also clear that this was the first time she had walked up
there for more than thirty years – an amazing achievement in view of her
age and her arthritis.

    The relevant paragraphs from her letter make a very interesting
comparison with the Diary entry, and a fitting epilogue to this work.

> *There was a wonderful day three weeks ago next Tuesday, when the
> sunshine was golden all day with a soft balmy warmth, and a perfectly
> clear sky such as we so rarely see. I cut sandwiches (I was at Fron Goch)
> and went to Maengwynedd and parked by the sheepfold. It was so warm
> I had to take my cardigan off. I had lunch sitting against the wall facing
> the mountain. Then I got into my boots and set off. I thought I would
> just go as far as I could and then turn back. I took it slowly, but gradually
> worked up the slope towards the col. I then began to think about what
> would be visible if I got there, so I kept on. Sure enough, when I got to
> the top of the pass, there was Tryfan with its bristly hump and the masses
> of Glydr and Carnedd on each side of it. I went two or three hundred
> yards to the right and the Snowdon massif came into view, hidden
> from where I arrived up by the shoulder of Berwyn. I can't tell you how*

lovely it was – the whole range blue and clear-cut, a marvellous sight. The pleasure was increased by the fact that a big finger-stone which had stood on the pass to guide travellers from time immemorial, and which fell down about the end of my walking time up there about thirty years ago, had been set up again. It is a splendid stone, 8–9 feet high and slender, I greeted it like an old friend. It was warm to the touch. It was a miracle day. I had seriously thought I might never get up there again. What luck to have the time and the energy just on that marvellous day.

Omissions from the published Diaries

Full descriptions of the following have been omitted from the published Diaries

[Square brackets = names also omitted]   * Asterisk = drawings omitted

Mallorca: [Anchusa officinalis], [Antirrhinum orontium], [Asperula arvensis], [Borage], [Calendula arvensis*], Cakile maritima*, [Centaurea aspera], [Cirsium syriacum], Clematis, [Composite], [Composite], 'Cornflower', shrubby, Daucus aureus, Erica mediterranea, [Euphorbia], [Euphorbia, 3 spp*], [Euphorbia sulcata*], [Fumana ?procumbens*], [Geranium], Gladiolus illyricus, [Lathyrus cicera], [Lotus ornithopodioides*], [Melilotus ?sulcata], [Pallenis spinosa*], [Polygala], [Psoralea bituminosa], [Reseda alba], [Salvia horminum*], [Scandix pecten-veneris*], [Trefoil], [Trefoil], [Trifolium stellatum*], [Vetch], [Vicia notata].
S.W. Ireland: Euphorbia hyberna, Glaux maritima, Osmunda regalis, [Pedicularis sylvatica], Saxifraga spathularis.
Provence: [Composite], [Echinops ritro], [Erodium cicutarium], [Fumana], [Kohlrauschia prolifera], [Labiate], [Legumes, 2 spp], [Mallow], [Quercus coccifera], [Salvia], [Umbellifer], [Verbascum sinuatum].
Savoy: [Cephalanthera longifolia], [Dactylorhiza sambucina], [Orchis militaris], [Orchis pallens], [Orchis purpurea].
Great Britain: Acinos arvensis*, [Alchemilla vestita], [Anthriscus neglecta*], [Arabis hirsuta], [Arenaria leptoclados], Atriplex littoralis, [Calystegia soldanella], Campanula latifolia, Carlina vulgaris, Centaurium erythraea, [Convolvulus arvensis], [Crepis nicaeensis], [Doronicum pardalianches], Echium vulgare, [Epilobium pedunculare], Epipactis helleborine, Eryngium maritimum, Glaucium flavum, Helleborus foetidus, [Hieracium (Sagittata)*], [Hapericum dubium], [Hypericum hirsutum], [Hypericum montanum], [Hypericum perforatum], [Hypericum pulchrum], Hypochoeris radicata, Inula crithmoides, [Lathraea squamaria], [Lathyrus sylvestris], Lavatera arborea, Limonium binervosum, Lobelia dortmanna, Lychnis flos-cuculi, Lysimachia vulgaris, Narthecium ossifragum, Oenanthe aquatica, Ononis repens, Ophioglossum vulgatum, Paris quadrifolia, [Pentaglottis sempervirens], [Pimpinella saxifraga], Pyrola rotundifolia (*), Ranunculus lingua, Raphanus maritimus, [Rosa rubiginosa], [Rubia peregrina], Sagina subulata, [Sambucus ebulus], [Saxifraga hypnoides*], Saxifraga oppositifolia*, Scrophularia nodosa*, [Senecio viscosus], Serratula tinctoria, Spergularia marginata, Spergularia rupicola, [Spergularia salina], [Spiranthes spiralis], Suaeda maritima, Trifolium arvense, [Verbascum nigrum*], [Viburnum lantana], [Vicia orobus].

SELECTED FACSIMILE PAGES

1961

March 22nd
Wed.

In the end we set out for Santa Ponsa, which was just as well, because the hill-village must have been Capdella and we could never have reached it. The hotel provided us with four huevos, meat, cheese and the usual hunks of bread, and we set out, first to Paguera, and from there on the main road to Palma. Soon I was making terrific loops which we were able to short-cut across the difficult in the pinewood. Any little hollow that had accumulated enough soil, had been cleared of wild trees and planted with olives or almonds. the olives always seemed to have been mutilated: as soon as a limb reached a reasonable size, it was lopped off, so that the trees were in all sorts of contorted shapes, & often no more than twisted half-hollow boles; like the holly-forest on the Stiperstones, they had rock-like bodies of a thousand years which still could clothe themselves in a farm short young shoots persisting leaves, silvers & stirring, but always unchanging lustre flush and promise.

Just as we were beginning to tire, a hotel bus came along, and an Englishwoman in it arranged a lift. In this way, we were whisked along about five miles, into entirely different scenery. Where three roads met, we decided to get out, & a tip to the driver settled the question of fares.

We were now among the largest fields we had seen yet. The pine-covered hills had retreated into the background and we were in a region of rich red soil. The fields had widely-spaced rows of almond trees, so that other crops could be grown in between. The almonds, which had half grown fruit, some pink buds, were in full bloom and have been and white side fruit; in January they were and opposite sides. The road south led to Santa Ponsa. In the angle between this and the Palma road was a brown mas, with several tall date-palms waving over it. In the opposite corner was a mound, & on it a disused round windmill without sails. Near this was a sunny bank on which we decided to have lunch, after making sure there were no snakes.

212

1961

Bristly Ox-tongue (Picris echioides) – a plant of great character. It was clearly a biennial – there were several flowering plants & still more rosettes of basal leaves getting ready for next year. Leaves lanceolate, tapering off to a sharp point armed with a spine; wavy, rough, with bumps and boils and bristles all over, gall sizes. The larger with raised whitish circles at the root. Stem round with fine red ribs, covered with spines & bristles of almost transparent fish-bone colour and texture, & all sizes. All the spines on the stems branch at the very tip into three, turned outwards at right-angles. The stems branch frequently, & at each join there is a sessile leaf with cordate bases clasping the stem ferociously and reaching far back beyond it in a well-armed curve. Flower-stalks from these branchings are similarly ribbed & bristly, & carry sometimes one flower, but more often three: each of these has a stalk ½ – ¾ inches & then a set of terrific bracts looking more like a calyx than a set of five bracts. They are more or less heart-shaped but with a long fine point ending in a spine, a broad midrib & wide-based wings, all with bristles. Inside these is the normal calyx of long narrow segments also ending in prolonged bristly points. The flowers are yellow & I found two types – one inside only, with ligulate petals each with one stamen, thick and yellow at the base, black and two-branched at the top. The tips of the branches cling together when the middle have begun to separate, making a club-shaped organ with a gap in the middle. These male flowers had about five rows of petals, decreasing in size right down to the centre. The other type was hermaphrodite, with male ligules, for 3–4 rows, & a group of about a dozen female flowers in the middle. These were tubular and yellow of the usual disk-flower type though hardly numerous enough to make a disk. Such splendid, if spiny, curves and rugged individuality, called out to be drawn.

Hilda Murrell's unique amalgam of technical language with subjective impressions and poetic phrases is well illustrated in this masterly portrait of a handsome but rebarbative plant.

Opposite page
Hilda Murrell was a perfectionist. She worked over her comparison of the ancient Mallorcan olive-trees and the Stiperstones Hollies at home until the words fitted her vision.

Scotland 1971.

Sunday, September 19th

On the way to Aviemore, I made a détour to see Culloden. The site belongs to the National Trust for Scotland, and is beautifully cared for. A cottage of pre-1746 survived the battle and is now a small museum. The gables are built of peat-blocks and the roof is thatched with heather, held down by heather-ropes tied to poles at the eaves, and pegged into the peat across the gables. Inside, among other exhibits, was a spinning-wheel with three bobbins.

Soon after leaving Culloden there was a notice: "Stones of Clava", so I decided to go and look at them. I was very glad I did, for this was a numinous place. The "stones" were three splendid megalithic tombs of 1800-1500 B.C. in a line down the centre of a glade enclosed by beech-trees, rather gnarled and stunted, and with the lower branches sweeping the ground, making a high wall of seclusion round the whole site. Footsteps were muted by deep soft moss, and the only sound was a slight sighing of the wind in the leaves. The great stones imposed their presence even more forcefully in this strange setting than others seen in vast spaces of open moor, or in the flat lands of Anglesey under huge skies.

The first and third were passage-graves. All had piles of smooth rounded rubble, like giant sea-washed shingle, between the inner mega-liths and their encasing circular walls, and were attended by outer rings of standing-stones. The middle tomb had three narrow ribs of rock set in the ground, equidistant radii from grave to circle. Near the last and grandest grave a noble menhir, a slender solitary watcher, not rough-hewn like the others, but beautifully dressed and squared at the top, brooded in its aloof significance, now known only to itself. I was alone with all this splendour, in gentle sunshine and total peace.

How I would love to roll back the film of time, and see these mighty chieftains in their prowess and their state, and then at the end of their days be a witness of the funeral rites which must have been as splendid as their tombs. These were no mere savage tribes, the grandeur of the geometry and the size of the stones speak for their powers of conception and construction, the nobility of their imagination. Who were these people?

I came out on the main road again at Daviot, and stopped at the Landmark centre at Carrbridge where I had lunch at one of the picnic tables. These, and places for car-parking, are scattered in an open pinewood in a very pleasant way. Moved into my room at Aviemore, & then went up to the small car-park at Coire na Ciste. I walked down to the stream and took to the path beside it on the opposite bank. There was plenty of fresh-cooking Alchemilla alpina, and I also found dwarf Cornel. I worked up on to the ridge where at about 2,500 ft. I found the Alpine Azalea (Loiseleuria procumbens) growing tight under a boulder. The vivid pink flowers caught my eye. This

Hilda Murrell's dense and individual hand belies the easy fluency of her narrative style: this lyrical realism was the outcome of much re-working and polishing. She sometimes 'wrote up' her rough drafts as much as a year later.

1983

September 26th. Llanymynech. There was solid fog early, yellowish at first in the low light, but soon turning paler & sinking in solid white bars along the valleys, leaving just the tips of the foothills visible. Berwyn was hidden in higher and denser cloud. I went up on the hill, but earlier would have been better, by the time I got to the crag, the white cotton-wool was dissolving into long grey wisps, which were driven along the river-valleys towards England by a steady south-west breeze. The really wonderful sight was not this, but the cobwebs, not the usual kind but three-dimensional ones, nearer fabric than thread, so close-woven was the gossamer. The dew had been heavy, and they were spangled with droplets so small that I counted twenty of them on a bare inch of thread, but though minute they were brilliant reflectors of pure celestial light. Miraculously, I had the sun behind me when I went to look at one of them, to find an inverted rainbow lying across it, very softly orange and green & blue, living specks of opal. The fineness of the filigree was breath-taking. These super-cobwebs were everywhere in hundreds. I only saw one of the more usual cartwheels but it was a superb structure.

This passage has a beauty and serenity of treatment and style all the more remarkable in the light of Hilda Murrell's current preoccupation with the nuclear power controversy.

REFERENCES

[Those in square brackets are cited in the Introduction or Notes only]
Initials in the left margin, '(CTW)', are abbreviations used in the Diaries.

(CTW)   CLAPHAM, A.R., TUTIN, T.G., & WARBURG, E.F. (1952, 1962) *Flora of the British Isles.* (Cambridge University Press)

CLAPHAM, A.R., TUTIN, T.G., & WARBURG, E.F. (1959, 1968, 1981) *Excursion Flora of the British Isles.* (Cambridge University Press)

DUPERREX, A. (1961) *Orchids of Europe.* (Blandford, London)

FITTER, R., FITTER, A., & BLAMEY, M. (1974) *The Wild Flowers of Britain and Northern Europe.* (Collins, London)

[FOWLER, H.W., *et al.*(Eds.) (1911 etc.) *Concise Oxford Dictionary.* (Oxford Univ. Press)]

FOURNIER, P. (1946, 1961) *Les Quatres Flores de la France.* (Paul Lechevalier, Paris)

[FRASER DARLING, F. (1947) *A Natural History of the Highlands and Islands.* (Collins, London)]

LLOYD, L.C., & RUTTER, E.M. (1957) *Handlist of the Shropshire Flora.* (Caradoc and Severn Valley Field Club, Shrewsbury)

MCCLINTOCK, D., & FITTER, R.S.R. (1956) *The Pocket Guide to Wild Flowers.* (Collins, London)

PERRING, F.H., & WALTERS, S.M. (1962, 1976, 1983) *Atlas of the British Flora.* (E.P. Publishing Ltd & BSBI, Wakefield)

ROBERTS, R.H. (1982) *The Flowering Plants and Ferns of Anglesey.* (National Museum of Wales, Cardiff)

(SRC)   ROSS-CRAIG, S. (1948–1974) *Drawings of British Plants.* (Bell, London)

[SINKER, C.A., PACKHAM, J.R., TRUEMAN, I.C., OSWALD, P.H., PERRING, F.H., & PRESTWOOD, W.V. (1985) *Ecological Flora of the Shropshire Region.* (STNC, Shrewsbury)]

STARK, F. (1968) *The Zodiac Arch.* (Murray, London)

[TRAHERNE, T. (1908, etc.) *Centuries of Meditations by Thomas Traherne (1636?–1674).* (Dobell, London)]

WITHERBY, H.F., JOURDAIN, F.C.R., TICEHURST, N.F., & TUCKER, B.W. (5 volumes) (1938–1941) *The Handbook of British Birds.* (Witherby, London)

INDEX OF PLACE-NAMES

Page numbers are for reference to places actually visited or seen (sometimes distantly) at the time described; or with which detailed comparison is made.

Spelling and hyphenation of Scottish and Welsh place-names are generally those shown on recent Ordnance Survey maps, where these differ from Hilda's usage.

INDEX OF PLANTS AND ANIMALS

Page numbers in italics indicate illustrations